Taste Berries™ for Teens

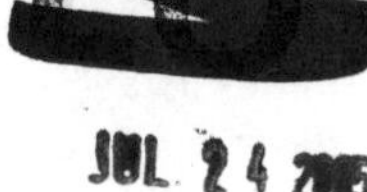

#4

Inspirational Short Stories and Encouragement on Being Cool, Caring & Courageous

contributions
teens for teens

Bettie B. Youngs, Ph.D., Ed.D.
Jennifer Leigh Youngs

Authors of the national bestselling *Taste Berries*™ *for Teens* series and *A Teen's Guide to Living Drug-Free*

Health Communications, Inc.
Deerfield Beach, Florida

www.hcibooks.com
www.tasteberriesforteens.com

We would like to acknowledge the following publishers and individuals for permission to reprint the following material. (Note: The stories that were penned anonymously, that are public domain or were previously unpublished stories written by Bettie B. Youngs or Jennifer Leigh Youngs are not included in this listing. Also not included in this listing but credited within the text are those stories contributed or based upon stories by teens.)

(Excerpted from the World Storytelling Prize award-winning book, Taste Berries for Teens #3: Inspirational Stories and Encouragement on Life, Love, Friends and the Face in the Mirror, *pages 173–176.)*

Library of Congress Cataloging-in-Publication Data

Taste berries for teens #4 : inspirational short stories and encouragement on being cool, caring & courageous / [compiled by] Bettie B. Youngs, Jennifer Leigh Youngs ; with contributions from teens for teens.
p. cm.
ISBN 0-7573-0223-8 (tp)
1. Teenagers—Conduct of life. I. Title: Taste berries for teens number 4. II. Title: Taste berries for teens number four. III. Youngs, Bettie B. IV. Youngs, Jennifer Leigh, 1974–

BJ1661.T362 2004
158.1'0835—dc22

2004047456

ISBN 0-7573-0223-8

Publisher: Health Communications, Inc.
3201 S.W. 15th Street
Deerfield Beach, FL 33442-8190

Cover illustration and design by Andrea Perrine Brower
Inside book typesetting by Dawn Von Strolley Grove

To

Natalie Kent,

a loving taste berry

and angel in our midst.

To: ____

who is cool, caring and courageous!

From: ____

Also by Bettie B. Youngs

Living the 10 Commandments in NEW Times: A Book for Young Adults (Faith Communications, Inc.)
12 Months of Faith: A Devotional Journal for Teens (Faith Communications, Inc.)
A Teen's Guide to Christian Living: Practical Answers to Tough Questions About God and Faith (Faith Communications, Inc.)
365 Days of Taste-Berry Inspiration for Teens (Health Communications, Inc.)
A Teen's Guide to Living Drug-Free (Health Communications, Inc.)
A Taste-Berry Teen's Guide to Setting & Achieving Goals (Health Communications, Inc.)
Taste Berries for Teens #3: Inspirational Short Stories on Life, Love, Friends and the Face in the Mirror (Health Communications, Inc.)
A Taste-Berry Teen's Guide to Managing the Stress and Pressures of Life (Health Communications, Inc.)
MORE Taste Berries for Teens: Inspirational Stories and Encouragement on Life, Love, Friendship and Tough Issues (Health Communications, Inc.)
Taste Berries for Teens Journal: My Thoughts on Life, Love and Making a Difference (Health Communications, Inc.)
Taste Berries for Teens: Inspirational Stories and Encouragement on Life, Love, Friendship and Tough Issues (Health Communications, Inc.)
Taste-Berry Tales: Stories to Lift the Spirit, Fill the Heart and Feed the Soul (Health Communications, Inc.)
A String of Pearls: Inspirational Stories Celebrating the Resiliency of the Human Spirit (Adams Media)
Gifts of the Heart: Stories That Celebrate Life's Defining Moments (Health Communications, Inc.)
Values from the Heartland (Health Communications, Inc.)
Stress & Your Child: Helping Kids Cope with the Strains & Pressures of Life (Random House)
Helping Your Child Succeed in School (Active Parenting)
Safeguarding Your Teenager from the Dragons of Life: A Guide to the Adolescent Years (Health Communications, Inc.)
Keeping Our Children Safe: A Guide to Emotional, Physical, Intellectual and Spiritual Wellness (Westminster/John Knox Press)
Getting Back Together: Repairing the Love in Your Life (Adams Media)

Also by Jennifer Leigh Youngs

12 Months of Faith: A Devotional Journal for Teens (Faith Communications, Inc.)
A Teen's Guide to Christian Living: Practical Answers to Tough Questions About God and Faith (Faith Communications, Inc.)
365 Days of Taste-Berry Inspiration for Teens (Health Communications, Inc.)
A Teen's Guide to Living Drug-Free (Health Communications, Inc.)
A Taste-Berry Teen's Guide to Setting & Achieving Goals (Health Communications, Inc.)
Taste Berries for Teens #3: Inspirational Short Stories on Life, Love, Friends and the Face in the Mirror (Health Communications, Inc.)
A Taste-Berry Teen's Guide to Managing the Stress and Pressures of Life (Health Communications, Inc.)
MORE Taste Berries for Teens: Inspirational Stories and Encouragement on Life, Love, Friendship and Tough Issues (Health Communications, Inc.)
Feeling Great, Looking Hot and Loving Yourself: Health, Fitness & Beauty for Teens (Health Communications, Inc.)
Taste Berries for Teens Journal: My Thoughts on Life, Love and Making a Difference (Health Communications, Inc.)
Taste Berries for Teens: Inspirational Short Stories on Life, Love, Friendship and Tough Issues (Health Communications, Inc.)

Contents

Part 2: Teen Poetry Contest: You Pick the $100 Winner!

Part 3: The Single Most Important Lesson I've Learned

Part 4: Standing Tall(er): Surviving the Loss of a Parent

Part 7: Cool Attitudes: The Art of Being Cool

Part 8: Dear Dr. Youngs, What Should I Do About . . .

Acknowledgments

We would like to thank the "taste berries" in the development of this book. First, to the many, many teens who were a part of this new addition in our *Taste Berries for Teens* series: Thank you for so generously sharing your experiences to help other teens see their lives in the most positive light possible. As always, you teach us the importance of living close to your heart and greeting each day with anticipated wonder. May we all be inspired to learn what you intuitively know and live.

We extend a heartfelt gratitude to our publisher, Peter Vegso, and the talented staff at Health Communications—most especially those with whom we work most closely: Bret Witter, Genene Hirschhorn, Lori Golden, Susan Heim, Randee Feldman, Doreen Hess, Terry Burke, Kelly Johnson Maragni, Tom Sand, Elisabeth Rinaldi, Paola Fernandez, Kim Weiss, Brian Peluso and the many others who play an intricate role in transporting our words into the hands and hearts of our readers.

A special thanks to Andrea Perrine Brower and Larissa Hise Henoch for the great cover design, as well as Lawna Perrine Oldfield, Anthony Clausi and Dawn Von Strolley Grove. We also extend a very special thanks to the school administrators and educators who so generously shared goodwill and allowed us to work with their students. A very, very special thank you to administrator Barrett Luketic and his staff and students; to administrator Carolyn Dowler, and to educator Vanessa Vega and her students as well as the many others with whom we worked on this very special undertaking. Their valuable input in this book is evident throughout. And to the many important taste berries in our lives, and to our many brothers and sisters everywhere in the world, thank you for sharing the journey and holding our hearts in such a touchingly human way.

As always, we give all glory to God from whom all blessings flow.

Introduction

Welcome to *Taste Berries for Teens #4: Inspirational Short Stories and Encouragement on Being Cool, Caring & Courageous,* the latest in our *Taste Berries for Teens* series. As with all books in the series, we worked with many real teens to bring you this wonderful compilation of their stories about coping with real life—hence the "taste berries" in the title.

For those of you joining us for the first time, a *taste berry* (also known as Richardella dulcisica) is a little fruit that, when eaten, mysteriously convinces the taste buds that all food—even something as bitter as a lemon—is sweet. This bright little berry has been used around the world for countless years to sweeten bitter foods. In our *Taste Berries for Teens* series, we use the taste berry as a metaphor for those people who help, inspire and encourage each other. Has someone reached out when you were suffering a disappointment, nursing a broken heart or felt overwhelmed or down-and-out? Has someone cheered you on to victory, said "Way to go!" when you've been a winner or simply told you how great you look today? If so, that person was acting as your taste berry.

In this book, you'll find stories by teens like yourself who are living to the fullest—being and doing their best. We are taste berries in people's lives when we feel honored to help them see things in a more positive light. On some days, we could all use a taste berry ourselves. These stories will inspire you and show you how to change or "sweeten" any situation you're facing!

You're about to read stories from fellow teens concerning eight key issues that matter to you the most. Here's how the book is organized: Each unit starts out with *A Word from the*

Authors, which gives you a head's up on what you're about to read, as well as a chance to let you know if we feel you should have any particular background on either the subject matter or specific content within the unit. The *Word from the Authors* section is followed by the stories from teens (or in the case of Part 2, poetry entries). This is then followed by a commentary (remarks) by yet other teens who want to share their views on the subject.

As you can see from the table of contents, we've started this book off with a unit called "What I've Learned About LOVE So Far . . . (As of Noon, Today)." As most teens will tell you, love is what makes the world go around—and around, and as such, it can create some of our most "dizzying" moments! Teens always enjoy reading how other teens are coping with both the elation and zaniness love brings, and you're sure to find their stories most interesting and insightful!

Part 2 features a poetry contest with twenty-three awesome entries! YOU, the reader, get to choose your Top-Three Favorite category winners, with the overall winner to receive a $100 cash prize. (The next *Taste Berries for Teens* book will also have a poetry contest, so don't forget to enter it!) You'll find everything you need to know about how to judge this contest, as well to enter the next one, within Part 2.

Part 3, "The Single Most Important Lesson I've Learned," features some really great stories on a variety of subjects. For this particular unit we asked teens to tell us what was a really, really important lesson they learned. We even have a story by someone so many of you greatly admire: TV actress Danica McKellar. Danica is not only a star, but a math genius who has authored a math theorem! Note that at the end of her story, she has generously invited you to contact her (what a taste berry for you!).

Part 4, "Standing Tall(er): Surviving the Loss of a Parent," is a most loving unit, one we decided to add because we receive so much mail from teens who suddenly face life without a mom or dad. No one can know, or possibly imagine, what it is like to be a young person who has lost a parent—which is exactly why you all will find this unit insightful. It was inspired by Amanda Martinez (a teen we've published in several of our books) when she sent us her "Not Even a Star Can Outdo the Moon!" story. We were so taken by her words, and because we get some three thousand stories a year from teens who have lost a parent, we decided it was time to share a collection of such "heart-to-hearts" with you. We also decided to reprint Kyle Ross's "All the Ways He Loved Me" story from our *Taste Berries for Teens #3: Inspirational Short Stories & Encouragement on Life, Love, Friends and the Face in the Mirror* (which by the way, is the 2003 World Story Telling Book-of-the-Year-for-Teens winner!). We receive so much mail on Kyle's beautiful and powerful story, we had to share it yet again. We know you will find the commentary, from teens who talk about the importance of helping a friend through this loss, to be insightful. As seventeen-year-old Ashley Strimple commented in a story she did when her thirty-seven-year-old mother was recovering from a heart attack: *"When my mother was in the hospital she was so missed. I learned that a mother is the heart of a family. Everything pivots around her."* Of course, everyone knows that a home pivots around Mom or Dad, but imagine the moment this insight dawns on you "for real." Such is the revelation you will find in this spectacular unit by your peers.

Part 5, "Courage: We're All Heroes in the Making," features one of your favorite teen authors, Mike Siciliano, with his exciting story, "An Acrophobic's Plunge," as well as a riveting story by Sergeant Jeff Struecker, 82nd Airborne. Note that Jeff, too, invites you to share with him what he's learned about "the most important courage." In these awesome stories, teens discuss moments in which they either saw courage, or took their own up a notch or two!

In Part 6, "Dying for Attention: A Candid Look at the Importance of Teen Self-Worth," we bring you selected pages of the diary from a teen who from sixth grade through her second year in college kept a journal on her own struggle with personal worth, one that led her into the jaws of an eating disorder. Also featured are some fifteen guys and girls who discuss body-image issues—be it with a struggle to keep their weight down because they're on their school's wrestling team or because "being thin" is seen as the key to acceptance. This is a most insightful unit, and we would love to hear from you on your own "image" issues. As teens learn, the degree to which we are accepting of ourselves—acne, bad hair days, the size and shape of our bone structure, mood swings and all—is an important contribution to our own self-worth. With bodies undergoing such rapid and dramatic change in adolescence, and because your peers are all-too-quick to "judge" the size and shape of bodies, teens are especially vulnerable to resorting to drastic measures to lose weight. Because eating disorders are dangerous and so prevalent among teens, we've chosen to include this subject in our book.

Part 7, "Cool Attitudes: The Art of Being 'Cool'," is a subject that occupies a great deal of daydreaming time in the teen years. Who knows the importance of being cool more than teens! In this unit, you'll learn what other teens say is the "how, when and where" route to being cool. You'll also get a chance to think about how cool you are, and why you feel this way.

In Part 8, "Dear Dr. Youngs, What Should I Do About . . . ," Dr. Youngs answers some of the mail we get from teens who ask for advice. We hope that by answering those we've selected—such as how to deal with a bully; how to earn back a good reputation after stealing or cheating; or how best to deal with being pressured for sex—you'll find support for dealing with your own similar issues. We did a very popular unit like this one in *Taste Berries for Teens #3,* and we hope you enjoy this one. As always, send us your questions and concerns you'd like us to answer in the next book.

So there you have it! We hope you will enjoy reading these

stories and be inspired by them. We invite you to send us your stories about people or situations that have shaped your views and touched your life. Send them to:

Taste-Berry Teen Team
3060 Racetrack View Drive, Suite 100-103
Del Mar, CA 92014

For more information on stories or books we're working on, visit *www.tasteberriesforteens.com.* You will also find a picture and a description of each of the books we've written for young adults on the Web site (as well as at the back of this book).

❤ *Taste berries to you, Bettie and Jennifer Youngs*

Part 1

What I've Learned About LOVE So Far . . . (As of Noon, Today!)

Know YOURSELF before you expect someone else to know you.

—Anonymous

The world is nothing but a school of love; our relationships with family and friends are the university in which we are meant to learn what love and devotion truly are.

—Swami Muktananda

Love is the way messengers from the mystery tell us things.

—Jelaluddin Rumi

There is only one happiness in life, to love and be loved.

—George Sand

The heart is forever inexperienced.

—Henry David Thoreau

Until we remember that our own capacity to love is what we truly seek, we are doomed to search for satisfaction in places where we will find only more longing.

—Marianne Williamson

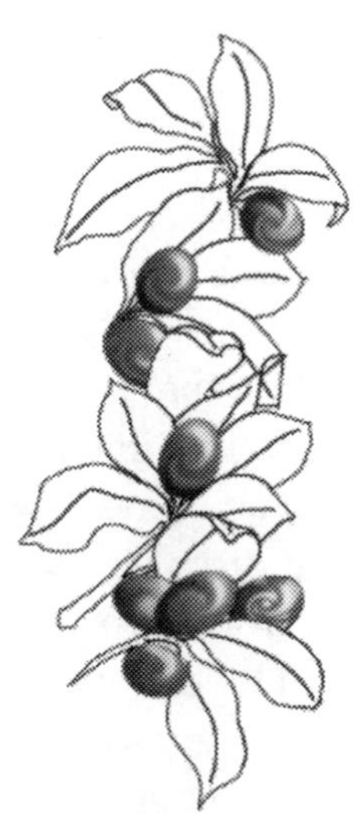

A Word from the Authors

Ah yes, love again! Love is never an old topic, is it? No "been there, done that" for this powerhouse of an energy. In every single one of the books in our *Taste Berries for Teens* series, we've included a unit about love. (In our *More Taste Berries for Teens,* we included two!) Always, always we receive "tons" of mail from teens telling us how much they enjoy reading stories by other teens who themselves have discovered this most awesome emotion, and how it fills their days with elation—and lunacy!

It's been said that love is the most potent force in the world. Perhaps it is: When love beckons, we are all—young and old alike—drawn in. When love alights, we're ever willing to follow, wanting to know what it has in store for us. When it comes to love, we are all students.

There is so much to learn! Always, there is a new day, and with it, a new way of looking through the eyes of one's heart. As teens everywhere discover, just when you think you have something figured out, along comes another lesson, or a new special someone, teaching something new. Whether it's just how different people can be in the way they express their affection or how treating different people in the same way can produce very different results, there is never anything boring—or ordinary—

about what we learn when love is on our minds and in our hearts.

From winning someone's heart, to the realization that someone has won yours; from telling a special someone it's time for you to move on, to having someone deliver that same message to you (or as teens say, "dumped"); always, we discover that Cupid is a master teacher. And oh, what a busy one! No one knows this better than teens, who will tell you that love is one of the biggest of their challenges! Of course, your mom and dad—even your grandpa and grandma—could have told you that. But who is listening to yesterday's news? Every teen knows that lessons of the heart are an individual and personal thing, and that you have to experience each one firsthand. Things such as, sometimes you have to wait for it to come knocking, while at other times, just when you've welcomed it into your life, it's already walking out the door. Or, just because love sends you shopping for a new outfit for the homecoming parade doesn't necessarily mean you'll be needing something red to wear for the Valentine's Day dance. Or maybe love will send a particular sweetie your way for homecoming and yet a different honey for the Valentine's dance. And yet another for the prom. And yet another to be your summer love. When it comes to love, only Cupid knows what's in store for you!

Whether Cupid brings you a special "one" or many special someones, either way, you're in for some lessons. Whether your heart leaps for a "one and only" or brings a series of heartthrobs, you can count on love to bring with it some highs, some lows, and some ups and downs. Yes, Cupid seems intent on teaching us that *just as love is about learning about the other person, it is also (if not more so) about learning about ourselves.*

How about you—what are you learning about love? Are you learning how to be a more loving and lovable person? Are you learning that how smoothly love goes is pretty much determined by how much you love and care about yourself? It is so important that we love others. It is even more important that we love ourselves. Certainly, these are among the many taste-berry lessons that teens learn in the name of love.

In gathering the stories for this unit, we asked teens to share an experience or situation in which they learned a valuable lesson about love. We took note that at the end of nearly every story we received, teens added something to the effect of, "This is what I've learned to date . . . so far." And sure enough, before the ink was dry on their letters, or the moment they'd clicked "send" and the e-mail was on its way, things had changed. Just when a teen admitted that love had swept him or her off their feet—and hence a letter professing undying love—it was only a matter of time when a letter or e-mail arrived saying, "PLEASE DO NOT PRINT MY STORY BECAUSE THAT RAT DUMPED ME (or I dumped him or her)." Sometimes this was then followed by a story telling of that heartbreak, complete with words trashing that no-good so-and-so. But alas! The very next week, the two had patched things up, and love was off and running once again. Fair enough! We'll honor that what you've learned about love so far may be as of noon today . . . and that this may well be different than what you've learned by day's end!

In bringing you this unit, at first we tried to get a handle on the kinds of lessons love brings, such as waiting for love: "Everyone has a boyfriend or girlfriend but me. I'm still waiting"; or discovery of feelings: "When I first saw so-and-so, my heart stopped . . ." or "I couldn't believe how much my heart ached when I was dumped." But the more we read, we quickly understood that in the teen years, there are roughly some 3,698,668,965 lessons, and so we decided to let you make the list for yourself! Space doesn't permit us to include a story on each of these lessons, but we've included those we think you'll relate to and enjoy the most! As you'll see, some lessons were about first discovery—how someone's heart felt when first awakened to love; while someone else discovered such feelings for the second, third or fourth time! While some teens learned what a broken heart felt like, others thought perhaps he or she had met the love of a lifetime. Other teens discovered that though they had invited love in, it was time to usher it out. Still others learned that while they thought their lives would be magically transformed "if only" they had a special someone, their lives had been transformed all right—but not in the way hoped for. While some teens saw a lesson most clearly when love walked out the door, others saw the real learning was not so much in "why" the person left the relationship, but in the way the person handled the leaving.

Ah, yes. Love is always a teacher, and no one knows this better than do teens. Just as teens know the frustrations of love, they also know the benefits of harnessing its power. As Teilhard de Chardin's famous phrase says: *"Someday, after we have mastered the winds, the waves, the tides and gravity, we will harness the energies of love. Then, for the second time in the history of the world, we will have discovered fire."* The energy of love compared to the importance of fire? Teens say YES! But then again, every mom or dad, or grandpa or grandma could have told us that!

So enjoy this unit, brought to you by your peers. And please take note that whenever we do a unit on love, often we receive mail from readers asking for someone's address. Even though well intentioned, "If so-and-so doesn't want him, I do!" or, "That happened to me. Please give me so-and-so's address, and I'll write that person and tell him or her how to handle things," know that we do not (for safety, security and legal reasons) give out anyone's name or address. Still, thanks for the taste berry of your concern and generosity. It's always nice to know that there are others out there who can coach, comfort and guide the rest of us as we continue to gain experience in learning valuable lessons in love.

❤ *Taste berries to you, Bettie and Jennifer Youngs*

Keeping Tabs on John

A memory of a loving moment is forever: Though a certain guy is no longer in my life, I can still feel him removing my glasses and kissing me.

—Tracey Seiple, 16

Secretly, I had a huge crush on John Joseph, and for nearly a whole year, I'd been keeping tabs on him. There were a couple of big hurdles to our getting together, however. The first was that he didn't know I existed. Still, the biggest hurdle was that we're in different circles at school. John is a jock. I'm a "band-o"—a band geek.

At my school jocks date ONLY cheerleaders. They're expected to. So a popular jock dating a band geek would be out of the question. So my heart and I watched John Joseph—from a distance—week in and week out. Finally, one day my heart asked me, *"What's to lose if we talked to him?"* Given that it was already October, I thought it was a fair question. My next step was to find a way to be in the same place he was—like maybe the library—and then go up to him and start talking. How was John J. ever going to know that I was alive and sharing the same earth as he if somebody didn't let him know?

That one day arrived.

I was entering the library, where I planned to return *Flowers for Algernon.* John was walking into the library at the same time! Spotting the book I was holding, he asked, "Are you returning that?"

"Yes," I replied. "I had to read it for creative writing."

"Oh, you must be taking Mrs. Wilson's class, too," he said. "Have you already done the paper on it? I haven't started. Well, that figures, 'cause I haven't even read the book! In fact, I've not even checked out the book."

And that's when I just said as coolly as I could, "Well, it's a great book but slow reading. It'll take you all of two days for sure."

"Really," he groaned. "I don't have two days. I've got an out-of-town game after school tomorrow, so Coach said it was going to be a long and late practice tonight." Then he looked at me and asked, "Where do you live? Are you pretty close, because maybe you could tell me the whole story and I could sort of write my paper from your, ummm, executive summary!" With this he laughed, and I realized the crush of my life just asked me to get together with him!

"I don't live too far from school," I answered, trying to think of what to say next, as a million and one questions went through my head: "Would Mom and Dad care if I had a boy over after dinner? Would Mom ban my little brother to his room so that he wouldn't pester us and so that I'd have private time with John? Was the house clean enough to have him over? Would he want snacks—what snacks? Would popcorn be okay, or would chips be better? What kind of chips—jalapeno, or just plain ones? No onions for sure. Dip? Would it be good to have dip with the chips? Coke or Pepsi? Can jocks do caffeinated drinks, or might John get drug-tested and then busted and be mad at me for offering him a soda with caffeine? Should I suggest he come over right after his football practice, or ask him to come over after he's done with dinner? If I put it off that long, might John call and suggest I just tell him the story over the phone? What if . . .?"

"Give me your address and I'll stop over right after practice," he said, interrupting my stress attack.

"Okay. Sure," I said, trying to sound as cool as I could under the circumstance. I gave him my address, phone number and cell number, and an alternative phone number in case he couldn't reach me on any of the others.

It was nearly six o'clock when he arrived—with a six-pack of Coke and a bag of Doritos in hand! I took him to the television room, shut the door and began telling him the story and reading him certain parts that I'd found really interesting. Every now and then John would ask a question. A couple of times he asked me to reread a certain paragraph. I could tell that he was really getting into the book. He especially had taken Charlie, the book's central character, to heart.

I had taken John Joseph to heart!

Because of the out-of-town game, John didn't come the following evening, but he did the night after that. I was just nearing the end of the book, where Gimpy is telling Charlie about the importance of friends, ". . . we want you to remember that you've got friends here . . . it's good to have friends. . . ," I read.

"It's good to have you," John said tenderly. Then, he took my glasses off and kissed me on the forehead.

I fell in love right then and there of course. "Want to go for a walk?" he asked. "Do you think your parents will mind if you leave the house for an hour?"

"Be right back, Mom!" I yelled, heading out the door with this gorgeous guy. Did I care that I didn't get my algebra done? Not in the least! We walked around the block in my neighborhood and then he left. I was in seventh heaven.

Unfortunately, as easy as the two days came, they passed without any more interaction between us. A couple of days later John was named our school's "Mr. Football"—our school's male equivalent to being voted homecoming queen. Homecoming was less than a week away, and as expected, John asked Tara Wells, a cheerleader. Three months have passed, and John is still dating Tara. But sometimes I'll look over in his direction and catch him glancing over in my direction. When that happens, I can just feel that kiss all over again. What I've discovered is that even a memory of a loving moment is forever: Whenever I look at him, I can still feel him removing my glasses and kissing me. It is so romantic—still. I'm not going to ever give up hope that one day he will do that again.

Tracey Seiple, 16

Your Boyfriend . . . Ought to be Mine!

Some guys make better boyfriends than do others.

—Daniella Chopra, 15

Ty Wilkins has green eyes, brown hair and the best smile in the whole world. From the moment I saw this guy, my heart dumped—for good, this time—my old boyfriend! I had never been so attracted to a guy before! But here's the problem: Ty is the boyfriend of my best friend, Samantha Milner—who just happens to also be my cousin—and we go to the same school!

I didn't plan on falling in love with my cousin's boyfriend.

What happened is that Sammy and I had made plans to go to the state fair together. At the very last minute she asked Ty (her boyfriend) to come along. They'd been a couple for about three months. Though I'd never met him, from everything she'd told me about him, I figured the two of them were really tight with each other. Some guys make better boyfriends than do others, and Sammy had described Ty as a cool guy. He sent her e-mails all the time while doing homework on the computer, and called her practically every night. He wrote her notes and put them in her pockets, books and other places where she would find them when she least expected it. He sat with her at lunch without being bashful like some guys are. And when there was a school dance, he bought the tickets. Stuff like that. Ty certainly sounded to me like a good boyfriend! I thought she was a lucky girl to have a boyfriend who really, really liked her.

So that's why I was so surprised that when the three of us met up at the entrance of the fair, there was an immediate attraction between Ty and me. Trying to calm down my fluttering heart, the moment we started walking I looked around to see if there was a stand where we could get some food. "Yum! Hamburgers on the grill," I said excitedly as we passed by one of the food stands. The moment I said that, I remembered that Sammy is a full-fledged vegetarian, strongly for PETA, and here I was, suggesting we eat meat! Immediately, Ty spoke up saying, "Awesome! They have elk burgers, too." I looked at Ty and he was grinning. We looked at each other, and as though we could read each other's mind, headed for that particular food stand.

So then Ty and I were ordering while Sammy chastised us for eating meat. As though he couldn't care less about her disgust over us eating meat, he said, "Two huge hamburgers, please." Then, while eating—Sammy, having french fries only—Ty chomps at the burger and says, "Oh man, nothing like red meat!" Personally, I thought his teasing her in that way was probably unnecessary, but I took it as flirting with her and just laughed along with him. As the three of us sat at the food stand, Ty commented that once, while on a trip to Florida with his parents, he'd tasted alligator meat. Well, I had a very similar experience when I'd been on a school trip and we'd visited an alligator farm. After the tour, we ate in the cafeteria, and it just so happened that alligator meat was on the menu. I ordered it. That both Ty and I had tried alligator meat seemed an interesting coincidence. "Alligator is really good," I said.

"It is. It's great. Better than chicken," Ty remarked. Sammy scrunched up her face and groaned, "Oh, gross!"

As we continued to talk, I discovered that Ty and I had a lot in common: We each had one brother and two sisters, and both of us were the oldest. We liked the same music; we both preferred casual to dressing up; and we both had the same kind of pet—a snake! We both played soccer and we're both Lutherans. That we were both so much alike was just incredible. We could have talked for hours. I'm not saying that Ty ignored Sammy. He was very affectionate toward her, and she toward him. Like when we would enter exhibits, he'd open the door for her or always ask if she wanted a Coke or ice cream or anything. Still, it seemed to me like they were mismatched. I mean, they didn't really talk between themselves.

We stayed at the fair for most of the afternoon and then left for home. On the way to Sammy's house I commented that my back was hurting. "Why does it hurt?" Ty asked. This prompted Sammy to tell him that I had done a flip on the trampoline in gym class and because I'd done it wrong, I'd wrenched my back. "I'll give you a back rub when we get to Sammy's house," Ty offered. And that's just what happened. Ty rubbed my shoulders, and because he was really strong, I commented, "You're really strong." Samantha picked right up on that and said, "Okay, enough for you. It's my turn." So Samantha and I traded places, and he started rubbing her shoulders.

Apparently, Sammy didn't appreciate his strong touch, because Ty had no more started massaging her shoulders when she complained that it was too hard. So then Sammy decided no more shoulder rubs and instead started to cuddle into him while sitting on the couch. He put his arm around her and cuddled back—but continued to look in my direction the whole time he was talking. He talked about how his brother had just gotten out of drug rehab and how worried he was for him because staying clean had been a real struggle. A friend of mine had just gotten out of rehab and I started talking about that. Once again, Ty and I were in a two-way conversation—with Samantha sitting quietly and not adding to the conversation.

Pretty soon I had to get home, and Ty offered to take me home. Samantha came along, of course. When we got to my house, I gave Samantha a hug and said good-bye to Ty. He gave me a quick hug, saying, "That was fun." Then he reached for me again and hugged me again—a hug that lasted a little longer than Sammy found comfortable. "C'mon, Ty," she prompted. "Let's go."

"Okay," he said, and then turning to me said, "Call me if you need to talk or anything." That was exactly what my heart wanted to do. I wanted to run into my room and dial him up the instant I thought he'd be home. Turning again to say good-bye to Samantha, I then saw the look of hurt in her eyes. It was clear that she understood that Ty had feelings for me. I had seen this look in her eyes one other time—the time her last boyfriend broke things off with her. And that's when everything registered for me. In that moment I realized that for the entire time the three of us had been together, Sammy had put up with the connection between Ty and me. Worse, her boyfriend had massaged my shoulders. It had to be an awful day for her!

I called her later that evening and apologized for talking so much to Ty. "Promise me you won't call him," she said. I gave her my word that I wouldn't—so I won't. Two weeks have passed, and so far I've kept my word. But I've still got really strong feelings for Ty. I'm hoping that Samantha and Ty break up. Still, I've decided that until the two of them break up, I'll just be patient. I do think it's just a matter of time until they do. But like I said, my heart also feels for Samantha knowing Ty and I "clicked" as we did. But a promise is a promise, and I'm not going to hurt my friend by "stealing" her boyfriend. I had that happen to me once, and I learned that to be betrayed by a best friend hurts more than does having someone leave you for another. I'll wait for Ty to come to me. It's just a matter of waiting on love.

Daniella Chopra, 15

"We've Got to Talk . . . NOW!"

Here's the thing about love: It makes you a bit crazy. Whether you've just fallen in love—or you've just been dumped—either way, you do and say some silly, and sometimes pretty stupid, things.

—Lindsey Rubia, 16

What was so important that my boyfriend of four months had given my best friend a note telling me to meet him "Right now, because we've got to talk"? I asked the teacher for a restroom pass and headed for the back hall where we always met up. As I watched my boyfriend approach me—looking his usual cool—I looked to see if he'd turn on his "puppy dog" look—something he always did when he saw me.

He didn't.

As hard as I tried not to feel insecure, I was. Was Dylan delivering good news—or not? We'd been a couple for four months, though the last few weeks hadn't gone so well. There had been the fight over Monica Green—which was her own fault because she had started a rumor that Dylan was breaking up with me. And Dylan and I had fought over his not calling three nights ago—as he'd promised. He'd been especially quiet the last two days. And just yesterday he stood me up rather than walking me to class. But most disturbing was that when I called his house last night, his mom said he couldn't come to the phone. That wasn't a good sign.

Trying to get a quick read on things, I noticed that Dylan was walking fast—and not smiling. What was he upset about? I tried to think positive. I smiled. I tried not to look as nervous as I was.

"Hi, honey!" I offered, reaching for his hand. He did not offer his.

"Lindsey," he said, not saying hello or asking how I was, "You've got to stop calling my house and stop writing me notes."

"But we always do," I said in self-defense.

"I know, but not again," he countered. "Things are over between you and me."

"What?" I asked, stunned and then stammered, "Why?"

"Because I have feelings for someone else."

Like that. Just like that. That's how things ended between us. He said he was sure things between us couldn't be "worked out." Well that made sense: He had "FEELINGS FOR SOMEONE ELSE"!

I was stunned. Blindsided is more like it. Surely this couldn't be happening. I looked into his eyes and knew he meant it. Four days ago—in the back row at the movies—he'd held my hand, played with my hair and kissed my neck. But that was four days ago! Can four days change things this fast? I demanded an explanation, of course! Impatient, and sensing a "scene," he told me to "relax" and that we could "still be friends." Friends? Friends? After four entire months of being boyfriend and girlfriend we were now going to be "friends"? Who tells these guys to say such stupid things? By now I was sobbing. But Dylan stood there as if the sun was shining. How could he? I was in tears, my heart ripped out. All our plans evaporated. What about our plans for the dance on Friday and the prom in the spring? We'd planned everything out, from how the color of the ribbon on his boutonniere would match the ribbon on my wrist corsage, to which couples we would ask to help share the expense of a limo.

What about all those plans—were they going to be "just friends," too? Can love be canceled so fast? How could all we had thought was so special about the two of us now be special only to me? Was I just another girl . . . like all the others I'd seen on his "photo wall"?

"Can I have my jacket back, please?" he asked. I was worried about our lives, and he was worried about his jacket? I was wearing it, so I ripped it off and as hard as I could I threw it at his feet. "Just take your bleeping jacket and get lost!" I screamed, stomping on his jacket.

"That's it! It's really, really over!" he said, making a point of using my being out of control as a reason his decision to leave was a good one. Calmly, obviously feeling vindicated, Dylan picked up his jacket, brushed it off and off he went. Into the sunset. I stood there. Feeling discarded. Devastated. Worse, I'd returned his letter jacket, and he'd probably give it to the new girl to wear.

That was a month ago. I'm better now. My heart doesn't hurt as much as it did in the first days and weeks. And I don't feel so panicky when I sometimes see Dylan in the halls—though I have to admit that it helps that the new girlfriend has already dumped him! Now she's the girlfriend of Dylan's best friend—which makes me feel even better.

I think about all this—how love comes and goes. I find it amazing that the heart feels so blessed when loves comes, and so devastated when it leaves. But here's the thing: It'll feel the same the next time around.

And here's something else I've discovered: There's no way around your feelings. You're going to have them. Whether you've just fallen in love or you've just been dumped, either way, you're going to do and say some silly, and sometimes pretty stupid, things. You won't get to decide how you feel; only your heart knows. All you can do is trust yourself to not get too bent out of shape about things. So that's where I'm at for now with the love thing. Hoping that each time when love comes—or goes (and knowing it will), I won't act too weird or crazy.

Lindsey Rubia, 16

Do You Love Me: Yes or No?

I love being in love! It's so much drama sometimes.

—Dana Giordano, 16

I love being in love! It's so much drama sometimes. There are really good times. And sometimes you have to prepare for a few days of tears. Not that I have everything figured out. But I'm learning a lot.

My first lesson in love was in the eighth grade. In English class, Billy Thornton passed me a note that read, "Do you like me? Circle 'yes' or 'no.'" Well, I didn't really know for sure. I'd never had a boyfriend. And I hadn't thought about Billy Thornton as a candidate to be my first one. But two of my friends had already had boyfriends, so I circled "yes," walked to the front of the room to sharpen my pencil and on the way past Billy's desk, dropped the note on his desk. That was how I came to have my first boyfriend.

Our being boyfriend and girlfriend was mostly a secret, though. From across the rows of desks in Mrs. Walton's class, Billy would clear his throat to get my attention. Then, with his eyes darting to and fro, he'd alert me to the fact that he had written me a note. It was my job to retrieve the note, which also meant that I had the sharpest pencils in class! Always, these notes were about what a "doad" the teacher was. But what else does one write about in eighth grade? That being my first experience with love, I thought it was romantic. One day Mrs. Walton caught on to our little game and confiscated a note. So that was the last of our romance, one that had lasted all of eleven school days.

For my next boyfriend, I moved on to Brandon Wilkerson. Brandon was my first kiss, my first dance and my first holding-hands sort of love. We had three classes together, which meant we could walk to class together and sit together in class if we were working on a group project. We even went to a dance, to a school play and to a baseball game together. It was great fun. Brandon was my sun, my moon and stars. Still, he frustrated me so much. He was argumentative and sometimes he would yell at me for no reason. That seemed like a really dumb thing to do with someone who is your girlfriend. So after three months of that I had to tell him I needed a better class of boyfriend.

My next experience with love came when I accepted a date to go to a dance with a really popular boy, Sid Metzler. For as cute as Sid was, we never really clicked. I think the reason was because my heart still belonged to Billy and Brandon. I was okay with it, though, because I could tell Sid was a little too experienced for me. He thought it was okay to put his hands on my butt when we danced, and that was a little scary to me.

In my next experience, I thought I hit the jackpot. One morning, standing at my locker with a group of friends, this incredible guy walked over and started talking to my friends. But he kept looking at me, so I knew he was checking me out. His name was Luis Michael Bustillos. He was two grades ahead of me, which is why I'd never seen him up close. We instantly clicked and instantly became an item. Each and every morning we would meet up in the student center and just sit and stare into each other's eyes. All day long we'd write each other notes and pass them off to each other. It was so wonderful. Because of him, I learned what "love at first sight" feels like. It's totally wonderful, and I recommend it highly. But on the morning of our third week as "an item," he replaced me with a girl in his own class. So that was that. I cried and cried. It was the first time I'd cried over love gone wrong.

So then I decided to give love a rest. Or at least that's the way things turned out. For one full school year I had a real dry spell as far as boys were concerned. Luckily, summer changed my luck. What happened was, a friend had invited me to her barbecue party. I'd been dancing and decided to get some food. I loaded up my plate, and while looking around for a place to sit, spotted Billy Thornton sitting by the firepit. He was staring at me. He motioned for me to come join him, and I went over and sat next to him. We sat there together for the next full hour—talking about everything under the stars! He asked me if he could drive me home, and since I'd come with friends, I said yes. Once to my house, we sat in the car and talked for almost another whole hour. If my dad hadn't flipped the porch light on and off several times, we'd probably still be there! Then, the minute Billy got to his house, we talked to each other by e-mail for another half hour. It was so much fun. That weekend he asked me over to his house to help him wash his car. After that, we watched a corny movie, snuggling on his futon. Right in the middle of the movie, I instinctively kissed him as I turned my head. It was so beautiful, because that kiss told us how each felt about the other. We both knew true love had struck.

The next weekend we went to the movies and then we went for a pizza. The next Friday he invited me to watch a Josh Groban concert on television with his family. The weekend after that he came to watch me sing in a choir concert. He'd driven me there, and just before we got out of the car, he reached in the backseat to get the flowers he'd brought me. There were two white roses and a red one. The card read, "Do you love me? 'Yes' or 'no?'"

"Definitely!" I answered. I just love it when a guy steals your heart! Well, that was six months ago. I'm still in love and I expect to feel this way about Billy Thornton for the rest of my life!

Dana Giordano, 16

That Was Your "Sister"?—Yeah, Right!

I guess I'd classify the kind of love I'm in as the "puppy love" version, because it wore off faster than lip gloss in a kissing contest.

—Tina Convoy, 14

My first experience with love was when I was twelve. His name was Adam Morgan. We weren't really in love, though I thought so at the time. But it was not the kind of love where nothing else in the entire world matters. It was not the kind of love where you can think of nothing all day and night long but that one person. Two of my friends are in love that way, and from talking to them, it sounds like the best kind of love to have. So comparing the kind of love I was in with Adam Morgan to the kind my friends had, I guess I'd classify mine as the "puppy love" version, because it wore off faster than lip gloss in a kissing contest. Still, I was happy with Adam while it lasted.

The big problem between Adam and me had mostly to do with his splitting his time between his parents. His parents were divorced and living in different towns. His dad lived in my town, but his mom lived twenty miles away. Adam lived with his mom during the week and attended school there, and then spent weekends with his father. I got to see Adam only on the weekends. This meant we were apart all week. He didn't have a computer, so we couldn't e-mail each other during the week. And after racking up a huge long-distance phone bill in the first week we met, neither of our parents would allow us to call the other again. So when we got together on the weekends, it was like we had to start all over again, from nerves to not knowing what to say. Still, I happily considered him my boyfriend.

One Sunday afternoon as we were playing miniature golf, the bomb dropped. We were having a good time, laughing and sharing a Coke from the same can, when Adam told me he loved me. I think he was scared the moment he said these words. I don't think he planned on saying them. I think they just slipped out of his mouth because we were having such a good time. Probably, he should have said, "I like being with you," or something like that. To tell you the truth, "I love you" freaked me out a little, too, because I didn't know what was supposed to happen next.

What did happen was that Adam began to act weird. Like the next weekend we were supposed to hang out at the mall and play games in the arcade. Because he was an hour late, I called his house. A girl answered the phone. "I need to talk to Adam," I said wondering who the girl was. "Adam can't come to the phone," she said and hung up on me. That made me mad, so I called back and demanded, "Put Adam on the phone!"

"Oh, you again," she said, adding, "Don't you have homework to do or something?" Again she hung up. I pressed redial and waited for someone to answer. On the three-hundredth ring Adam answered. "Yeah, what?" he asked, obviously irritated. "Who was that girl who answered the phone?" I demanded. "My sister," he said and then sort of laughed. I could hear laughter in the background, so I knew it wasn't just him and his "sister." So then I started to get paranoid because I'm pretty sure Adam does not have a sister. At least he never told me he did. We always talked about his family and he never once mentioned anything about a sister. And you just don't forget to say you've got a sister! So I felt really strange about things. "You're late! Come pick me up right now!" I demanded.

"Hey, I can't get over there today," he said all too coolly. "I'll talk to you next weekend." Then he hung up.

I sat there with the phone still to my ear listening to the dial tone for nearly a minute. Then I just bawled. Fifteen minutes later, feeling really mad, I called his house again. Once again his "sister" answered. "Tell Adam I'm dumping him," I told her and then hung up. But the moment I hung up, I called right back and blurted, "And tell Adam I think he's a real jerk." I hung up again and cried some more.

I had no way to get to his dad's house or I would have gone over. But since I couldn't get there, I just waited until the next weekend, knowing he'd call. He didn't. So I called him. "Have you been cheating on me?" I blurted. "Yeah, sure," he laughed. "I'm going steady with Britney Spears!"

"Yeah, right," I said. "In your dreams!" So I hung up knowing I had to dump him for good. So that was the end of my first love, my puppy love. I hurt for a long time over that. So what that shows is that even puppy love, when it's over, is a painful thing. Next time, I'm going to skip the puppy love kind and go for something better. I'm new at this, but my friends tell me it doesn't matter if it's your first or last love, because you "Win a few and lose a few, but you have to suit up for them all." So I've decided not to be bitter. I'll just take this in stride and when the next love comes along, I'll "suit up" again! One thing is for sure: I'm going to choose someone who doesn't live out of the city, because it's too hard to keep an eye on him! And one of the first things I'm going to ask him is the names and ages of all his sisters.

Tina Convoy, 14

"I Dare You to Ask Him to Dance . . ."

If you think you know everything there is to know about love, love will prove you wrong!

—Alaina Ramey, 14

I had just dumped my boyfriend of four months and was feeling really lousy. When my friends suggested I go with them to the Valentine's Day Sweetheart Dance at school, I said no. But Christine, Bethy, Tamara, Lindsey, Meredith, Jennifer and Holly talked me into going. So I did.

Not long after we got there, Bethy dared me to go up to Justin Latta—the most popular boy at school—and ask him to dance with me. "No, way. You're totally crazy!" I told her.

Justin is the coolest guy in the universe, and everyone knows it. Even he knows it! There is no way I was fool enough to do something so stupid! My friends and I pretty much just all stood around and talked about the couples dancing. Some of my friends got asked to dance, and sometimes they just danced with each other, especially if a great tune was played. About a half-hour into the dance, still not one single person had asked me to dance, which I pretty much expected. Practically everyone likes my ex-boyfriend, so it's not like they want to be seen asking his former girlfriend to dance. Besides, some kids didn't even know my boyfriend and I had broken up, so they weren't about to ask me to dance, either. I just knew my being there was a hopeless cause.

But my friends convinced me to stay anyway. Then Lindsey came up with the bright idea that she was going to go around to ask if there was anyone who might like to dance with me. I was mortified and begged her not to. She went anyway. I watched as she made her way through the crowd, asking a zillion boys—all of whom obviously said "no." Then she got to Justin Latta. I thought I would die! Well, soon I see Justin looking in my direction, and I'm thinking he's going to die laughing. But no, he starts walking in my direction. "I didn't know you'd broken up with Seth," he said to me. "I can't say that I'm sorry to hear that! Would you like to dance?"

I thought I was going to faint. I reached out and took his hand, and he led me onto the dance floor. We were the very last couple to leave the dance! We've been dating now for seventeen days. So if you think you know everything there is to know about love, love will prove you wrong! I'm betting there isn't one person in the entire universe who can say she knows everything there is to know about love.

Alaina Ramey, 14

The Grim Reaper

They say you never forget your first love. I'm sure of it.

—Shire Feingold, 16

The room was pitch-black. Standing in the dark, I listened as the door creaked open ever so slowly. Then, like a comet, something swooshed into the pitch-black room. All I could hear was the flapping of wings as tiny creatures—like bats or something—screeched loudly. Frozen in my tracks, I then heard a blood-curdling scream followed by my little sister's "Little Bo Peep" dress ruffling along the ground. The scream made her scream and then call out, "Oh my God! It's a skeleton!" In the same instant something grabbed my foot. I screamed and jumped back, almost tripping over my floor-length yellow Renaissance dress. Then someone grabbed my arm. It was too strong to be my sister. Terrified, and fighting it off, I strained to see who could possibly be gripping my arm.

This was the most fun haunted house ever!

As the lights came up, I saw all the commotion was caused by the Grim Reaper! And then came the apology: "I am so sorry to have scared you. Are you okay?" At this I started laughing!

His name was Michele. We walked outside, found a seat and started talking. Anything to be together. I could just feel the chemistry between us. We didn't move for the next half hour. In that time we'd covered so many topics, everything from school to our love for music; from writing to sports; and from friends to family. All this time together—and not one awkward moment. It was amazing! Well, there was one disturbance—Little Bo Peep—my little sister kept coming over to me wanting me to take her back into the haunted house. I tried to fend her off, telling her everything from "Little Bo Peep, go find your sheep" to "Bryce, Dad is looking for you" (it was a family-style party). Finally, my dad came to the rescue, and Michele and I were alone again.

Michele had still not removed his mask. I couldn't help wondering what he looked like, and yet I didn't want to ask him to remove it. "What a great buffet," he said. "Let's get some food." So we went from table to table, loading up our plates, finally returning to our spot to eat. And that's when Michele reached up to remove his mask. I held my breath, hoping he'd be good-looking. He was! Under that mask was the most amazing face! I was mesmerized!

The haunted house was emptying out and Michele asked me if I wanted to talk somewhere "more private." He said I looked cold, and so he put his arm around me. We walked over to the porch, away from the crowd. As we stood talking, I felt like a princess in a fairy tale: me standing there with my Prince Charming, my long hair and flowing dress just blowing in the wind. The moon was out. The stars were twinkling. It was just so romantic. Then as a slow song came on from indoors, Michele asked me to dance. Dancing close, he leaned down and kissed me. Giddy just by being in his arms, I just stood there holding my breath. Even after the song had ended, we both stood there swaying back and forth. Neither of us wanted to let the other out of our arms. So that was my first experience with love. I'd never known the definition of "romance"—until this night. But surely this was it. For me, it was better than any romance novel I'd ever read; better than any love movie I'd ever seen.

But just as the song ended, so did this night. I've never seen Michele again. But I'll never forget him. They say you never forget your first love. I'm sure of it.

Shire Feingold, 16

They Call Us "The Cutest Couple at School"

He was the model boyfriend: smart, friendly and courteous.

—Tara Cutshaw, 18

In my junior year my family moved from Palm Springs to Washington State, then to Carlsbad, California, where I finally settled into yet a third high school. With no friends—once again—I was lonely and, quite frankly, really tired of being the "new girl." I was really looking forward to having friends, and a boyfriend! Everyone, it seemed, had love in their lives. I didn't even have friends, except for my sister—who was not only in love, but engaged and getting married!

As soon as I settled in this new school, I looked around to see if any of the boys had potential. There were a few, but wouldn't you know all the good-looking ones were taken! Always on the lookout for love, I couldn't help but notice a couple who seemed absolutely perfect for each other. Peter and Janis were so cute together. Everyone liked them and referred to them as "the cutest couple at school." Whenever I saw either of them, sure enough, there was the other. Janis was adorable, but Peter, well, not only was Peter nice looking, but he was the model boyfriend: smart, friendly and courteous.

So Peter became my ideal. I really wanted a boyfriend like Peter. But I knew I'd have to "pay my dues." How was I going to find my Prince Peter Charming if I didn't get involved in school activities? So I started being "social." This led to my going out with Michael, a really nice guy, but well, it was more boring than watching grass grow. I did go out a few times with other guys, but my heart never really came along.

The year came to an end—and surprisingly, so did Peter and Janis's relationship.

My senior year started and I began dating someone who was really nice, but I couldn't get Peter off my mind. Much to my surprise, Peter was in three of my classes. We got to know each other and started talking. A really good friend of mine, Jodie, was best friends with Peter (I'm pretty sure she secretly had a crush on him), but luckily, she had met a new guy, Nathan, and the two of them really clicked. As it turned out, Nathan was also a really good friend of Peter's. This was just great because it meant the four of us could hang out together and really enjoy our time together as a foursome. Jodie talked to Peter about me, and I talked to Nathan about Jodie, and everything was going well. For the homecoming dance, Peter asked me and Nathan asked Jodie at the same time. That's when things started to heat up. To make a long story short, Peter and I have been going out for a while now. Nathan and Jodie are still going out, too! If someone were to tell me oh-so-many months ago that my boyfriend was going be Peter, I would never have believed it.

We're getting ready to graduate now and know that the future—and the way we feel about each other—is something we have to discuss. What we've decided is that we hope to be in each other's lives, if not forever, then at least for a long, long time. Peter wants to go to a college out of state, and I want to stay home and attend a college here in town for a few years then possibly transfer somewhere closer to him. I hope that our love will last our lifetimes. I feel that it can. But I also know that the years ahead will have their challenging times as well. I talk with friends who are in college, and many of them have been through the situation I'm facing. Not too many relationships survive when couples go to separate schools. So I know it will be hard. Still, my heart tells me that I am willing to do what I can to see if our relationship can be a forever one. Only time will tell. I do know that I've never cared for anyone so much before.

So that's my experience with "true love." I couldn't have been more surprised by "who" came into my life. Nor could I have been more surprised by how much we loved, and cared for and about each other. But love is that way; you really don't know what is in store for you. And that's the exciting part. You just have to believe that love will come into your life—even if you don't know when. Once there, you have to trust that there is a reason for its being—even if in the beginning you aren't exactly sure what that is. And you have to trust that however it transforms—however it changes—you will be accepting of it. In the end, I believe, you just have to treat it like a gift, a gift that comes from a sacred place. And sometimes that is enough. As for Peter and me, we trust that whatever the future holds is right for the two of us.

Tara Cutshaw, 18

Undercover

When someone says she has eyes only for you, but then flirts with someone else, that's not a good sign.

—Geoff Granbury, 18

I wish I could say that my first experience with loving someone was totally spectacular, but I can't. In fact, it turned out to be the most awful experience in my life so far. Worse, I've been jailed as a result.

I found a wonderful girl when I was sixteen. I had never had a girlfriend, but this particular girl showed a lot of interest in me. Every time I noticed her she was looking at me. And always she smiled at me so sweetlike. So I knew she was very interested. This gave me the courage to ask her out. About one month into going out, we were standing in line at the movies when I caught her looking at another guy. She saw that I noticed and quickly reassured me that I was her guy. Her only guy. "I only have eyes for you," she said. That sounded real good to me. I fell madly in love with her.

We dated for a couple of months, and it seemed to me that we were a happy couple. But maybe it was all in my mind. I guess I didn't see it coming, because one day right in front of me, she flirted with someone else. I tried not to be jealous, but it really upset me. When someone says she "only has eyes for you" and then flirts with someone else, that's not a good sign. Within the next couple of weeks, she did this a lot. It was like she no longer cared if it hurt my feelings or not. I wondered what was up, so I started watching her more closely. That's when I discovered that she was into smoking pot. I confronted her about it and she admitted it. I had never done drugs, so I told her that she had to stop or else I'd break up with her. "Whatever," she said, like she didn't care one way or the other. I didn't want to lose her, so I told her she could smoke, but not around me. Well, because I didn't break things off as I had threatened, she knew that I was "okay" about her smoking. So then she smoked in front of me whenever she wanted. It bothered me but I said nothing—because I didn't want to lose her.

One day when we were standing in line at the movies she saw a friend of hers also in line. She called him out of line and together they went to stand beside a parked car where they lit up a reefer. I went over. It was obvious the two of them knew each other very well. I guess I was feeling insecure because when she held out the reefer to me, I took it.

Feeling like I'd lose her if I didn't do pot, I started smoking pot, too. Then, because we were smoking together, it suddenly became my responsibility to have it on hand for us. Never having done drugs, I didn't know where to buy the stuff. So I asked around to some of the potheads at school. Well, though I didn't know it, the school had an undercover narcotics agent posing as a student. My search for buying pot led to him, and buying some pot one day from him got me arrested. Due to the amount I was buying, and the fact that I had solicited pot from the agent for the fourth time, I was sentenced to twenty-two months in jail. I've since served sixteen months of that time. My girlfriend instantly left me. I assume she took up with the guy she smoked with in the parking lot.

I'd like to say that because of her not sticking by me while I'm in here that I just turned off my feelings for her. While I'm really disappointed that she could so coolly leave me (to say nothing of how mad I am at myself for making the decision to smoke pot in the first place!), my heart has not shut her out. I'm still not over her. Some days are better than others. On some days I'm jealous and upset and disgusted and just plain mad at her (and me!) for smoking pot in the first place. Other days I just long to talk to her and even ask her to please come back and be my girl. But I won't. And I know she wouldn't, even if I asked her to. So I'm here serving time. And all because I didn't think about what I was doing.

So what I've learned about love is that it's all too easy to do stupid things in the name of love. Still, those first months she and I had together were the sweetest I've ever known. So much so that it is what I'll look for again when I'm ready to find new love. For now, I've got to take care of myself and try to complete my education credits so I don't screw up my life ever again. Time for a little "self-love" as they say!

Geoff Granbury, 18

He Said I Was "Beautiful"

What is love? Is it an overused word or one of life's best-kept, yet sweetest, mysteries?

—Lia Sardo, 18

Many of my friends had been lucky to find love; I only stood on the outside waiting for it to happen to me. Then one day someone did notice me! From across the room, a certain special someone noticed me. He looked at me as if I were the only girl in the room.

We began dating. Love, I discovered, is a truly awesome feeling. Everything in life changes. When I was with him—or even thought about him—the sun came out and the moon was always full. Stuff like that. For me, the feeling was even grander than the outer world suddenly being filled with sunshine, blooming flowers and shooting stars. I felt alive, too. The feeling was indescribable, other than to say that it felt as though there was nothing I couldn't do, which is a powerful feeling. What I especially liked was that before love, I was in the "hoping seat"—hoping that someone would want me to be his girl. But once someone had expressed an interest in me, finally the roles changed. I was wanted, and I was the one who had the power to choose, or not! I was the one who could let our feelings grow and become something—or not.

Well, I guess I really didn't have all the power, because within no time, his love totally captivated me and I melted. But who wouldn't? Love is totally fun! One beautiful thing after another. Always the phone ringing and it's for you—how long do you wait for that? Making plans for the Saturday coming up—how cool! Going out to dinner—how romantic! "You're soooooo beautiful," he told me one spectacular evening. To hear these enticing words was such an aphrodisiac! Always, always things that just swept me off my feet.

Perhaps my mind did a meltdown along with my heart, because did I bother to think he was only a poet with great words and a way with looks? No. We were in love and nothing like that could ever happen! Cupid had found and blessed me! The only thing I cared about was being his—and his alone.

But slowly his feelings of love for me dwindled. And one gloomy day, they went away. The phone calls stopped. The gazes that were once just for me began to drift around. What was happening? Had love come and gone so quickly? Was what we had all in my head: Was it merely lovely lines or worse, candy-coated lies? I discovered the answer as I watched him use the same approach to manipulate love's next victim. Off he went, making her feel special and loved. All this leaves me asking, what is love? Is it an overused word or is it one of life's best-kept, yet sweetest, mysteries? The answer, I've discovered, is both—which means that I'm available once again. I am, once again, waiting for love to come knocking. But I'm a veteran now; I'm no longer standing on the outside. I know the feel of love.

Lia Sardo, 18

All It Took Was a Smile

Once you've felt the power of love, you're sure that no one should ever be without it.

—Alison Hudak, 15

At the dinner table two years ago, my parents announced "we" were going to adopt a baby. I wasn't quite sure why we were doing this. There were already three kids in my family. Why would my parents want another kid? It wasn't like they couldn't have children of their own. It was my mother's idea. She'd found out about international adoptions from a lady at work. She thought about it, and that was that. So "we" were going to adopt a little girl from China.

I was flabbergasted! Mad, too. And really upset at my mother. I didn't want to have someone in my family who wasn't really a part of my family. I told my mother so, too. She said we wouldn't be getting the little girl for a year or so, so there would be plenty of time to think about things. *Thank God,* I thought! But within no time, we received a picture of the "new sister." I didn't mean to judge, but I thought she was very strange-looking. She had a large head and huge eyes that seemed cross-eyed. I told my mom that at least we should pick a prettier kid, and this isn't the one we want. She ignored me and sent word that the baby known as Qin Li Chun would now be Kara Qin Li Hudak. I was going to have a Chinese sister.

Then, we were notified that my mom had been picked to go on the next trip to China. My whole family and even some of my extended family went with her to the airport to send Mom off and wish her a safe trip. Not me! I was still totally opposed to this whole thing! I pleaded and pleaded with my dad to stay home. More than a year had passed since the "family announcement," but I still didn't want this baby. Everyone knew this. I had informed everyone that this was a really stupid idea, and that we'd all be sorry we were actually doing this. Over and over, Mom tried to "warm" me to the idea and said that in time, she hoped I'd be excited about it—like everyone else was. I was certain I'd never be okay with it! Dad said if that was my choice, I could stay home.

It was nice to have Mom gone on the trip. It was a really fun time because Dad was very lenient and we got away with things—like not doing our chores or cleaning our rooms. Then reality hit! Mom called, and I could hear "Kara" screaming in the background. I told my mom that if that was the kid she was bringing home, she should reconsider because already it sounded like the huge mistake I knew it was. But she "retrieved" this kid. And she did bring her home! This time I tagged along with the family to get her from the airport. I was excited to see Mom, not excited to meet my new ten-month-old "sister." When I saw Mom, I hugged her. I only looked at the baby, but I didn't want to hold it. Right away I could tell Kara was "her" baby, and that was all she cared about at that very moment. I thought Mom didn't have enough time to split between three kids. How could she ever do it with four? I knew that this baby, being an infant and also adopted, would get all the attention from everyone around her. I disliked this kid even more—if that was possible! To me, she was simply a total intrusion on my family.

Kara didn't say a peep in the first half hour we met her. But that's the only time this girl would ever be quiet again. The moment we put her in that car seat, she screamed, and I mean screamed. I've never heard anything so piercing in my life. I put my hood up and tried best to think of a happy place and what life was like before this terror was brought here.

Things went downhill from there. Kara was the most annoying creature that God had put on the planet. She was ALWAYS crying about something or another. She had no clue what we were saying, of course, because she didn't speak English. I wanted absolutely nothing to do with the child. I wouldn't play with her or hold her. If my mom needed help, I would try to get out of it any way I could. My mom was so disappointed in me that I was being this way and not accepting my new sister. It seemed to me that the new baby took over our family. It was Kara this, Kara that. One day, I couldn't take it anymore. I sat in my room and just cried and cried. I even prayed. "God," I pleaded, "pleeeeease make things better, because I can't stand the way things are!"

I guess you could say my prayers were answered—though not in the way I expected. I mean, the adoption agency didn't recall this crying creature, nor did my parents tire of loving or soothing her. School was out, so I was home a lot more. One day, as I was sitting in my room, Kara came dashing in, bear-hugged my legs and then, looking up at me, gave me the biggest smile. It was just so evident that she totally loved me. I totally melted right then and there. Suddenly, like a flash of lightning, I just loved her. I can't even account for the change in me. But that's all it took. The hug and huge smile changed my entire attitude toward her. In that moment, I just fell in love with a little girl who had come halfway around the world to have a family to call her own.

I've become a sister to Kara. She is my baby, my baby sister, and I love her.

I now realize how Kara is blessed to have us take her in. But we are so blessed by her presence. All this makes me love my mother even more. If it weren't for her, Kara might still be in an orphanage with no family to call her own. My mother—her heart big enough to love even more than three children—had reached out to a little child who didn't deserve to be alone. I criticized my mom for doing this "stupid" thing, when in fact she had brought a little angel to our home. Mom had created a miracle for this little girl. And it's become one for us, as well.

Someday, I would like to adopt a child. I'm sure of it. The

sense of love and satisfaction of helping someone who needs a home is a beautiful feeling beyond description. Yes, Kara is a lucky little girl that she has a home. But I am even luckier to have a sister as special as Kara. Love is like that. Once you've felt the power of love, you're sure that no one should ever be without it. Everyone needs someone to love them in the way I've learned to love my little sister. My mother has given our family the chance to learn this. Thank you, Mom.

Alison Hudak, 15

AUTHORS' NOTE: *When Alison sent us her story, she was so proud of her "new" little sister that she included a picture of Kara. Alison, like your mother and family, you've discovered the truest essence of what it means to be a taste berry in the life of another. You are cool, caring and courageous!*

The Day I Fell in Love—for Real

Seeing how people are fickle creatures, waiting for someone to say "I love you" so as to feel loved and lovable, is limited thinking. You've got to be your own number-one love.

—Diana Seretis, 16

"Diana! Diana! DIANA!!!!!" My eyes flew open and tried to adjust to the light covering every single inch of my stark white-walled room. "What? Who? Huh? Okay! Okay—I'm up!" It was 7:45 A.M. and I was going to be late for school—again. As I stumbled into the shower with the warm water running over my face, I can remember thinking, "Oh no. Another day of school. Same old, same old. BORING!"

I got into my car, put on the most "rev me up" CD I could find and blasted it the whole way to school. Surely by then I'd be awake. I got to school a bit late (okay, so that's an understatement!) and practically ran to my first-period class, Algebra II (loads of fun at eight in the morning!). Groggy and not all that interested in math at eight in the morning, I took no notice of anyone in the class or the fact that they were looking at me a tad weird—because this was a Diana they'd not seen before. Not only was I a half hour late, but also my hair was soaking wet and not combed. This from a girl with the best hair in the entire school! On this day, I was in jeans and a sweatshirt. I had no makeup on—"highly unusual," considering I could never go ANYWHERE without full-scale makeup. Always self-conscious, I always looked my very best. In fact, my life revolved around looking good. Everyone expected it from me. And I never let them down.

So here I am, sitting in class, wet hair, no makeup, ordinary clothes. I had to think about that. So would everyone stop liking me and thinking I was a nice person? No. Would they think I was no longer smart or funny? No. Hey, I'm running late: I have wet hair and no makeup—so? I am not my wardrobe; I am not my makeup. Yes, I love all those things, but they no longer define me!

As Louise Hay says, "Loving ourselves works miracles in our lives." How true that is. And on this day, I "got it"—what it means to be "comfortable in your own skin." And for some reason, everything fell into place. I was going to stop working so hard at fitting someone else's ideal. It was one of the most liberating days in my life. Seeing how people are fickle creatures, always waiting for someone else to say "I love you" so as to feel loved and lovable, is limited thinking and not such a good plan. You've got to be your own number-one love. Always, you want someone to love you, that's for sure. But I don't need someone to say "I love you" in order for me to feel loved. I'm over that limited thinking. Finally, I know what "true" love means. Finally, I've fallen in love with myself. And it's a totally awesome and comforting feeling.

Diana Seretis, 16

Teen Talk: My Experience with Love . . .

How Do You Know—for Sure—If It's Love at First Sight?

Monica Wells, 15: My girlfriend and I were driving around and she needed gas. We turned into a 7–11. While she pumped gas, I went into the store to get us Cokes. A cute guy was in the checkout lane in front of me, fumbling in his pockets for money. Either he was short a dime or he was flirting, because when he noticed me behind him, he smiled really nice and then asked, "Do you by chance have a dime I can borrow?" My heart fluttering, I dug around the bottom of my purse for a dime, found one and handed it over. He paid for his things and then handed me a pen and his receipt saying, "Give me your phone number. Maybe we can hang out sometime." "Sure, okay," I said, happily writing down my name and number for him. "Great!" he said, smiling. It wasn't until I'd watched him disappear from sight that I realized in my nervousness, I'd forgotten to ask him his name. For the next week I waited by the phone. No call. Two weeks passed—still no call. Four weeks later, still no call. I've even gone back to that same 7–11 hoping I'd see him, but haven't. So that's it. Short and sweet. Well, short at least. I don't recommend waiting by the phone, especially when you don't even know the name of the person you're expecting a call from. I'm not sure if what I felt was "love at first sight," or if it was just my imagination. I do know, however, that the experience was worth the ten cents!

No Matter What Your Age, Being Dumped Hurts

Crane Adams, 17: I never really knew how much it hurt to be "left" until a girlfriend of five months dumped me. Man, did my heart hurt. In fact, it just ached. So that got me to thinking about how my mother must have felt when my dad left her for another woman. When that happened, Mom cried and cried. I was really upset, too, but my feelings were more about anger than tears. Not having any experience in "losing" at love prior to when my girlfriend left me, I'd say that I really couldn't empathize with my mom as she went through the separation and divorce ordeal. It might even be fair to say that I was angry with her—thinking if she'd done something different, then she and Dad wouldn't be splitting up. But looking back, now that I know what a broken heart feels like, I can see that my mother was heartbroken. And what a terrible time that must have been for her. Because now I do know how that feels. So that's probably the biggest lesson I've learned about love: how it hurts to have your heart broken. But what I don't understand is how someone can leave a person he once loved so passionately. I mean, how is it possible to fall out of love so fast? Just one week before my girlfriend left me, she told me she loved me. And I'm positive that my parents must have been very much in love at one time. So what I least understand about love is why it's not a more permanent thing. I mean, if you chose someone for all the right reasons, then why can't it last? If love is really that fickle, then how can you ever know for sure if you're choosing the right person? One thing is for sure: No matter what your age, it hurts when love ends.

What Proof Do You Have That He Loves You?

Jalette Daye, 17: What I've learned about love is that you can give away too much of yourself. It's been my experience that when you do that, it changes things—and not always for the best. As a result of trusting someone's words, "I love you," I went too far. I'd never do that again. I believe that a few guys—not all guys—will say almost anything to get you to go all the way with them. I think that when a guy tells you he loves you, before you fall head-over-heels in love with him, you should make him prove he loves you. Ask him to ask you for a date (as opposed to just meeting him somewhere). Ask him to pick you up from your house and to ask your parents what time they expect him to bring you home. However he responds will be good "proof" of how much he loves you. Try it. You'll see.

What Does It Mean When a Girl Calls You a "Bad Boyfriend"?

Danny Power, 16: A girl I really liked and thought was special told me I was a "bad boyfriend." I don't know what that means. Nor do I have any idea what I did (or didn't do) to deserve being labeled as such. I don't want to be a bad boyfriend, but what is a "bad boyfriend"? I did ask her, but she told me if I had to ask, I was "too dense" and therefore not worth the explanation. So the next girlfriend I had I treated really, really nice. I wanted to make sure I did everything just right. After going out for two months, she told me I was really boring. So I'm confused. I'd say that right now I'm not exactly sure how girls want a guy to act, but I want to know. Right now I don't have a girlfriend—but I want one. Probably I should get girls figured out first—which is a difficult thing to do because they all act so differently. So I'd say I don't really understand love just yet. Or maybe I just don't understand girls.

Love Can Complicate Your Life

Maria Diona, 17: I'm in love. I consider my boyfriend my high-school sweetheart. I've been going out with him since I was a freshman. My parents like him, and his parents like me. Having a boyfriend definitely has its advantages and disadvantages. It's great to feel you love someone and to know that person loves you. Even so, I sometimes I think I am too young to be committed to one person. I think a relationship is a lot of work. Even though I can't imagine being without my boyfriend, it sort of scares me that I depend on him to make me happy. Like when I'm without him, I feel unhappy. Or if we have an argument, then my heart aches and I'm sad, and feel incredibly out of balance. But I also find that even being as much in love as I am makes me feel "out of balance." I find myself really wanting to be with my boyfriend, and then when I do spend a lot of time with him, I feel like I need some space. And having a boyfriend doesn't mean your loneliness goes away. Sometimes I feel lonely—even when I'm with him. And what else troubles me is that I want him to want to date just me—still, I sometimes want to date others. But I don't want him to be free to date others. So what I've learned most about love is that it is not the answer to everything. That's a real eye-opener because when everyone has a boyfriend except you, you think that everyone is happier and has a better time than you. But then you get a boyfriend, and you find that while, yes, it's wonderful to be in love, it's only one thing—and not your whole life. Does that make sense? I guess I'm saying that I thought when I had a boyfriend, life would be better. It's not. In fact, I'd say having a boyfriend makes things complicated.

Being Shy Puts a Damper on Breaking Into the Social Scene

Tammara McNamara, 14: I'm really shy; it's just my nature. I do think it may be one big reason that I don't have a boyfriend. Maybe if I were a little more outgoing I would attract a boyfriend. But until I learn to be outgoing, it's probably not going to happen. So what I've learned about love is that it doesn't always come knocking on your door. You have to look and act like someone who is wanting to have someone in your life. So that's what I'm working on: looking for ways to be more friendly and social. I've decided that since I'm shy, rather than making boys my number-one priority, I'd start by making more friends with girls. My strategy is that with girlfriends to hang out with, the boys will follow. So then I'll work on being more friendly and outgoing with them. I haven't made much headway on my plan yet, because I still don't really know how to approach girls, either. But at least it's a goal. My bigger goal is to be breaking into the social scene with boys at least a good month before the prom!

The Love of My Life . . . Is Here with Me Now

Rachel Garza, 16: It's amazing what we'll do for love. Like everyone else, I wanted to be in love. When I was dating, I worried about being cool enough. How's my hair? My weight? My clothes? Now my priorities have changed; now I have more important things to worry about. Today I worry about my one-year-old son and our future. I don't go to every football game, and I'm not trying out for the cheerleading squad. I'm not into the latest fashion. In fact, these days most of the clothes I buy aren't for me; they're for my little son. I'm not looking for a party to go to on the weekend. I'm changing diapers, doing my homework and applying to colleges. I know that it's up to me to set a good example for my son. While others my age are looking for love, I'm at home caring for someone I love. Five years from now, no one in my class will care how I styled my hair or remember what I wore to what. My son, however, will always remember how hard I worked to provide a good life for him. He will know that his mom has a college degree, and she is why he has a good life and a safe place to live. Love, for me, is about the quality of future I can create for my son and me. What I've learned about love is that when you know what it is, really, you'll be absolutely responsible for every single one of your actions. Until then, you can't call it love. I'd like to tell you a little more, but I can't right now. The love of my life is crying; responsibility calls.

A Hickey Is Not an Indication You're Going Steady

Ronda LaMont, 15: "You should be totally ashamed of yourself," my mother said when she discovered the hickeys all over my neck as I was leaving for school. I was embarrassed that she saw them—but I was in love and so the hickeys were my badge of honor. So what if I'd only known the great kisser all of two hours—a boy from another school who I'd hooked up with after meeting at the concession stand at the football game. The next day, immediately after school, I raced home to phone the love of my life. "Who?" he asked, and, "Where'd I meet you?" When I reminded him where we'd met, he said, "Oh." I told him how excited I would be to see him again, and he said simply, "Look, please don't call here again. It ties up the fax line." I always heard there were "consequences" to love, but I don't remember feeling lower than dirt was one of them. I've discovered that just because someone is willing to give you hickeys may not mean that he's thinking of going steady.

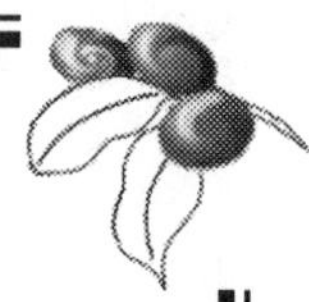

Part 2

Teen Poetry Contest: You Pick the $100 Winner!

When power narrows the areas of man's concern, poetry reminds him of the richness and diversity of his existence. When power corrupts, poetry cleanses.

—John F. Kennedy

Poetry is the suggestion by the imagination of noble grounds for the noble emotions.

—John Ruskin

A poet is a nightingale, who sits in darkness and sings to cheer its own solitude with sweet sounds.

—Percy Bysshe Shelley

Poetry is the opening and closing of a door, leaving those who look through to guess about what is seen during a moment.

—Carl Sandburg

We make out of the quarrel with others, rhetoric; but of the quarrel with ourselves, poetry.

—W. B. Yeats

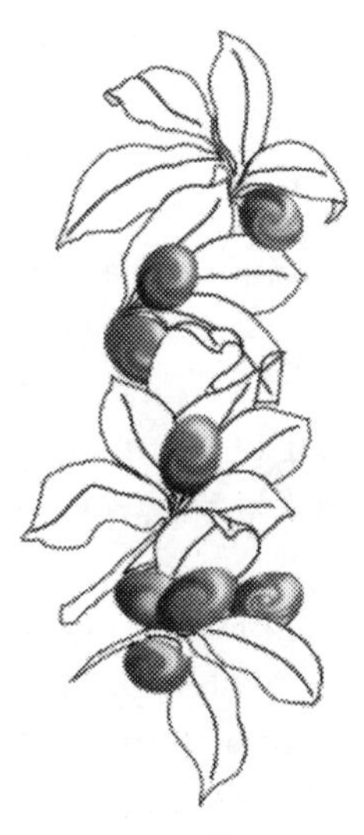

A Word from the Authors

There is no question that teens are natural poets. And there is so much to write about! What awesome and history-making times we live in! We can clone our cat, "cyberchat" a friend all the way around the globe and buy real estate on the moon real soon. There is nothing dull about living in the twenty-first century. It is absolutely worth writing about!

But aside from living in a world that is undergoing full-scale renovation, on a personal front, YOU are in the midst of an incredible transformation yourself! Your body is growing and your hormones are raging, and your inner child is getting a "makeover," too. Your mind is expanding and your heart is awakening—to first longings or learning how to comfort your own broken heart. Day by day you become more familiar with yourself—gaining a deeper understanding of your interests, needs, aptitudes and desires. All give way to your asserting yourself, to asking for a bigger say in the decisions that affect your life. To put everyone on alert that it is your time in the sun, you turn pent-up feelings into sun-kissed words!

Speaking up and speaking out is in your heart and on your mind. You know that the boundary of a country can separate one region from another, but it can never keep one loving soul from caring for another. It's simply the purpose of having a heart in the first place! You are fast becoming world-wise and people-wise too. From expanding boundaries to bending the rules, you are learning that replacing the childish demeanor of "demand" with the more mutually supportive "collaborate" is the way to go. And you write to explain yourself.

In gaining wisdom, you are growing compassionate. Having experienced disappointments, heartaches, and a mistake or two of your own, you're able to empathize with people wherever they may live: in your house, down the street or across the globe. You've discovered that your parents, like you, are learning as they go, doing the best they can and working through issues as they arise. Maybe you have already reached the stage of appreciating their love and support, and can better see how they sometimes must work through their own unresolved hurts and traumas from their past before they embrace new ideals. This, you conclude, is just another importance of "family": each member being afforded a safe place in which to learn and grow—and change. And so you write about the experience of "family."

Relationships on the home front aren't the only ones worth your words. Friendships are never hassle-free, something you learned in elementary school (and so kept a diary!), but now you're more willing and able to evaluate who gets your friendship and why. Friendship, you find, IS conditional: It is based on fair play and everyone's willingness to be a taste berry to the other. No more one-sided compromises or the "I'll do anything for you" if it means you end up with the short end of the stick. Friendships, you decide, are expendable if they are not mutually supportive. And so on and on you write, scolding your friends, pleading with them and thanking them, too.

From finding your own place in the world to wanting a place of your own, from school assignments to the world as your classroom, as a teen, you are opening yourself to becoming a student of life and a true child of the universe. All is a part of the fabric that makes up the incredible tapestry of teen life. Oh yes, you could fill journal after journal after journal with all that is going on in your life. And you often do!

Not a day goes by in which our office doesn't receive stacks of mail from our readers. Story after story, e-mail after e-mail, teens have much to say about life. Many times your entries are in story form, but many times they are written in verse. With topics ranging from "I love you and want to tell you," to "You deserve to be dumped and now you are"; to "I long for one close friend," to "Thank you being the truest friend in all the world," you wish to express yourself. From "My life would great if it weren't for curfew and rules," to "Thank you, Mom and Dad, for all that you do"; to "God, can you please bring me a date for the dance?" to "Thank you for all the blessings," teens know that poetry is, as John Ruskin so elegantly pointed out, "grounds for the noble emotions." This is what you'll find in this unit: incredibly noble emotions.

Always in our *Taste Berries for Teens* series we include poetry within each book. In *Taste Berries for Teens #4* we continue that tradition, but with a twist: We're holding a **contest** in which you get to decide which of your peers has the most "noble of emotions"! If you'd like to be a judge in this contest, read each of the poetry selections in this unit, then on page 89, select your favorite in each of three categories: Best Title of Poem, Most Interesting Subject Matter and Overall Best Poet. *(Note: You will also find a copy of the voting form in Appendix A in case you would like to use that page to send in, or to share with a friend who would also like to vote for his or her favorite poet.)*

Send your entry to us at Taste Berries for Teens Poetry Contest, Box 2588, Del Mar, CA 92014. Your entry ballot must be postmarked no later than December 30, 2004. The winners in each of the three categories will be notified by mail on or before January 15, 2005. (The person with the most votes in the BEST OVERALL POET category will receive a $100 cash prize!) We will also post the names of the winners at *www.tasteberriesforteens.com*. This announcement will be posted from January 15, 2005, through December 28, 2005.

If you are reading this and that date has passed, but would like to enter the next contest, no problem! We're always looking for good poetry, so if you've written something you would like us to consider for an upcoming book or future contest in our *Taste Berries for Teens* series, send it to us.

Good luck, Teen Poets!

❤ *Taste berries to you, Bettie and Jennifer Youngs*

Set Me Free

Whenever I am melancholy
or angry
or lonely . . . like now
I walk the beach
tasting the salt
as the mist from the ocean plays in the air,
sprinkling my face
like angel breath.
Deep and mysterious, dark yet blue
Maybe the ocean is lonely, too?
I can almost hear its long, slow moans
as it heaves its wrath against the rocks . . .
I love it that it can be so angry—but never at me.
The mighty ocean . . .
so willing to mope with me
cope with me.
Instinctively it knows my feelings, the
unspoken words of my heart.
The glorious ocean,
not angered by anything I say
not frustrated by anything I do
saving its fury to hurl at the world
for its many faults—but never at me.
For in its eyes I am perfect,
loved as its own.
The ocean, my friend . . .
always there for me.
Whenever I am in need,
I walk the beach
tasting the salt air
letting it set my spirit free.

Diana Seretis, 16

She Was MY Girl—My Entire World

She was my girl, my entire world
We had so much fun together
Didn't matter what it was,
Could've been whatever.
I wanted to be around her,
Wanted to help her with everything,
Learn to drive or open a jar.
I just loved being with that girl
She was MY girl, my entire world.
But the waters began to get choppy,
And oh so hard to navigate
I thought we could get through it,
I prayed that it be our fate.
I made some mistakes, ones I will claim
And it was me who let her go.
She begged, cried and pleaded
Too proud and too bigheaded,
I told her, "No, I just need some space.
Gotta chill; it's time for me to go."
I was surprised how I felt without her,
So I called and said, "Come back."
She was reluctant and then tentative
But eventually said yes to a second chance.
Guess I hadn't learned my lesson, though
'Cause I failed her yet again,
Said careless and hurtful things
Then walked out on her again.
Told myself it was time to cruise again
But soon learned I'd be setting sail without my heart,
She owned it of course.
It was hers, and hers alone to keep.

Now I'm standing here wondering what's wrong with me
And why it's so doggone hard to move on.
Just something about that girl still gets to me,
I may never be the same.
I choke up thinking about the good times.
Downplaying and dismissing the bad
I just loved being with that girl—MY girl, my entire world.
We had some really bad times,
But at least I was with her.
I didn't think I'd feel so cracked up over this,
Don't know if I'll ever get over her,
I guess only time will tell.
It's hard to not feel broken,
Considering the distance I fell.
I want us to get back together,
but I know she's gone for good.
I just wish I'd recognized it sooner,
That she was more than my girl,
She was my world,
My entire world.

Brent Queck, 19

I Dream About You Every Night

I dream about you every night
Each and every one the same
I try to imagine everything about you
Yet I know nothing but your name.

I find a table in the cafeteria
Where I stare from across the room
Watch as you laugh and talk with friends
Bigger than life you loom.

You seem like such a cool girl
Perfect in every way
Could it happen between us?
Will I find the words to say?

Night and day I dream the dream
There is a you, me and an "us"
I'm wishing, hoping and wanting this
In a clandestine vision I put my trust.

I dream about us on a date
And sharing a good-night kiss
I see us at the homecoming dance
You holding me close; it's bliss.

I dream about us doing homework
Sharing moments washing my car
We're in the show ring at the fair
I hope such times are near, not far.

I see us going steady
Laughing and holding hands as we walk
along
You've got your arms around me
As we sing to our favorite song.

I dream about us hanging out
Talking and laughing as natural as we
might
Kicking back, laying in the park together
Making plans for sweetly promised nights.

I dream about you every night,
Each and every one the same
I imagine that I know everything about you
Yet I know nothing but your name.

Sean Sanders, 16

Life Support in Room 204

Lying in a bed, in room 204
Is my very best friend,
So young, so cool, "old soul."
Such a great friend . . . loyal, lovely and true
Intelligent, thoughtful, so amazingly bold.
Now she lay likened to a "vegetable."
"Nothing's in her head"
The medical establishment say,
"Nothing we can do now, so sorry," and
"Time for sweet good-byes."
Easy for you to say
That is my BEST FRIEND
Lying there in a hospital bed!
I look to her mother and father,
So much pain yet hope in their eyes,
They refuse to understand, too.
It's sprinkling outside but pouring in here
I look away, because I know it's true
My friend and I
Are losing our bond,
unsticking the glue.
I'm feeling abandoned,
but she's all alone, too.
The time has come to let her go,
I wish it wasn't but I know it's so.
The Life Support in room 204
Is all you hear; nothing more
It gives her one last breath,
Then she reaches to the world beyond
I feel like my life is draining away, too.
The hospital room is quiet now,

That room up there on second floor,
The lights are off;
they've closed the door.
Her journey here is over.
I need to believe she's in heaven now,
Watching down on me, smiling
As I stand here at her gravestone
Placing upon the angel's hand
A flower from our secret garden
Hoping she'll never forget
All that we shared
The secrets, the plans
For dancing to life and the latest band . . .
You are my life support. Still.

Steph Lloyd, 14

No Crap, Low Blows or Name-Calling . . .

I like who I am
Not willing to change
I've accepted myself
No more parts to rearrange.

I'll no longer be crying
While you sit by and poke fun
I've no intentions to leave
my new place in the sun.

Sent my insecurities packing
Gave up emotional free-falling
Not taking any crap,
low blows or name-calling.

No more unwarranted tears
I'm totally free
No more black holes
I'm back to respecting me.

Embracing new friends
Getting rid of the old
Negativity is out
I've let go of your hold.

Time for fresh air
And letting go of the past
I'm building new dreams
Cleaning house at long last.

Finally found my courage
Redefined mentally fit
Giving up negative people
Don't s'pect me to babysit.

Returning to my values
Sorry that it took me awhile
But hey, I'm willing and ready
To sport a new—and real—smile.

Good-bye drama-mamas
Get lost heartaches and tears
I'm tired of misery
And unjustifiable fears.

Time to grow up and
Get on with new plans
Love who I am,
I've become my own fan.

Been forgiving myself
Getting good at it too
Feeling confident this is a love
To whom I'll stay true.

Renee Charles, 16

To Dance with the Man in the Moon

I close my eyes and dream of a place
Where sadness doesn't exist
Harm isn't a real word
And tears come only from happiness.

I close my eyes and dream of a place
Where stars are the floor to heaven,
A place where young and old can live
And wishes are granted in lots of seven.

I close my eyes and dream of a place
Where love is the only currency needed
Where thoughts and notions are all evolved
And flowerbeds are forever seeded.

I close my eyes and dream of a place
Where I can dance arm in arm with the man in the moon
And the wind can have a conversation with me
And the sun shines at the sound of a tune.

I close my eyes and dream of a place
A world where people are rooting for each other
Knowing that if we wanted—you, me, each of us
In a heartbeat, together, we could create it.

Angelina Cardinale, 19

Blonde Girl . . . Big Feet

Who am I to you, God . . .
. . . blonde girl with big feet
. . . her dad's eyes and
. . . her mom's smile?
Is it that simple to you?
Is it supposed to be a complicated
top secret to me?
If so, you've succeeded
Because
I feel confusion
Over who I am versus who I can be
I'm so filled with conflicting ideals
. . . the good versus the bad,
Always doing battle
. . . conscience versus matter
A questioning mind,
. . . an unsure heart
Always running into
. . . the wall to my soul
. . . the mysteries of heart
Is that the plan, God,
. . . that it be a secret to me?
Or wait . . .
It's not about me . . . but rather,
YOU . . .
Are you watching me play . . .
. . . play out who you've destined me to be?

Heather McHale, 17

Feelings We Once Had . . .

Poetic verse she said "To fill my heart"
A simple rhyme, a place to start
Maybe witty or filled with mirth
With fiery passion, or just down-to-earth.

Elegant words with which to dream
Of tender times of thoughts redeemed
Of days gone by in memory's lane
Or strong emotions old loves that waned.

Or maybe clever words entwined with truths
And old-world words to wit-forsooth
Make me laugh or make me cry
Or both at once with longing sigh.

"I need to feel once more," she pined
Lost emotions that once were mine
I feel so empty in my soul
Give me now some words to hold.

I'm feeling down and a little sad
I miss those feelings we once had
Just out of reach they still remain
I try to touch them just the same.

To share loves warm, soft kiss anew
To glow and sing and dance with you
With untamed glee to play and tease
And laugh out loud with childlike ease.

While I know we can't begin again
At least let's start where we were then
Before the doubts in angry words
Became the only sounds we heard.

Before the stars within your eyes
Became the tears you try to hide
Before the pain depressed our souls
Before the anger took its toll.

When hearts and hands were ours to hold
Where joy and love and kindness flowed
Where we were together and not apart
Where we were two yet still one heart.

Let's journey there not, too far past
Together once again at last
I need to love and hold you so
Not stand aside and watch you go.

Our lives were destined and thus entwined
For reasons yet unknown, opined
As yet two souls to meld in life
Free-fall in love for all we might.

Gerald Lee Kuiper, 18

Carousel Ride

Why do I cry these tears?
My life spins like a never-ending carousel ride,
The wooden horses are images of those around me
Their dark, rough eyes stare soullessly,
Their hard, tough bodies unbreakable as stone.
They all stand the same,
Criticizing . . .
Gossiping . . .
Judging . . .
Their eyes glare
As they announce their insults
Their insensitive remarks
Falling upon my ears
Coursing my body
Piercing my heart
Destroying my confidence.
They watch as I deteriorate
My world shattered
My soul saddened
Injured
Their dreams come true
I feel so strange
Like a victim
of crude personalities
Lost to a world of spinning carousels,
I stand,
crying.

Jade Tamborello, 17

Frostbitten Love

Our love budded in early spring,
Shy at first to this new fling.
Love letters followed, wafting perfume in the air
The gift of giddy emotions, so amazingly rare.

Our love grew stronger as summer came,
With you in my life, I was never the same.
Lying on green grass beneath Cirrus clouds in July,
We'd fallen in love; two hearts willingly complied.

Autumn arrived and with it a cool breeze blew,
Doubt struck, two pained hearts knew.
As one by one the leaves began to fall,
Hearts in a slump, no more standing tall.

The nights grew colder for winter was here,
A frostbitten love, the ending so near.
Two dreams dying, faith covered in frost,
First love had come but now, alas, all lost.

Jean Burres, 16

Barbies, Boys and Malls

From dress-up and dolls
To boys and malls,
You're the finest friend of all
You've been that special someone when I needed to spill it all.

We've talked about our dreams for the future
Sorted and categorized our fears
Schemed how to break curfew and a few rules,
Held each other through alligator tears.

I'm so glad to have been in these "places" with you
Best friends for so many incredible years
More than a good friend, you are the sister I never had,
We squabble, share clothes and work through being mad.

Though our world of Barbie and make-believe is gone
And college days and adult times lay just ahead
Husbands, kids, careers may come and go,
But we'll stay best friends forever, till the end.

Cassandra Kollath, 17

AUTHOR'S NOTE: *This teen poet wrote an original version of this selection for her best friend, Juli Zelasney, and had it inscribed on a key chain for her as a present! How cool is that!*

Should I Take You Back?

Did I make a mistake to leave you
Should I take you back
Would that be wise or foolish
Do I need to cut you a little slack?

So much happened, so much went down
Yet you love me . . . and I love you
But how can I forget what happened?
We did things we shouldn't do.

And how do I trust you now?
It was you who shut that door
I let many, many things go . . .
And then finally couldn't ignore.

Two broken and now regretting hearts
Was it worth it—for sure it wasn't fair
I'm so disappointed that we've broken up
I know that we both still care.

Now here we are trying be "just friends"
And we can if we're standing ten miles apart . . .
As long as we're not in each other's sight . . .
It's the only way I can control my aching heart.

We went to the movies as "just two friends"
You sat close, our hands touched; didn't realize I cared so much
A total journey back in time . . .
As long as I didn't tell a single friend of mine.

So very conflicted but what am I to do
Like when you came to see me the very next day

You asked if I was surprised to see you . . .
I love you but with all that is between us, what am I to say?

I'm involved with someone new now
I can't forget yet I need to move on
My feelings for you so deep, yet hidden away
But I still cry when I hear our song.

He makes me smile and I need that,
So I'm giving the new guy a chance
Need to forget about everything—especially you
It's hard; nothing compares to our romance.

So two still-in-love hearts will be moving on,
Telling ourselves we'll be just friends
Will we succeed in that or will we find
That two hearts in love can never end?

Kacey Stepanek, 17

The Way You Made Me Feel . . .

I remember the way I felt: warm, safe, wanted . . .
Like the world revolved around us
So in a space of our own
In my adoring eyes, you were so perfect.

I remember the way I felt: trying to get your approval . . .
Searching for a nod that never came
Wanting to feel I measured up
Even for a second.

I remember the way I felt: your every praise paired with criticism . . .
Words that in the draw of one breath
Could bolster my tiny dreams
And reaffirm my insecurities.

I remember the way I felt: reality began to cloud your perfection . . .
I filtered your truth for fault
And found your judgment lapsing
Your cover was falling.

I remember the way I felt: the sound of your voice echoing . . .
Off my eardrum
The undying devotion I felt for you
Crossing with deep lines of resentment.

I remember the way I felt: holding the knob in my hand . . .
The noise the door made as it shut behind me
The smell of the night that changed everything
Finally I'd got your attention: My world no longer revolves around you!

Kelly Chakeen, 17

Scandalous Mementos

Mildew in the air
Gleaming dust hanging in the light
There in a grimy box of brown photos
My teenaged father looks up at me
Sporting bangs nearly to his eyes
Most assuredly scandalous at the time.

College memorabilia
A sweater proudly bearing
Bold letters of their alma mater
They fell in love there
A picture of them cuddling
Under a tree makes me smile.

And now photos of years later
Still cuddling on their Golden Anniversary
  beneath a lovely weeping willow
I can hear their comfortable laughter, but then
A huge silence seizes the room, a reminder of how much
  I miss them
Taking comfort in knowing they share an eternal bed.

A fatal twist of metal
Stole any hope of a normal life from me
At such an early age, I had no guide
They left too fast for me to say it
So I repeat the words endlessly
To lifeless mementos of your beautiful life.

Never blinking, while tears fall down
I consider my life and what it's become
What shall I do without you until the day
My life becomes photographs and sweaters
The day I join you under the willow
And tell you in person, "You left too soon"?

Tom Hatfield, 17

Homeboy

Mocking he said, "Not to worry,
My driving is fine, besides, we're in a hurry,"
We were late so raced through the stop sign . . .
Therein lies fate . . . his . . . and mine.

There were sudden jolts
And the sound of popping bolts
And the car began flipping
To the sound of metal ripping.

As I rolled around inside
Not a single fear could I hide
In slow motion my life flashed before my eyes
My heart doing a checklist of final good-byes.

I awaited and awaited the final blow
The one where I'd finally and totally know
Then with a candid and sordid crack
All was eerily quiet and . . . deathly black.

Seconds later out of a fog I awoke
Was this reality or was it pure hoax?
On my knees I climbed out, surveying around
There lay scattered pieces of metal all over the ground . . .
  and a tiny body

We were just a few miles from home; it wasn't far
But we'd be going nowhere in this totaled car.
That night a young tiny child had died
And all because my homeboy wanted to get high.

The stoned and reckless driver is now in jail
Living out his life without possibility of bail
Sadly he was soon to wed himself a wife
Now he's looking at fifteen to life.

I feel remorse, guilt, regret and sorrow
It'll be with me for many, many tomorrows
A deadly accident and oh how it cost
Anguish, pain and a little one's life lost.

Casey Casto Ybañez, 17

Will You Marry Me?

If only we could be together
Forever and a day
I'd be eternally grateful
If only there was a way.

Let's talk of life together
Let's create a world where we're totally free
To love and grow a future
One that belongs to just you and me.

Let's lie on the grass and count the stars
And talk to the man in the moon
Let's talk about this dream of ours
And of a wedding we'll plan real soon.

Tommy Luketic, 18

Given Up

I was put up for adoption sixteen years ago,
Given up at birth for "a better place to grow."

Did you think I'd be fine without her?
That I'd never want to know?

So many days she fought heartache and tears,
Her life turning into long and suffering years.

Who can tell a young mother what is best for her child?
Who has the right to put a heart to such a torturous test?

Everyone said, "Let it go. Just let things be,"
But the void in my heart had quite another plea.

A voice within said to not let more years go by,
Didn't know what to do but knew I must try.

Then one day, years after my quest had begun,
I discovered where she lived; my search was soon done.

Now came the hard part: making the call
My heart on the line, my soul pinned to a wall.

I dialed, she answered, and I told her my name,
I held my breath then heard the tears of joy that came.

Said she'd longed for my voice, my smile, my touch,
That not a day went by she didn't miss me so much.

We got together, sharing an immediate embrace,
She shook and trembled as her hand touched my face.

We spoke of the past and the years gone by
Both the good and the bad, and this made both of us cry.

We're together now, never again will we be apart
Two souls reunited; mother-daughter, one heart.

Mary Beth Burke, 19

Meet Your Rival, Bub!

Did you believe I'd fool so easy,
Buy into everything I heard,
Did you think of me as clueless
Not able to decode your slippery words?

Did you think I was short on common sense,
Easily overwhelmed by disarming charm,
Unable to sort truth from fiction,
Gullible regardless of its harm?

What gives you such a big head
To think I'd get in so deep?
What makes you think I'd be open,
To take a foolish, futile leap?

Do you think you can mislead me,
Toss caution to the wind,
Cast your net of immoral slippery tricks
Regardless of the claim, cost or sin?

I know your crooked, cunning ways,
Your lust to deceive is true,
But where will all your bravado go
When the new guy—your rival—is confronting you?

Marie Laree Taggert, 15

Awkward Glory

How can you still love me, God,
When so often I turn away from you,
Always skating in the fast-line
Chasing the good life,
Even when I know
It's a never-ending headache
A cycle of chaos and easy lies.
I say I know you.
I say I love you and that I follow your teachings.
Then I meet him—and I forget about you,
I compromise my values,
I jeopardize my morals,
I denigrate myself.
I fall. I cry. I return to you.
But then I meet another, and the pattern returns:
I trust, I believe,
I give, I am deceived.
I fall. I cry. I return to you.
Do you never tire of my antics, God,
Or wince at my coming to You with excuses and tears . . .
Distrust my coming only when in need?
You must love me,
I deserve less; instead you offer more.
To live and breathe and wake each day
Is nothing less than your grace
In awkward glorious movement.

Emily-Jane Robinson, 16

Who Teaches Guys to Smile That Way?

I love it when you smile
The way you always do
It's the one that makes me melt,
And gives me something to hold onto.

I love it when you grip my hand
Can it mean there'll never be heartbreak or tears
Or that whenever I'm lonely, worried or insecure
That you'll chase away ill-tempered fears?

I love the way you hold me
Like I'm a china doll of glass
So afraid you'll hurt or break me
Like I'm precious and first-class.

I love the way you kiss me
On the hands, lips and cheek
I think about it day and night
Even thoughts make knees go weak.

I love the way my heart feels
When you glance at me in that special way
It seems to say a million things
Is it merely amusement, or does it imply you'll stay?

So many things I love about you
From your nose down to your toes
But if you want to know how to get to me
It's all about the way you hold me close.

Spectacular is how I'd describe your smile
The one the best guys always do
It always makes me melt and lets me know
I'm going to hold onto you.

Morgan Redding, 14

Only One

We're all lost,
We're all found,
We're all the same.
Just one heart
With different names.

Laura Campanelli, 20

Anticipated Night

Dress shopping hours on end
Finding the perfect one.
Shoes to match.
Purse to match.
Nails to match,
Hair appointment to schedule and keep,
Place an order and pick up the boutonniere,
Change clothes,
Find your shoes,
An hour for makeup,
Get ready.
Excitement,
Joy,
Nervousness,
All the same.
Waiting, waiting
Anxiously.
Here he comes.
The doorbell rings.
Heart beating fast,
Black shirt, silver tie,
Very classy.
Looking great.
Off we go, homecoming dance
What a night—
. . . One I've been waiting for!

Kylie Lynn, 16

Reflection on the Nail

He created a most exquisite world, decking
it out far beyond anyone's wildest imagination
His goodness and righteousness evident everywhere,
Blessings blanketing the lives of His children,
Even though I don't always deserve it
Contentment and grace unworthy but granted
Then I sin.

He wants for us an interesting life
Filled with meaning, purpose and puzzle
God's creations dazzle—and boggle—even the minds of
Cleric, scholars and scientists
His omnipotence far beyond what the human heart can fathom
He is so majestic, so loving, all-promising,
Then I sin.

He suffers pain and anguish
For my corrupt soul's deliverance
Well aware, I thank Him for His grace and mercy
Tell Him I will follow and devote myself
I watch His arms and feet be pinned to the cross
I shudder as I see my reflection on the nail
Still, I sin.

Melissa Miller, 18

Teen Talk: "Best of the Best" Contest—Vote for Your Favorite Teen Poet!

Here's how to be a judge in this contest:

The poems below are shown in order as they appear in this unit. Vote for your favorite in each of three categories: Best Title of Poem, Most Interesting Subject Matter and Overall Best Poet. Send your entry to us at *Taste Berries for Teens* Poetry Contest, Box 2588, Del Mar, CA 92014. Your entry ballot must be postmarked no later than December 30, 2004. The winners in each of the three categories will be notified by mail on or before January 15, 2005. The person with the most votes in the BEST OVERALL POET category will receive a $100 cash prize! We will also post the names of the winners at *www.tasteberriesforteens.com.* This announcement will be posted from January 15, 2005, through December 28, 2005. If you are reading this and that date has passed, simply enter the next contest!

- ❤ _____ *Set Me Free,* by Diana Seretis
- ❤ _____ *She Was MY Girl—My Entire World,* by Brent Queck
- ❤ _____ *I Dream About You Every Night,* by Sean Sanders
- ❤ _____ *Life Support in Room 204,* by Steph Lloyd
- ❤ _____ *No Crap, Low Blows or Name-Calling . . .* by Renee Charles
- ❤ _____ *To Dance with the Man in the Moon,* by Angelina Cardinale
- ❤ _____ *Blonde Girl . . . Big Feet,* by Heather McHale
- ❤ _____ *Feelings We Once Had . . .,* by Gerald Lee Kuiper
- ❤ _____ *Carousel Ride,* by Jade Tamborello
- ❤ _____ *Frostbitten Love,* by Jean Burres
- ❤ _____ *Barbies, Boys and Malls,* by Cassandra Kollath
- ❤ _____ *Should I Take You Back?* by Kacey Stepanek

- ❤ _____ *The Way You Made Me Feel . . . ,* by Kelly Chakeen
- ❤ _____ *Scandalous Mementos,* by Tom Hatfield
- ❤ _____ *Homeboy,* by Casey Casto Ybañez
- ❤ _____ *Will You Marry Me?* by Tommy Luketic
- ❤ _____ *Given Up,* by Mary Beth Burke
- ❤ _____ *Meet Your Rival, Bub!* by Marie Laree Taggert
- ❤ _____ *Awkward Glory,* by Emily-Jane Robinson
- ❤ _____ *Who Teaches Guys to Smile That Way?* by Morgan Redding
- ❤ _____ *Only One,* by Laura Campanelli
- ❤ _____ *Anticipated Night,* by Kylie Lynn
- ❤ _____ *Reflection on the Nail,* by Melissa Miller

Fill out the form on page 89 or Appendix A and send in.

How to Enter the Next Teen Poetry Contest:

Want to enter the next Teen Poetry Contest? We're always looking for good poetry, so if you've written something you would like us to consider for an upcoming book or contest in our *Taste Berries for Teens* series, send it to us.

Taste Berries for Teens Poetry Contest
Box 2588
Del Mar, CA 92014

For details or for more information, visit www.tasteberriesforteens.com.

WHO GETS YOUR VOTE FOR:

Best TITLE of Poem: ____________________

____

____

Most Interesting Subject Matter: ____________________________

____

____

____

Overall BEST POET—$100 cash prize winner: ______________

____

____

After you've voted, send this form to:

Taste Berries for Teens Poetry Contest
Box 2588
Del Mar, CA 92014

All entries must be received by December 15, 2004, to be eligible. To find out the winners, visit our Web site: *tasteberriesforteens .com*.

Tell us who you are:

Name ____

E-mail ________________________________

Age__________________________________

Street Address ____

____

State _______________ Zip code ______________________

Part 3

The Single Most Important Lesson I've Learned

Learning is when you suddenly understand something you've understood all your life, but in a new way.

—Doris Lessing

You cannot dream yourself into a character; you must hammer and forge yourself one.

—James A. Froude

I am not afraid of storms for I am learning how to sail my ship.

—Louisa May Alcott

Everything is funny as long as it is happening to somebody else.

—Will Rogers

Everything is connected . . . no one thing can change by itself.

—Paul Hawken

The fragrance always remains in the hand that gives the rose.

—Heda Bejar

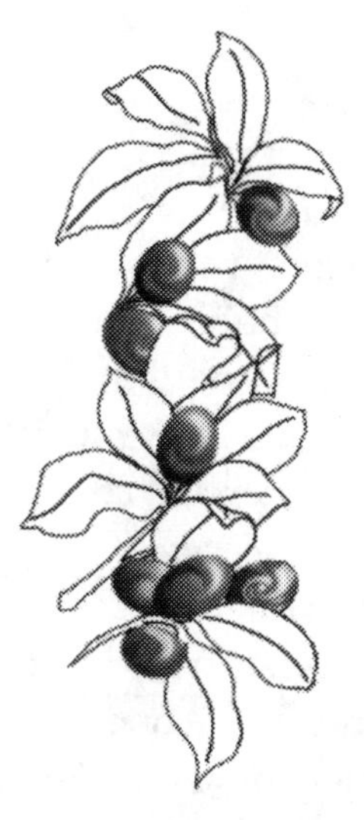

A Word from the Authors

You and a friend are playing a round of golf. Your friend, who thinks his ball went into the rough, goes to search for it. After several minutes, he calls out that he's found it. You know he is lying—because you have been standing on his ball for the past three minutes! You have a predicament on your hands. Your moral dilemma is: You can't call your friend on his lie without revealing (because you've been standing on the ball) that you've just cheated, too!

Lessons do come in the most unexpected ways, don't they?

The teen years naturally are a time of many lessons. It's a time of many "firsts," a time when you are stretching your wings to see exactly how far and wide they will carry you. That you are willing to try out your wings is good. As you practice your flying skills, you learn what works and what doesn't. You also learn that while there will be some mishaps, with each flight you gain experience. Translated: You've learned. Yes, life is all about learning, gaining experience to grow wiser so as to become even more cool, caring and courageous.

For this unit, teens were asked to share a time in which a certain experience caused them to see the world, or themselves, in a new way. As you will discover when reading the stories profiled here, sometimes the learning experience was private and personal, and sometimes it was a cause of public embarrassment. Lessons ranged anywhere from discovering that one must be willing to take risks, to learning that sometimes it is simply not smart to risk (maybe because of a certain consequence that was sure to follow). While some teens learned that it can be dangerous—even illegal—to simply do whatever someone asks you to do, still others discovered it can be smart to listen to those around you. Of all the lessons learned, the one that stood out above all the others was that of fairness or justice. Yes, our competitive society puts a premium on winning. But we also put a premium on winning fairly. Think about the fall from grace by athletes, politicians, business leaders and others who have gone from hero to goat when their cheating to get ahead was found out. Whether they used a corked bat to hit longer home runs, or raved about other people's low morals while hiding a gambling habit that cost them or their business a good name or money, when they were finally caught, their self-esteem and respect were greatly reduced by a less adoring public.

Our own sense of fairness demands that people play by the rules, live within the law and abide by the same standards to which they hold others accountable. It may be tempting to bend the rules to gain an unfair advantage, but the costs aren't worth it. And by costs, we don't just mean getting caught. Even if you cheat and get away with it, you can never really feel good about the victory. Consider again the two golfers at the beginning of this section. When the two friends leave the golf course, can either really feel good about his or her score? Not really. After all, if in your heart YOU know you didn't really earn your score, then the price you pay is lost self-esteem for the deception.

The desire for justice and fair play runs so deep in our culture that it may very well be innate. In other words, you and I may be born wanting to balance things in a way that seems fair to us. Any infringement on our perception of justice clicks on a deep sense of outrage. In this unit you'll find a story called "No Plea Bargains," by Danny Morse. When you read Danny's story, you'll no doubt feel a sense of injustice about all that happened. Maybe you'll think that the principal should have cut Danny more slack for confessing. Maybe you'll think Danny was unfair to his friends by getting them into trouble by confessing. Maybe you even think Danny got off too easy. The point is, we humans always have our antennae out for signs of injustice as we see it.

Because fair play and justice are so critical to human motivation and the results it can bring, we humans have developed elaborate systems of law and order. Whether it is referees in a soccer game or judges in a legal system, we have found that rules are necessary for the benefit of all. Breaking rules carries with it penalties. Danny found this out when he and his friends vandalized the school. He learned that going along with a crowd that is going the wrong way carries with it some concrete consequences. He learned that when you make bad choices, you often experience bad results.

Can you relate? We have all made choices that we later regretted. Maybe we didn't want some kids not to like us, so we let someone like Drake or, in Cliff Chapell's case, his neighborhood gang, lead us down a path we knew wasn't good. Maybe we cared too much about winning and tried to gain an unfair advantage—and learned that while no one found out, our hearts knew, and that was far too big of a price to pay. We learn that the older we get, the more we need to "think, think, think." The older we get, the less often we can say, "Just kidding!"

Think about your own life for a minute. How many times have you felt a sense of outrage for being treated unfairly? Maybe a friend slighted you in some way or a teacher asked a question on a test that you thought was unfair. Or maybe your parents will let you drive the family car to school—provided you drop off and pick up your younger brother or sister—and it is exactly what you don't want (to be seen with a child in the car with you)! Maybe it was something bigger. Perhaps your parents divorced and you felt that you unfairly had to suffer. Maybe you're dealing with a disability that makes it difficult to do "normal" teen activities. Maybe you've even been the victim of a crime.

Teens often believe that the world may not be fair, but that it ought to be. As so many teens discovered, as we work toward justice for others and ourselves, good character follows. Character allows us to stand up against other injustice when we see it. We can speak out against injustice when we hear about it. And we can accept justice when it sometimes means our not getting what we want. That's the power of a lesson: Learning takes us to a whole new place!

Yes, our journey in the world is all about lessons. Our relationships with family and friends are the "university" in which we are meant to learn the importance of being a taste berry to each other. So welcome to this unit, filled with stories and accounts from your peers about some of the best insights they've gained—and how, as a result, they've been changed for the better.

❤ *Taste berries to you, Bettie and Jennifer Youngs*

Movie Star; Math Genius

Sometimes it takes someone else believing in you before you can believe in yourself.

—Danica McKellar, 29

I had always been an A student, and I was starting junior high with expectations. But I had enrolled in the honors math class and found myself struggling just to keep up. I had always done well in math in elementary school; why was this so different? Things got progressively worse; I couldn't understand a thing our teacher was telling us! I remember wrestling with homework assignments for hours on end, and my grades were slowly but surely sliding downward.

Midway through the year, the school switched our teacher and we were given Mrs. Jacobson to finish out the course. She was friendly and helpful, but at that point I was convinced that I simply would never understand math. Things continued to get worse for me—it looked like I might actually fail the class.

And then came the day for the dreaded quiz. Mrs. Jacobson had handed out the quiz, and as I sat there reading it, I could have sworn it was written in some other language. I had NO IDEA how to proceed. The page remained blank for the entire time, and the only thoughts going through my head were, *"I can't do this!"* and *"I don't belong here!"*

The recess bell rang, and my page was still blank. I remember holding back the tears, trying so hard not to cry. Other students all stood up and turned in their quizzes. I just couldn't move. How could I turn in a blank test?

After everyone else had left, Mrs. Jacobson walked over to me and said, "Why don't you keep working on the quiz through recess?" I stared up at her through my watery gaze, and she just nodded at me and sat down at her desk. What did this mean?

She wanted me to work on the quiz during recess? She would do that for me? Grateful and energized, I got to work on the math problems in front of me. Inspired by the opportunity for a second chance, my brain started to open up. Suddenly some of the questions began to make some sense. I was finding some success with it! When recess was over, I handed the quiz back to her and went on to my next class. We never spoke about it again.

I got a C on that quiz—75 percent. Somehow in that fifteen minutes of recess, I managed to get 75 percent of the answers correct! How had it happened? Why did she do that for me, and why was I suddenly able to think clearly? As my grades in that class quickly began to improve, and I finished out the year with an A, I finally realized something: The teacher gave me the extra time that day because she believed in me—when I couldn't believe in myself. It made all the difference.

I recently graduated UCLA summa cum laude with a degree in mathematics, where I also tutored calculus for two years. Since then, I've spoken to Congress on the importance of women in mathematics. I am now a published mathematician, after coauthoring a new theorem. I am also a spokesperson for a middle-school math organization called *Figure This!* (*www.figurethis.org*), which helps middle-school students with math. I also answer math questions on my Web site, *www.danicamckellar.com.* Today, although I now work primarily as an actress, my hobby of mathematics continues to be a source of joy and intellectual thriving. And I love sharing my passion for math with others.

I don't know if this all would've happened if not for Mrs. Jacobson, but I do know that in that moment when she had a little faith in me, I believed that I was worth that faith. From this experience I learned that sometimes it takes someone else believing in you before you can believe in yourself. What a taste berry!

Just as Mrs. Jacobson was there for me, I can be there for you, too. Math really can be a fun subject, and I encourage all of you to face it without fear. If any of you would like some help, please visit my Web site, and be sure to mention that you got my address from this book, *Taste Berries for Teens #4: Short Stories and Encouragement on Being Cool, Caring and Courageous.* I always enjoy passing along any gift that was once given to me!

Danica McKellar, actress from
television's *The Wonder Years* and *The West Wing*

"No Plea Bargains"

I've learned that justice may be hard to accept when it lands on us personally, but it's fair, and it's impartial. So now, I think about the consequences of my actions—beforehand!

—Danny Morse, 16

I sat waiting for the principal to see me—scared as only a thirteen-year-old who knows he's in some serious trouble can be. I only came to the office because I believed I'd be caught sooner or later, and I figured things would go better for me if I confessed instead of waiting to be caught. It seemed like a good idea just a few hours ago. Now, sitting here thinking things over, I wondered just how to explain it so that Mr. Camp would understand—and give me a break.

What happened was this: On Saturday night I'd been invited to spend the night at Shane's house. He's my best friend. I got there as planned, around six o'clock. We started out watching *Star Wars* and then played video games. Around nine o'clock we decided it would be fun to set up his tent and camp out in the backyard. We'd just hauled the tent into the backyard when Shane's older brother, Drake, came home from an evening out with his friends. He asked what we were doing, we told him, and he said he'd help us. So the three of us put up the tent and then carried out sleeping bags, pillows, a flashlight, sodas, a boom box, popcorn and chips. You would have thought we were going to camp out for a week! About an hour into our "camp out," we got tired of eating and listening to music and went back into the house to hang out with Drake, who was watching television in the family room. When he asked us why we were in the house, we told him we were bored and were trying to think of something fun to do. Drake suggested all three of us take a walk over to our school grounds. So off we went.

It was almost 10:30 when we arrived at Potter Junior High. "Let's see if we can get in," Drake said, checking to see if any of the lower windows would open. The third one he tried was unlocked. Drake gave Shane a leg up through the open window, and then me. Shane somehow made it up on his own. We all fell into a pile on the floor of the classroom inside, laughing, partly at our own pileup and partly to hide our nervousness. The room looked weird in the dark, especially since the security lights outside cast just enough light to make out the chairs and desks in the room. "This is Miss Murray's room," I said. "She's my English teacher."

"Geez, I hate that woman," Shane remarked. The next thing I knew, we were emptying the contents of her desk drawers all over the floor. We ripped down the papers and posters from the bulletin boards, pulled books off the shelves and kicked the desks all over the room. Egging each other on only made us want to do more. "Let's do old Foley's room," Drake suggested. "I used to give him so much crap! I can't believe he's still here. Well, actually, I can. He'll teach until the day he dies!" We were off, and when we had trashed it, we hit my "most-hated" teacher, Mrs. Henderson. Minutes later we were scrambling up and out the window we'd entered. Our adrenaline pumping, we ran the entire way home. Once home, you would have thought we'd talk and laugh about things, but we were all pretty quiet.

As morning dawned, I laid awake back in the tent—already worried. *What's going to happen if I'm caught? Somebody could have seen us! I wonder if they'll do fingerprints! What if there was a security camera! Why did I do something so stupid—what was I thinking?* The next three days and three nights were the most miserable of my life. I couldn't sleep and whenever a teacher looked at me in class, I was sure he or she knew I'd been a part of the destruction—or maybe even that I'd done it all. By Wednesday I was such a wreck I thought it would be a relief to confess. So here I sat waiting for Mr. Camp. Just then he opened his door. "You want to see me, Danny?" he asked, looking friendly and concerned. *Not really*, I thought, knowing the friendly look would be wiped away in moments. But it was too late to turn back. "Yes," I said, taking a deep breath and rising slowly to my feet. "What's up?" he asked, taking his chair and pointing for me to sit back down.

It took all the courage I had, but I blurted the words I had rehearsed. "Mr. Camp, I was involved in the vandalism Saturday night." He sat back in his chair and just looked at me and then said, "Suppose you tell me what happened, from beginning to end." I launched into the story, trying my best to make it sound like a harmless prank gone awry. I ended my confession by assuring him, "We didn't have it planned. It just sorta happened."

"'Just sorta happened?'" Mr. Camp repeated. "Desks turned over. Drawers emptied. Property destroyed. And it 'just sorta happened'? I don't think so." He paused, obviously planning his move. "Well, Danny, the first thing I'm going to do is call your parents. Then I'm going to call the police. Your vandalism wasn't just a childish prank; it was a crime, a felony. They'll come and take you to the station, where you'll be booked. Eventually, you'll go to trial; I feel sure the judge will hand you a stiff sentence. If you're lucky, he'll give you probation and hundreds of hours of community service. If you're not, you'll go to a juvenile detention center. What you've done is very serious."

My head was spinning. "But," I said, trying to defend myself, "I confessed. Doesn't that count for something? I admitted what I did and I'm really sorry about it. Please don't call my parents. Why do you have to call the police?" I started to cry.

"Danny," Mr. Camp responded. "I am very encouraged that you came to me and confessed. That took a lot of guts, and I respect you for that. However, you must realize that your confession in no way diminishes the wrong you've done. There are consequences to wrong behavior, and you need to learn that now."

"But when criminals confess, they get a lighter sentence," I pleaded. "Why shouldn't I?"

"That's known as a plea bargain," Mr. Camp explained. "It happens when a DA (district attorney) agrees to a lighter sentence in exchange for a confession or information. There are no plea bargains here." Confused and wishing I was anywhere but here turning myself in, I groaned, "But that's not fair."

"Let me explain 'fair,'" Mr. Camp said, folding his hands on his desk, leaning forward to meet my eyes more closely. "I care about you and believe that you are basically a good kid. I do not want to call your parents or the police. However, I'm going to because I am more interested in building your character than I am in making you feel like it's no big deal that you've done something gravely wrong. This is a basic truth: *Our actions result in consequences.* My calling your parents and the police isn't 'punishment' for the sake of revenge; it's a consequence of your bad choices. You've started to turn things around by making the right choice in confessing. Now let's see if you can face the penalty with the same integrity."

I sat stunned at the turn of events, crying as Mr. Camp made his phone calls—my stomach churning as I thought of all the trouble I'd made for myself. It was the worst day of my life, but, in a twisted way, it was also the best, because I learned something that will serve me for the rest of my life: Justice may be hard to accept when it lands on us personally, but it's fair, and it's impartial. Mr. Camp was right. Justice is the line between right and wrong, and when we learn that, it can help us choose which side of the line we want to be on. I kept reminding myself of that as I faced my parents and appeared before the judge and did my thousands of hours of community service and worked to repay my one-third of the damage we three had done.

That was three years ago—the time it took me to complete my service hours, after which my record was cleared. It's over and done with now. Though I wouldn't recommend learning the hard way, as I did, I do know that we are free to choose whether or not we'll just follow the crowd—or do our own thinking. As for me, I do my own thinking, always considering the consequences of my actions—beforehand!

Danny Morse, 16

Up to My Neck in Alligators

Consequences are a two-way street!
—Andria McGhee, 16

My name is Andria McGhee. I'm trying to get my life together. When I was fourteen (just three weeks before Christmas), I assaulted a police officer while being taken to a juvenile detention center. That was just the beginning of my problems, and boy, you cannot believe all the grief I've caused myself. When I went to court, the judge flipped through the pages and pages of charges filed against me and shook his head. Then, peering over his glasses, he looked at me and said, "Looks to me as though you're up to your neck in alligators, Miss." Put simply, I've got a lot of jail time ahead me.

I know I've got problems. And I really want to fix them. Like if I don't do something about my bad temper, I'll mess up my life even more than I already have. The first thing I'm going to try to do is to learn how to manage stress. I think that can help me a lot. About the tenth month of being locked up, I had so much stress—especially from thinking about all that I'd done and how long I was going to be locked up because of it—that I got eczema. Eczema is an ugly, scaly and really, really itchy rash. Doctors told me I had a "Type-A chronic case." Well, that's for sure: the rash was up and down my entire arms and legs, all over my chest and back, on my stomach and even in my navel. My face was totally covered—and so was my butt. I even had it on my eyelids!

When I stress out, my body starts the rash-reaction thing and I break out. Boy, the rash is really an incentive to learn how to manage stress, because when I break out, it itches so bad that sometimes I can't sleep. And if I scratch it, then it gets infected. If it gets infected, it spreads even more. So it all comes back to my bad temper. What I've learned is that there are consequences to everything. Like if I hadn't been joyriding that day, I wouldn't have been taken to juvenile hall. If I hadn't kicked the officer, I wouldn't have been charged with assault. If I didn't have the charges I do, I wouldn't be facing jail time.

But consequences, I learned, are a two-way street: If I learn how to manage stress, I won't trigger the rash. If I learn to manage my temper, I might get out of jail earlier than if I don't. If I keep working at not having such a bad temper, then I can prevent myself from being up to my neck in alligators.

Andria McGhee, 16

Piggyback Ride

The most profound lesson I've learned is that because I place my faith at the center of my life, everything else falls into place.

—Hallie Bezold, 16

It was the last day of camp, a warm and beautiful day in the Big Bear Mountains. I'd been at a youth camp for one full—and awesome—week. Like so many others, I'd been a part of some really positive experiences, one of which was the blessing of making new friends. Still, the most profound "lesson" came during our group session on that last morning. In the closing session, a favorite camp counselor spoke to us about the importance of living our lives with faith at the center of all we do. He asked us a couple of really important questions: "Is your faith your own, or are you taking a 'piggyback' ride? Do you consider yourself to be a Christian because your parents are or simply because you regularly go to church? If you attend a Christian school, does that mean you are living your faith? Is your relationship with God *your own*—really and truly your very own?"

I found this line of questioning startling because to tell the truth, I'd never given it much thought. I did consider myself a Christian. I'd been raised in a Christian home. I went to church most every Sunday. I even attend a Christian school. But was I *simply taking* a spiritual piggyback ride: Was my relationship with God my "very own—really and truly"? I went for a long walk to think about whether or not I knew God "personally." I came to the conclusion I was doing as the youth-camp counselor had suggested. My faith was mostly about association: I went to church, attended a Christian school and knew myself as a Christian because my parents were. But, I didn't have the Spirit of Christ for myself.

I do now.

So I am thankful for the camp counselor's line of questioning that day. It has caused me to learn the most profound lesson of all: Because faith is at the center of my life, everything else falls into place.

Hallie Bezold, 16

Summer Love

That your heart can feel so wounded one minute and then happy the next is an amazing discovery. Even when love ends, life goes on. The heart will always be looking around to help you find happiness again.

—Katie Ionata, 17

When a guy by the name of Chris asked me out, I was shocked, scared and overjoyed. Shocked because I didn't think he saw me as anything more than a friend. Scared because the last thing I wanted was to take the chance that having a love relationship would end our friendship. Overjoyed because, well, after he asked me out, I realized that I was crazy about him.

He was a guy with a really strong personality. One of the things I liked about him was that he wasn't all that preoccupied with what other people thought of him. That was refreshing, and so different from the guys I'd dated who worried about what everyone thought about them. And Chris had this beautiful long hair that I loved. And he was really great looking—which didn't hurt either.

We dated all that summer. I was mesmerized, just totally entranced by him. So what if I could hardly get a word in edgewise? So what if I always measured my words, making sure I didn't say anything that might upset him because then he'd sulk for the rest of the evening? So what if he didn't seem all that interested in my opinions? So what if, depending on his always-changing moods, he would be nice to me one minute, and then short and impatient the next? So what if when we were with friends he mostly ignored me? So what if he often was late in picking me up? So what if he wasn't sensitive to the fact that I didn't care for the food at the fast-food stand where we often ate? So what if I spent hours getting ready but he seemed to never notice? I always wanted to tell him how I felt about this treatment, but didn't.

Then summer came to an end, and so did our relationship. Breaking up wasn't my idea. It was his. The first couple of days after we broke up, I was devastated. To try to soothe myself, I went through all the things about us—especially the injustices that didn't sit well with me, to help me think breaking up was an okay thing. Don't you just hate it when you discover that all the reasons for not being with someone were there all along and you just chose to ignore them? I knew that being with Chris wasn't good for me, and that I deserved better. Though I was hurting, the truth was that no matter how great-looking he was or how shiny and long his beautiful hair, he wasn't right for me.

After a couple of weeks of moping, a friend invited me to a birthday party. At first I was tempted to say no, so as to stay home and further drown in my sorrow. In the end though, I decided to go to the party and try to have a good time. Once there, even though I didn't know anyone, everyone was really nice, and slowly I emerged from my bad mood. And then, about an hour after I'd arrived, a guy walked in, a guy who absolutely took my breath away. He was incredibly good-looking, seemed really friendly and sweet, and said "hi" to everyone. He had a smile on his face the whole time. Oh, yeah, and he had really gorgeous long hair, which didn't hurt. In that moment, you couldn't believe how happy I was that Chris and I had broken up! And just an hour before I was sorting through how I didn't think I could make it through another day without Chris. And now I was feeling like, "Chris who?"

Making his way around the room, the gorgeous new guy came up to me. "Hi," he said with a heart-stopping smile, "I'm Shawn." As it turned out, Shawn and I had a surprising amount of things in common, from our mutual favorite bands to our hobby of making tie-dye shirts. By the end of the party, Shawn had asked me to an upcoming dance at his school. Well, it was an incredible date—and I'm happy to report that he and I are still going out.

That your heart can feel so wounded one minute and then happy the next is an amazing discovery. I know that before I get married, there are probably going to be any number of boyfriends in my life, and my heart is probably going to hurt every time love ends. But while love ends, life goes on. The heart will always be looking around to help you find happiness again. What a lesson. My heart was really hurting when Chris and I broke up. Chris had not even been a good boyfriend; he didn't treat me all that well—and still my heart did a number. That means that one's heart probably hurts any time and every time love ends. So knowing this, I'm going to try to not be so down on myself, or put so much emphasis on the pain part of it. Because my sense is that's just the way love works. The other day a friend reminded me of an old saying that goes, "When one door closes, another one opens." This is very true. If Chris and I hadn't broken up, I might not have met Shawn. So it's okay when a door closes. Another will open. Believe it. I do now!

Katie Ionata, 17

A Weird Situation

I've learned that sometimes situations aren't as bad as you think they're going to be. And sometimes, they're even better than expected.

—BreAnna McDermott, 13

My parents have been divorced for seven years and now live in different cities. One day this past this summer, my dad called my mom at seven in the morning—which was weird, because first of all, he rarely calls, and never that early in the morning. He asked Mom if I could come and visit him—which was also weird since I hadn't seen him for two years. Mom told me to get on the phone. My dad said he really wanted my sister and I to come stay at his house for the summer—which was too weird, since we'd never visited his house since he'd been remarried four years ago. But the weirdest thing of all was his saying, "Everyone here wants you and your sister to come, especially Alicia." I found that more than a little difficult to believe. I mean, how could Alicia want us to come so badly—she had never even met us, and we'd never met her. How could a twelve-year-old be "happy" about sharing her house—and her own mother—with two "strangers" for an *entire* summer? But nothing topped "weird" more than Dad's next statement, "Your new stepmom is really looking forward to your coming. She really loves you guys." She loves us? Well, that just can't be true—she's only seen us in pictures; we'd never even once spoken to her by phone.

Everyone decided my sister and I would go to visit my dad—and for the entire summer. I wasn't all that sure I wanted to be gone from Mom for such a long time, and knew I'd miss my friends and my room. And I wasn't sure what to expect once I got there. I mean, it did seem like a lot of time to spend with people we hadn't met before (other than my dad, of course).

What if we got there and the stepmother and her daughter didn't like us? Then what? Would we get to come home, or would she lock us up in the basement or something? I just couldn't see how any of this would be any fun either for my sister or for me—especially my sister who is "promised" to her new boyfriend.

Dad and everyone picked us up at the airport, and we all went out for ice cream and then we went to their house. We watched a movie, and I fell asleep on the couch but woke up in a bed in Alicia's room. I got up, made my bed and just waited in the room until, finally, Dad knocked on the door, asking if I was up. I tried being polite and quiet. Because I didn't want to make Dad's new wife mad at my sister and me, I tried to do everything just right. Like every day that first week, I made sure I washed and dried my water glass if I got up to get a glass of water late at night. And I always made sure I put the empty soda cans in the right recycling container in their garage. They had a recycling container for glass, one for paper, and one for tin cans. In the beginning I didn't know which one was which. But finally, I figured out that the blue one was for paper, the black one on the right was for glass and the black one on the left was for tin cans. I also hung up my clothes and made my bed every day—which I don't always do at home. My mom gives us girls an allowance for keeping our rooms neat, and if I don't need the money, I sometimes just let things lay around. But when here, every day I picked everything up.

So then two weeks had passed and everything was still okay. No hard feelings, and nobody had yelled at anyone. And no sign of the possibility of being locked in the basement (they didn't even have one). So then I relaxed a little. Sometimes I didn't always pick up after myself. Still, no one said anything, and still Dad's new wife smiled a lot. So then I dropped a little of my "always polite" demeanor and started making small demands, like asking if my sister and I could watch our favorite TV programs, too. Until then, I just sat in front of the television, politely going along with whatever Alicia wanted to watch. But even when I started making a few more demands, still, everyone was cheerful. Then one day, I accidentally dropped a glass in the kitchen. The floor was tile, and the glass shattered. I was mortified because it really was an accident, and my stepmom was in the kitchen at the same time. I apologized and almost started to cry because I thought maybe she thought I did it to be mean or something. Instead she said, "It's only a glass. No big deal." I could tell she meant her words. She even helped me clean up the glass. So that was cool.

With her being so nice, I started to slowly let my guard down even more. What shocked me was that she still liked me. She even asked me about important things, like who my friends were and if they were nice. I told her about a couple of girls at my school whom I don't like very much because they started a terrible rumor about me. So then she told me how once when she was in school, some mean girls started a rumor about her having stolen money from someone's locker. This made some of the other girls shun her, and other ones dropped her as a friend. So then she gave me some advice on how I should handle my situation. I thought her advice was pretty good. So now I like her. In fact, I'm starting to think she's pretty cool. Not as cool as my mother, of course, but pretty close.

So all in all, I had a pretty good time. I'm even looking forward to going back and visiting there again. What I learned is that sometimes situations aren't as bad as you think they're going to be. And sometimes, they're even better than expected.

BreAnna McDermott, 13

The Kiss in the Orchard

It really is "all about people."

—Laramie Stone, 17

Recently, we moved into a really old and ugly house. It needs repair really, really badly. Practically every single screen door and many of the windows need to be replaced. I'm embarrassed to say—but it's true—that I was ashamed of it to the point of being envious of other kids who live in nicer houses. My parents say this house is a "good investment" and that in time we'll get everything fixed up. Right now, we have a big monthly mortgage and so we can't afford to give the house, as they call it, "a face-lift."

The only thing nice about the house is the orchard—it has many fruit and flower trees. When they're in bloom (a totally incredible sight!), the whole neighborhood smells wonderful. Still, the orchard doesn't make up for the tattered appearance of the house. Which is why I've never had any of my friends over.

One day when my dad was remarking how pretty the fruit trees and roses looked in bloom, I couldn't resist remarking, "Well, no amount of great aroma from the orchard is going to help me become Karen Parks's new best friend!" Karen Parks is the most popular girl at school and the most cool. I'd like to be in her circle—me and about a million other kids at school. For sure I hoped she never saw my house—or I'd definitely never get invited to hang out with her. Karen is what you might say very "status" conscious. If someone isn't really cool according to her standards, well, then Karen Parks isn't much interested in gracing that person with her presence.

The remark hurt my dad's feeling. Then he asked me if that's why I'd never invited anyone over. "I think I'll wait until the house gets its face-lift, Dad," I replied. My dad was quiet for a moment and then in his usual thoughtful demeanor said, "It's all about people. If you create an atmosphere where everyone enjoys themselves, then that's going to be more important to them than the appearance of the house. They'll understand that we just moved in and haven't as yet started repairs." Then he suggested I have a little party in the orchard and to do that in the coming weeks since everything was in full bloom and looked and smelled so nice. He explained how we could run an extension cord from the house to the orchard so I could have electricity for music, lights and a hotplate for foods and snacks. He said that for about $75 I could have "quite a little get-together" and that he and Mom would be willing to set aside $75 from the budget so I could buy some of the things I needed for the party. He said that if I were to add to that from my allowance and babysitting jobs, it would cover anything else I needed.

His laying out the possible party plans made me feel ashamed for making the remark I had. I thought it over and then got to work making a flyer to distribute around the neighborhood advertising my looking for babysitting jobs. The flyer worked, and a month later I invited ten friends. Only eight came. Just enough—especially since Julian Lee, who wasn't among the ones I'd invited, came with Stan Boley, who was. Julian is a guy from school and considered a really neat guy. I thought so too.

It was a great party and easy to tell that everyone else thought so. Because the house sits on nearly a full acre, we didn't have to be concerned about disturbing the neighbors, so we cranked the music up and played it at full blast. It was great! Everybody danced the entire time. Dancing under the stars, amid beautiful blooms that filled the air with this incredible fragrance. It was magical.

So magical that Julian Lee kissed me!

I fell in love with Julian that night, and he with me. As you can imagine, falling in love makes any party "the best ever"! I considered the party a huge success! Still, Dad had been right—it's all about people. That night, the eight of us dancing under the stars in the orchard could have been at the best prom in all the world, but it wouldn't have topped the mood we created in the orchard. And you know, no one mentioned the appearance of the house, but everyone did comment on what a cool family I had. And of course, everyone said that we should party again very soon—and in the orchard.

Word got around at school that everyone had missed the "party of the century." So I took that to mean that maybe Julian and I weren't the only ones who kissed in the moonlight. Beth Mitchell and Kenny Groves became a couple the very next day! And Lindsey Evans and Chad Lockwood did the next week. I don't know if it was my imagination, but it seemed to me that after that, I'd become pretty popular. Even Karen Parks came up to me and said how sorry she was to have missed the party (she wasn't invited!), even suggesting that "we" have another one there very soon.

And maybe I will. One thing is for sure: I won't be waiting until the house gets its face-lift. Not for the party, or to have Julian Lee over.

Laramie Stone, 17

Two Years . . . to Go

Do not be so dumb as to believe that others will like you more just because you're willing to be their doormat.

—Cliff Chapell, 19

For the past five years, I've been behind bars for a crime I did at the age of fourteen. I've had lots of time on my hands to think about how I got into this situation and why I am where I am. At first I searched for a reason to blame others for my predicament. Here's what I came up with: My father died when I was thirteen—so I didn't have a positive male role model in my life. Which is why I started doing drugs. Which is why I was always getting into fights. Which is why my school kicked me out. Which is why I don't have a high school diploma. Always working, Mom was never home—which is why I craved attention from others. Which is why I sought it from thugs and gangs in my neighborhood. Which is I why I did what they asked of me.

I really want to add, "Which is why I'm here (prison)." But the reason I can't is that sooner or later you've got to give up your excuses. In my case, I can build the case against Dad and Mom, but the truth is, I am responsible for what I did, period. The more I thought about things, the more these excuses stopped making sense. I'm where I am because I allowed myself to be led astray. Yes, I did it for attention, but still, I did it. Because I was willing to do whatever it took to be "important" to the older "dudes" in my neighborhood, they saw how gullible I was. So it comes as no surprise that they saw me as someone they could "use." So they did. One day they told me they wanted me to do something for them. I was excited because that meant I would be made important in their eyes. They told me to take their gun, run by a certain house, and shoot at the windows. I did.

They told me the house was empty. It wasn't.

A young boy died as a result of my actions.

Pretty stupid. Pretty tragic. As a result of my foolish thinking—and illegal actions—someone's life ended. All just because I wanted others to think I was game for anything. I still have nightmares about what I did. I can barely utter the words: "I took someone's life." I can only hope that God will forgive me. I can never say I'm sorry to the boy I killed. I can never make it right to his family and friends. Nothing I can do will bring him back. I do talk to the parents of the "deceased," even though no amount of my being sorry or apologizing to them can give them back their son. The parents visit me, and have told me they have "forgiven" me. I'm not sure if I can forgive myself, but I am grateful they have forgiven me. That must be really hard to do: forgive someone who has cheated them out of their own child. They are really caring people, and I hope that God is good to them, because they have suffered so much because their son is dead.

I should tell you that the parents of the boy I killed asked me to share my story with you. For this I am most grateful, because I really want to tell you that regardless of the circumstances in your life, you don't have to go down the wrong path. You really don't. Even if your parents aren't around, or should they have messed up their own lives to the point of not being able to help you with yours—or whatever else you think is a reason for some tough times—then find someone else to help you. You really can find others who are willing to be a positive influence on you. You really can find others who will give you a reason and a chance to turn your life around. Maybe it's a favorite teacher, a counselor, an aunt or uncle or grandma or grandpa. Whoever it is, just don't be hardheaded. Listen to them. And don't drink or take drugs. Doing that will turn you into someone who is unable to make good choices. You won't care because when you're under the influence of chemicals, you're not in your right mind.

So for goodness sakes, think about what you're doing and why. Do not be so dumb as to believe that others will love or like you more if you are their doormat. Wanting acceptance from others at the risk of doing stupid or dangerous things can't lead to anything good. And it can lead to incarceration. This I can tell you from firsthand experience.

Life behind bars is not a way to live. It's a hard life, and an emotionally cruel one. Not that that seems to be stopping others from coming in here. Every day I see a truckload of young people coming in here. I can see myself in them. I try and talk with them about getting out of gang life and learning to care about themselves and their families. They listen sometimes—especially when they are by themselves—because they really do know how hard life is on the streets. Still, when they get together in groups, I can see the "big man" attitude setting in. Too bad. I know they just don't want to be seen as weak. They try to look strong, but really they're just lost. Like I was.

Believing that what someone else thought of me was more important than what I thought of me is a lesson I've learned the hard way. I hope you can learn it just by reading about it. Being someone's cellmate doesn't have to become your reality. Think. Think. Think . . . about all the things you love and care about. Don't ever be willing to lose it, and don't ever be willing to take it away from another human being.

Cliff Chapell, 19

Denmark Girl in America

It is possible to outgrow even your best friend—especially if you find yourselves living different values!

—Marie-Louise Thyssing, 17

I live in Denmark. I am seventeen years old. I had always wanted to go abroad as an exchange student. I applied, and then nervously waited. I did get accepted, as well as get the country of my choice, which was America. So then my nervousness turned from "Will I get accepted?" to "Will it be a good experience?" and "Will everyone like me?"

So while I was excited I was also a bit afraid. I didn't have a huge amount of experience in traveling, and I'd never been to America. Everyone knows that going to America is the most wonderful thing ever, a chance of a lifetime for a teenager. But everyone here talks about how different it is from life in my own country. Even before I left I began to miss my family and especially my best friend, Camilla. Camilla was very supportive of the idea—and happy for me that I was accepted, but, understandably, she was also sad that I was leaving for an entire year! That is a long time to be away from your very best friend, especially since for so long we'd been as close as sisters. It was really hard saying good-bye to her, in fact, almost depressing! But we promised to stay in touch, and made plans for being together the moment I returned from America.

So off I went to America, to a small town in Washington state. All I can say is that it was great and I had a blast! There were lots of new experiences, lots of "firsts." As an example, in Denmark I was used to having only one best friend. So everything pretty much revolved around Camilla. I discovered that in America teenagers hang out in groups—which was really fun. Being with a lot of kids, rather than just one, means you get to break an experience down and see it from a lot of different angles. I think this is good because that way you don't get so biased. You really have to think about what you believe, because discussing something means that you have new information, and this can change your mind about how you see something. I loved hanging out with my new—and many—friends. I got to do new things as well—things I'd never done before. As an example, I got to drive a car—which was new and exciting because in Denmark we can't get our license until we turn eighteen (I was sixteen at the time!).

While in America, I did write and e-mail Camilla as often as I could. Even so, it felt like we were growing apart. We decided it was because we were so far apart, and that the moment I got back, we'd plan some fun things and that would get us back in the swing of our friendship. She told me that shortly after my return date, her parents were leaving for a family vacation in Turkey, and that her parents said it was okay for me to come along. We were very excited about this. My year in America came to an end, and I returned to Denmark. Now just as leaving Denmark for America had been tough, leaving America for my return to Denmark was tough! Talk about confusing. It was hard leaving my new best friends.

Camilla was at the airport waiting for me. It was so good to see her and I was really looking forward to being together. But within moments I could feel the distance between us. But we both knew that we needed to be patient with each other and counted on the trip to Turkey as a great way to "re-bond"—to get our friendship back to the way it was before I left for America. Well, we almost didn't make it. For the next couple of weeks everything we did was a power struggle. Everything each of us did bugged the other. Even the little things, like I'd want to rent a movie, make popcorn and hang out together at my house or her house so we could talk and listen to our favorite music—and to catch up on all that had happened when we were apart. But she would want to go out and look up a party. It was like she was on a mission to party—it seemed weird. She just couldn't sit still. Nor could we agree on anything. Like if we did decide to go rent a movie, we'd argue over what to rent. Sometimes, we'd leave the store mad at each other—and without a movie! Or if we had to meet up somewhere, we would fight because I thought one place was easier and her, the other.

It was one thing after another. Not only had our tastes changed but so had our values. I was always up for a party—but not during the school nights. Camilla was up for a party, period. It didn't matter when, where or whose party it was. I worked at a hospital, and getting good grades was important to me, so I could not party like she did. Plus, I didn't drink—and didn't think it was smart that she did. But then I learned that not only did she drink; she had begun to drink a lot. One time we went out and she got really drunk and hooked up with some guy she didn't even know. It was pretty weird. She started doing this more and more. It wouldn't even matter to her that we'd gone to the party together; I'd end up going home by myself. Not only did I worry about her, but it was a breach of the promise we'd made to each other never to leave without the other in tow. The "old Camilla" would have never done that. It was like we'd become two very different people. Even so, off we went with her parents on the family vacation to Turkey.

The vacation was a real turning point. In Turkey, we realized we'd grown apart more than we could handle. It was almost like spending time with a total stranger, and one I didn't like all that much. I'm sure she felt the same. Still, I tried to be understanding. Because I had experienced so much in America and I talked so much about the American experience, I thought maybe she was a bit jealous. So I made a special point to talk less about America and the friends I'd made there, and instead let her lead the way in conversations. Even that made no difference. We were now different people, liking and needing different things. I couldn't believe that one year could make such a difference.

So the lesson in all this is that people do change. Even if I'd spent the year with Camilla as opposed to America, I wouldn't have transformed into such a different person. And she did. I loved America, and it was so different from my own culture, but it didn't change me. I learned and I've grown from the experience, but my values have not changed. Camilla's values have changed. When you've grown in different directions, it's time to move on. It is possible to outgrow even your best friend—especially if you find yourselves living different values!

Marie-Louise Thyssing, 17

The "Lauren Club"

So many times I'd sit in class worrying about who did or didn't like me. I don't go there anymore. I've learned that I can remain true to myself, refusing to buy into any of the cliques at school, and still be liked.

—Lauren Gay, 14

When I was in elementary school I had a very close group of friends. We had been together for six years, kindergarten through fifth grade (some of us had even gone to preschool together). We were all in the same classes together year after year. We played games and sports together. We went on skiing and snowboarding trips to neat new places (even out of state!) like Colorado and Idaho. We went backpacking and on fishing trips. We went on church retreats. Everybody was invited to everyone's birthday parties. We helped each other do homework. We stood up for each other. Our parents carpooled. We were more like a family than just classmates. For sure, most all of us considered ourselves to be each other's friends.

Then came middle school. I didn't expect things to change, but they did. Within weeks different kids began forming cliques. My old friends and I were no different. We formed one, too. I wasn't all that surprised that we were seen as the most cool because we were: We were smart and funny, very social, had quick wits, dressed nice and listened to the latest music. So we emerged as the "most popular" group. As for the girls in the group, we were the girls other girls wanted to be like.

I enjoyed being part of this group—it was great. At least in the beginning. But, it wasn't long before this group, my old friends, began to change. For example, one day two of my old friends, two of the "most popular" girls, walked up to another kid and began saying sarcastic things to him, calling him "a nerd" and "a loser." They called him other things, too, nasty things that I can't put in writing. I was shocked they were so mean to someone. It really made me uncomfortable, and I was embarrassed. It got worse. Within no time, this sort of thing began to happen a lot. Pretty soon it became a normal thing that happened all the time. Suddenly, in our group name-calling, cruelty and profanity were "in." If you weren't in the group, not only were you "not cool," but you were fair game for these attacks. I was sure it must have been awful to be confronted by members of our group. We weren't all that great to each other, either. We got so used to dumping on other kids that we started doing it to each other, too, sometimes even when outsiders were around. I was really feeling stressed out: I knew the way our group was treating other kids, and even ourselves, wasn't right. And yet, I didn't want to give up the benefits and status I had because I was part of this group. It felt nice to be envied and thought of as the "best" or "coolest." I know that sounds terrible, but I'd be lying if I didn't admit that it was true.

Then, fate sort of just stepped in. As it turned out, I didn't have many classes with my old group of friends and so I was meeting a lot of new kids, and a lot of us were becoming friends. Little by little I began spending more time with this new group, a group that was pretty much thought of as a "class act." Like the "most popular" group, they were smart, had fun parties, wore neat clothes, listened to popular music and were good athletes. They had everything going for them my old friends did, except they were nicer. They didn't get their kicks by making other kids feel bad so that they could feel better or more important. Best of all, they were hardly ever mean to anyone.

What a relief. It was such a big change from the "most popular" group. And a good feeling. I liked being with them because it felt like the old days when everyone supported each other. How different this was from my old friends. They always had a new rumor to spread, always a new victim to harass, always a teacher they were out to get. For all the benefits I got from being part of the "most popular" group, as exciting as it was, as flattering as it was, and for all the "bonding" with the coolest kids it produced, it was also stressful, tiring and time-consuming. And, of course, to make things worse, I knew a lot of what we were doing was not only mean, it was wrong.

So here I am, one foot in the "most popular" clique, and one foot in the "class act" group, but needing (and wanting) to choose to belong to either one or the other. While stressing out over it, I tried to understand why some kids, like my old friends, were more popular than others. They didn't dress any differently, weren't any prettier, smarter or better athletes. So why did other girls, including some of my new friends, envy my old friends, and want to be like them and accepted by them? All of a sudden, it came to me. The "most popular" were most popular because they acted and advertised that they were! They just put it "out there" that they were the most popular, and so other kids thought so, too. It was that simple.

I learned something else: Cliques demand total loyalty and commitment, as well as conformity. While the members choose who can join, initially, the group then makes you choose to be "in" or "out." Not that they have to pressure you a whole lot to make a choice. It's really difficult, if not impossible, to "belong" to two (or more) groups at the same time. Each group is always doing different things, in different places, at the same time, and going to different parties at the same time. Who can be in two or more places at the same time? I couldn't. But even before the "most popular" group could force me to choose, my new friends, the "class act" club talked to me about it. Even my new friends thought I had to make a choice. How, they said, could I be doing things with them and with my old friends at the same time? They weren't mean about it; they just wanted to see me more often.

But it wasn't easy to pick one friend or friends over another. Yes, I really admired my new friends, the "class act" kids, but I'd spent practically my entire life with my old friends, who were still my friends even though I knew they weren't perfect, and besides, I had to admit, I liked being seen as one of the "most popular." Talk about stress! So I was forced to really think things through. The two groups, my old friends, and my new ones, were alike in a lot of ways, but they were really different in the way they treated people. One was mean and exclusive, the other friendly and supportive.

But I knew I didn't want to be mean to other kids, and I didn't want them to be mean to me. So I started leaning toward choosing my new friends over my old ones. I began by mostly hanging out more with my new friends. Still, a couple times a week I would spend time with my old friends, like have lunch with them, see them at church or play sports with them. It was hard giving them up as close friends, even though they were mean sometimes, because they could also be a lot of fun to be with and they did a lot of fun things. Still, being part of both groups was confusing, to me and to them. No one, including myself, knew where I belonged, and you were supposed to know where you belonged—everyone was supposed to know where you belonged.

So I began to think that maybe it wasn't impossible to belong to two groups at once. We had been able to have a lot of different friends before we got to middle school. Why couldn't we do it again? Maybe I could make it work. What if I refused to join either group? What if I remained true to myself, and what I thought was right, refusing to buy into "membership" at all? Could I be myself, be with all sorts of kids, and still be liked and accepted? Would the "Lauren Club of One" mean that I'd be left out and home alone or could I be the "Lauren Club of One and Many," the one being me and the many being both my old friends and my new ones. A lot of kids thought I was crazy, and I was confused and unsure, but I decided to take a chance and to find out. So I did.

I couldn't believe what happened. I hoped it would work

out, but honestly had my doubts! I thought I would end up the "Lauren Club of One" with no friends. But the "Lauren Club of One and Many" is working out, and it has been accepted! It's great. My old friends and I still get to do a lot of things together, as do my new friends and I. And because I'm seen as me and not just as a member of a group where everyone is pretty much viewed as being the same, I get to be myself. I've really learned a lot.

Looking back at all the time I spent sitting in class wondering and worrying about who would like me and who wouldn't, now I don't go there anymore. I'm not saying I still don't face challenge and uncertainty, or that maybe things will change and I'll get a different lesson in friendship and membership in cliques a week or a month or a year from now. I'm just saying that I'm happy with my decision. What started out as such a big deal worked out really well, and I'm no longer totally stressed. Now I can hang with my newer friends at school and do stuff with them, but I still see my old friends around and we still do stuff together, too. It turned out great.

Lauren Gay, 14

How to Recognize a Miracle

A mother is "the heart" of a family. Everything pivots around her.

—Ashley Strimple, 17

I knew something was terribly wrong when the school gave me the message that my dad was picking me up from school "any minute now." Sure enough, within minutes, Dad did show up. There was pain in his eyes. "What? What's happened, Dad?"

"Mom's had a heart attack!" he blurted out. "She'll be fine, but she's in intensive care." These were incredible words to hear. "That can't be, Dad. Thirty-seven-year-olds don't have heart attacks," I informed him, trying to picture my mother in an intensive care unit struggling to hold onto life. If you knew my mom, you'd realize how her having a heart attack seemed so totally out of the question. My mother is one of the strongest and healthiest people I know. She doesn't get sick; I mean, a major flu bug could be going around, but my mother would be the one person who didn't catch it! Mom is a runner who is in excellent shape. She loves her job (she's a respiratory therapist at a hospital). She never stresses out. She loves her family. She loves life. So how could a heart attack happen to her?

As hard as it was to believe, it was true.

She could have died. People can and do die from heart attacks, no matter how young—or seemingly healthy—they may be. But like I said, my mother is fine now. Several months have passed. But it is a time filled with some of the most important lessons I've learned. Some of the lessons were simple, yet profound. Perhaps the most important lesson was that until she was hospitalized, I never considered just how much a mother is "the heart" of a family. Everything pivots around her. Certainly, our house just didn't seem to function the same without our mother there.

I also learned that there is much truth in what they say about life being "a gift." Because a heart attack can claim a life in the blink of an eye, I learned—firsthand—how fragile life is. I love my mother. Her brush with death made me want to never forget to tell—and show—her that I do.

And, that fateful day taught me that miracles—which I consider to be the hand of God at work—do happen. As it relates to my mother's ordeal, here are three that happened that day.

Miracle one: The heart attack happened while my mother—who works in a hospital—was at work! When she started having severe chest pains, she immediately went to the emergency room. The attending physician diagnosed her condition (a heart attack) instantly, so she received medical care at the very onset of her attack.

Miracle two: Mom got to the emergency room at 2:30 P.M., the exact time my dad routinely leaves for his coaching practice (which meant no one would have been able to reach him by phone). But on this particular day, my dad was running late, so when the emergency call came in, he received it. As a result, my dad was able to rush to the hospital to be there for my mother.

Miracle three: As the result of tests, it was discovered that a secondary blood clot had formed in one of the main arteries of my mother's heart. She was rushed to the cardiac cauterization laboratory, where a procedure called an angiogram was performed. This was followed by an angioplasty to reopen her blood supply to the heart. This early diagnosis could have prevented my mother from having a stroke, or worse. Early detection also meant she could stop further damage to her body. The doctors surmised that the blood clot was caused by the birth control pills my mom had been taking—a possible side effect of using oral contraceptives. The ironic thing is my mom had just seen the doctor two months before, and they told her that she should stay on the birth control pills because she was not at risk: She was healthy, a nonsmoker and was not overweight.

The heart attack is behind us now. Everyone in the family is pretty much back to life as usual, with one exception: We never let even one day go by without being totally grateful for it.

Ashley Strimple, 17

Stepping Up to Dreams

I've learned that I'm not alone in the universe. I don't have to always rely only on myself.

—Matthew Oden, 17

One night, at around three o'clock in the morning, I sat straight up in bed. Something was really wrong, or at least out of sync, but what? All I knew is that here I was, wide awake and feeling anxious in the middle of the night, trying to figure out what this "Something's wrong, but what?" feeling meant. I quickly did a rundown of what it could be. Had I forgotten to do something: Had I turned in all-important papers? Was a library book overdue? Had I mailed all of the college applications in on time? Was it a mistake to have told my girlfriend I didn't want to be as committed to the amount of time we spent going out? Had I forgotten anyone's birthday?

But I could think of nothing; everything seemed to be as it should. So then I began to mentally run down the things that were coming up. What was I going to do if I didn't get accepted into the college of my choice, then what? What if I didn't get the scholarship I needed? Should I keep my car on the college campus next fall, or wait until I get there to see if I really need it or if it would only be one more added expense? Should I take a part-time job, or was the time better spent working toward getting good grades? Like a detective, once again I searched for any and all possible clues as to what was bothering me to the point of waking me up in the middle of the night.

But once again I came up empty-handed. Then, looking over at the clock, upon seeing my Bible laying on my bed stand, I decided I'd flip it open and let whatever phrase was staring me in the eye "speak to me." It was Jeremiah 17:7–8, which says, *"Blessed is the man who trusts in the LORD, and whose hope is the*

LORD. For he shall be like a tree planted by the waters, which spreads out its roots by the river, and will not fear when heat comes; but its leaf will be green, and will not be anxious in the year of drought, nor will cease from yielding fruit." I read it again, wondering how it could apply to my "what's wrong?" feeling. And then it struck me that these words were full of promise. I was to trust. I must have faith. I must allow God to be a part of things. I've since done just that.

Here's what I've learned: I am not alone in the universe. God didn't drop me off and say, "There you go. Welcome to earth. Have a nice time." He didn't abandon me, which means I don't have to figure everything out for myself. I'm not saying that I don't take responsibility for my life. I expect to forge ahead and to live life for all it's worth. I do intend to set great goals and achieve great things. I'm just saying that when I bring God into the picture, I can better decipher if the "what's wrong?" feeling is about something I've put off or if He is trying to get my attention, whether to steer me in a direction or present me with a better opportunity than what I may have come up with on my own. Or, maybe it's to get me to listen to someone who has a better take on something than I do.

So now I don't lose sleep over things anymore. When I get that "something's missing" feeling, or even when life gets too crazy or out of control, I just turn it over to Him. These days, all my nights are about peace-filled sleep.

Matthew Oden, 17

Eternal Optimist

The pessimist may be proved right, but the optimist has a better time on the trip.

—Melissa Miller, 18

I am an eternal optimist! An eternal optimist is someone who finds the glass half full—as opposed to half empty. This, I have discovered, is a great key to living a great life. (I would know, because I have a lot of friends who see it mostly as half empty!) One of my favorite quotes is this one by Reverend Robert Schuller: *It takes but one positive thought when given a chance to survive and thrive to overpower an entire army of negative thoughts.* I believe that. I think it is possible "when doled lemons, to make lemonade." Not everyone believes this, of course, but it has been my discovery that optimism is one of the great taste berries of life. In other words, an optimistic attitude can make even a rain-drenched homecoming a fun experience.

Take the other day. My alarm went off really early and the moment my feet hit the floor, there was a smile on my face! This was going to be a very exciting day: It was homecoming! Was that a rain cloud in the sky? So? I pulled on my bright red-and-gold cheerleading uniform, raised my ponytail as high as I could and, for effect, sprinkled some red glitter in my hair and tied it with our special red homecoming bow. As I drove to the game that morning, the sky looked dreary and black, and the air felt cold. Rain is never a good thing when you are on a cheer squad. Not only do we wear skirts as we cheer, but there is no easy way to stunt and cheer when the ground is slick and shoes are wet and muddy. Girls just go flying (but not in the good way)!

We had been practicing for the halftime show for three-and-a-half months, and we were more than ecstatic to perform our routine in front of the energized fans for this all-important game! I arrived at school—only to be greeted by a friend who is an eternal pessimist. "Everything's ruined," she groaned. "Wouldn't you know it would rain on the most important day of the year!"

"Might as well go stretch and practice in the gym," I smiled. "Who knows, the sun could come out!"

"Our routine is history," she said, pouting. Doesn't hearing a "downer" just make you want to slump in disappointment, too? Exactly. Which is why you have to be very careful not to hang out with too many downers. Downers can really sap your optimism.

As though Mother Nature felt the gloom and doom, it rained. In fact, it was the first time in many years that it hailed in San Diego County! But of course, the game must go on! And it did. And you know what, we had a blast cheering in the rain. We even performed our halftime routine in the rain! Every stunt seemed to fall down, the routine seemed to be imperfectly polished and still, we never had so much fun. For one, all pressure was off. Not one person in the stands could fault us—for sure they had no way to know if our slipping and sliding was or wasn't a part of our cheers. As a squad of cheerleaders, we never had more fun, nor bonded so closely as a result. All petty behavior was put aside, and we all just sort of coped. And that's my point, as well. You always just have to do the best you can with whatever situation is at hand. And that's all that really matters. So when I am confronted by a bad situation, I try to perceive it as a challenge and try harder, letting it keep me on my toes.

It may sound outrageous, maybe even impossible, but I believe that everyone can be optimistic. Of course, no one, except for maybe a full-time saint, can be 100 percent happy all the time. But everyone is capable of thinking affirmative thoughts instead of negative ones. No need to let insignificant circumstances make you miserable—which is to say that the best lesson I've learned is that the pessimist may be proved right, but the optimist has a better time on the trip!

Melissa Miller, 18

Poisonous Beauty

Abundance is an attitude of appreciation that exists within our own hearts.

—Kelly Chakeen, 17

I was in Fiji, sitting in a tiny makeshift church on an unbelievably hot and humid day. Uncomfortable and totally bored, I looked around the room at the many faces. In spite of the heat, the eyes of the locals were utterly riveted to the minister who had, by now, gone on for four long, monotonous hours. But they were not bored; instead, they felt blessed for the time to listen to the Word. They had waited for Sunday all week.

The church made them a community; here they all gathered to share similar joys and common struggles. Here, once at church, they lay down their trials. Here, despite the past day's defeat, they were reborn, renewed and refreshed. I looked at the tattered walls, so desperate for a coat of paint. How so very different from my world of multimillion-dollar youth rooms and PowerPoint sermons. But to these eyes, the walls were just fine. They were the foundation for the church—which was the foundation of their lives. These walls represented hope and held the promise of eternal love.

I looked at the love and joy on their faces, and in that moment, I envied them. I looked at my carefully tanned skin and my pedicured feet, and wondered just exactly what it felt like to have that much faith.

Back home now, once again a part of the poisonous beauty of a country that is sure to head it into a downward plunge, the memory of rock-solid faith I had witnessed in Fiji is forever burned in my consciousness. Perhaps one of the most profound lessons I've ever learned is that "abundance" is best defined as the attitude of appreciation that exists within our own hearts. As for me, now, instead of complaining about the fact that I have to share a bathroom with a sibling, I am grateful I have clean water to bathe in.

Kelly Chakeen, 17

Teen Talk: Enlightened Perspective—I've Learned That . . .

I've learned that blinkers are important.

I've learned that brushing my girlfriend's hair is one of life's great pleasures.

I've learned that someone can love you a lot and not know how to show it.

I've learned that you can make someone's day by simply smiling.

I've learned that singing "Amazing Grace" can lift my spirits.

I've learned that you can tell a lot about how someone respects a date by the way he opens a door, calls when he's ten minutes away and leaves a tip at the restaurant.

I've learned that regardless of how much you argue with your parents, you miss them when you're on a trip.

I've learned that supermodels are not always as pretty as the girl sitting next to you in class.

I've learned not to pet porcupines.

I've learned that some questions ("Does this pimple look terrible?") should not be answered.

I've learned crying can make you feel better.

I've learned everyone comes into your life for a reason.

I've learned that not all locks are meant to be opened.

I've learned to forgive myself for not being born a genius.

I've learned there is no Santa Claus or Easter Bunny, and that my mother is not the Tooth Fairy.

I've learned that my parents sometimes lie to protect me from the pain of the truth.

I've learned that when the door says "push," I shouldn't pull.

I've learned that most pickup lines backfire.

I've learned that junior high and high school relationships are not forever.

I've learned that you shouldn't tailgate.

I've learned that when you speed over bumps, you can count on biting your tongue.

I've learned that police officers have little or no sense of humor.

I've learned that no one is perfect until you fall in love with him—and when you fall out of love, he's not perfect at all.

I've learned that I wish I could have told my dad that I love him one more time before he passed away.

I've learned that it's best to keep thinking about the words you say because tomorrow you may have to eat them.

I've learned that college is not for everyone.

I've learned that sometimes success is just making it through the day.

I've learned that light sockets are not made for paper clips.

I've learned dog kisses can make anything better.

I've learned parents make mistakes, too.

I've learned that just because you hide your vegetables at the table doesn't mean they're gone for good.

I've learned teachers don't always have the right answers.

I've learned it's better to be slow and careful than fast and careless.

I've learned lima beans are never delicious.

I've learned that not all love is forever.

I've learned that looking back on tears can make you laugh. Looking back on laughs can make you cry.

I've learned that sometimes "I'm sorry" just doesn't cut it.

I've learned sometimes the nerdy guy DOES get the girl.

I've learned that tomorrow will always remember what you put off doing today.

I've learned to worry less about what I have and concentrate on giving more.

I've learned that a bad experience can be a blessing in disguise.

I've learned to use my mistakes to my advantage.

I've learned being popular means you don't have to live by the same set of rules as everyone else.

I've learned love can make you crazy.

I've learned that no matter how old you are, body noises are funny.

I've learned a person can be ignorant but not stupid. On the other hand, a person can be intelligent and not smart.

I've learned that being book smart does not mean you have common sense.

I've learned manners can take you a long way.

I've learned to pay attention to the doors that have been opened for you.

I've learned that in the scheme of things, the little things really don't matter. BUT, it's the little things that can make your life miserable.

I've learned if you are going to dish it out, you better be able to take it.

I've learned that my dog doesn't like to wear sunglasses.

I've learned that cement is unforgiving.

I've learned that the "Matrix" is not real.

I've learned that a car accident can break my bones.

I've learned that traffic signs are not merely suggestions.

I've learned that bicycles are not bigger than cars.

I've learned that even when a girlfriend kisses your bruise, it still hurts.

I've learned that some secrets are not meant to be told.

I've learned that playing with fire will get me into trouble.

I've learned that 911 is for extreme emergencies only.

I've learned not to do things behind my parents' back.

I've learned never to embarrass my mom in public.

I've learned that a roll of toilet paper won't flush.

I've learned that just because someone smiles, it doesn't mean that he or she is happy.

I've learned that dressing up makes me feel better.

I've learned that playing hooky means you're going to end up in trouble.

I've learned that you should never jump into water when you can see the bottom.

I've learned that I like people when they sing the national anthem.

I've learned that our dog doesn't want to eat my broccoli either.

I've learned that when I wave to people, they wave back.

I've learned that if you want to cheer yourself up, cheer someone else up.

I've learned that life sometimes gives you a second chance.

I've learned that whenever I decide something with kindness, I usually make the right decision.

I've learned that everyone likes it when you say, "I'll keep you in my prayers."

I've learned that it pays to believe in miracles.

I've learned that people love a friendly pat on the back.

I've learned that I still have a lot to learn.

I've learned that being kind is more important than being right.

I've learned that sometimes all a person needs is a hand to hold and a heart to understand.

I've learned that when I'm upset with Mom or Dad, a walk around the block is all it takes to understand where they are coming from.

I've learned that under everyone's "tough kid" act is secret pain that hurts a lot.

I've learned that to ignore the facts does not change the facts.

I've learned that you shouldn't ignore the dragon if you live next to a dragon farm.

I've learned that when you plan to get even with someone, you are only letting that person continue to hurt you.

I've learned that I can't choose how I feel, but I can choose what I do about it.

I've learned that a smile is a great way to improve your looks.

I've learned that being nice to others not only brightens up their day, but sweetens mine as well.

Part 4

Standing Tall(er): Surviving the Loss of a Parent

I am sending an angel ahead of you
to guard you along the way.

—Exodus 23:20

Where you used to be, there is a hole in the world,
which I find myself walking around in the daytime
and falling into at night. I miss you so much.

—Edna St. Vincent Millay

It takes great courage and personal strength
to hold on to our center during times of great hurt.
When we are in the midst of loss, betrayal,
or crisis of any kind, there is power in the words,
"Be still and know I am."

—Marianne Williamson

It is not the years in your life,
but the life in your years that count.

—Adlai Stevenson

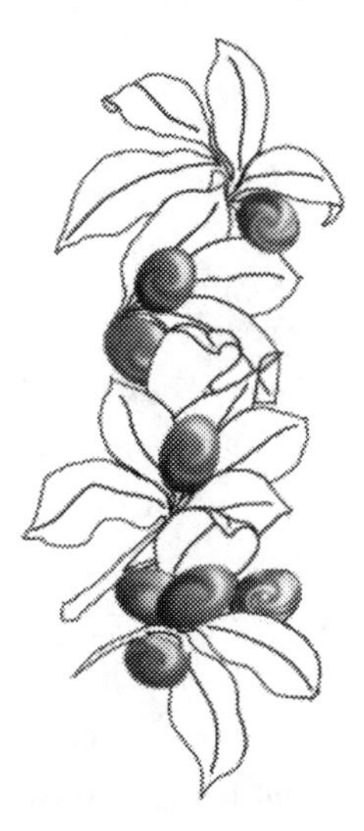

A Word from the Authors

Several months ago, I, Bettie, was a daughter. Today, I am not. I lost my mother two years ago. She was my most important friend, my number-one fan and the source I turned to when life got crazy—or as important, when I really, really needed a home-baked lemon-meringue pie. This past April, my father died. Agewise, he was eighty-three awesome years "old." Chronological years aside, to me both parents were ageless. Do children ever really take notice that Father Time is sneaking up on those who are the pillars of our lives? Probably not. Though I never took my parents for granted, I always took for granted that I'd be a daughter. But now I have to face a different reality: *I am no longer a "child" who has parents.* Do you know anyone for whom this is true?

That I had lost the two people who loved me more deeply and the most unconditionally of anyone who will ever love me in the course of my entire lifetime seemed surreal. The finality of each of their deaths, the "powerlessness" of it all, added to my sense of feeling hopelessly forlorn. The other day someone asked me how it felt to be without my parents. "Like an orphan," I replied. But this is not the only emotion seesawing its way through my mind and heart. Sometimes I am simply sad, while other times

I'm a little angry (about the fact that now I am "parentless"). On other days I pine and need to soothe myself and recall the special times, so I am grateful for the time we had together. And sometimes, I allow the memory of them to spur me on, as was true for the Green Bay Packers' Brett Favre one day after his father died. Brett threw a personal-best of 311 yards and four touchdowns in the first half alone, quickly turning a crucial game for the Packers' playoff hopes into a blowout victory. By all accounts, it was one of his greatest performances in his thirteen-year career. "Though it was just yesterday that I lost him, I knew my dad would want me to play," Favre said. "I love him so much, I didn't expect this kind of performance, but I know it was because he was watching tonight." This was a similar feeling shared by twenty-nine-year-old Dale Earnhardt Jr., who recently won the Daytona 500. His father, NASCAR legend Dale Sr., suffered a fatal crash during the Daytona 500's final lap three years ago. "How do you think your dad would feel about the win?" someone asked him at the victory lane. "He was riding in the car with me," Dale Jr. replied.

We may lose a parent, but we never lose the need to feel their love. So many teens can relate.

When we lose someone we love, understandably many of our feelings have to do with "grief." I am grieving. Jennifer is too. Grandparents are dearly beloved people—and for young people as well, their passing is extremely painful. Thousands and thousands of teens are grieving. Perhaps you, or a friend of yours, are one of them. If so, what you should know is that grief is a normal feeling, a somewhat predictable process people go through in coping with loss. Grieving is spirit-filled work. Moving through its stages is important—and serious—work. It is a bittersweet journey strewn with pain, love and confusion. It is about reminiscence—the good and the bad, as well as facing and making amends with any and all unfinished business with the people we once shared our lives with.

That we "process" grief in conscious ways is healthy. We must allow our hearts to be led through its stages. Should we "stuff" (deny) our feelings—by refusing to recognize our pain or resort to coping in negative ways (such as refusing to talk about our feelings, or to numb them with alcohol or drugs in the attempt to not face what has happened within our lives), then we run the risk of becoming bitter and angry. We only hurt ourselves more when we compulsively try to hurt less—such as through denial or avoidance. This can keep us from receiving the love and support from others who try to "be there for us" to comfort us as best they can. It can also keep us from attending to the daily tasks in our lives.

Does this mean that we "overcome" the loss of someone who has been so important to us? No. No one can, nor should they, "overcome" the influence of someone who has been an important part of their lives. Still, it is precisely because someone has had such a powerful role that we must allow the emotions of grieving to seep into and through our hearts, so that they might tenderize the hurt. Though it may not feel like it, our hearts can handle the anguish we feel. Like a hurricane, in time, powerful emotions will "spend" themselves, and we will then be more able to wear our loss as a badge of love and honor. It is then when we dry our tears and square our shoulders to the world—and stand taller. The loss of a parent transforms us.

That we are, like the young writers in this chapter, deep in the throes of grieving is just one of many reasons that working with teens who had themselves suffered the loss of a beloved mom or dad made this unit such an incredible undertaking. (Special note: We did not include the loss of a grandparent, sibling or friend, though many teens have experienced a loss of this nature, too, for space considerations, it was our decision to only include the loss of a parent.) You are about to read some remarkable and heartfelt revelations. As you will see, teens have much to say. Yes, their stories are about the loss of a parent, but it is more. It is also about the discovery of the *extent* of the "worth" of a parent's life within their own—and not just for the here and now, but for what this loss means for the years ahead. In the teen years especially, it can be easy to see "the parents" as the opposing team, the rival imposing boundaries and restrictions—those putting a halt to all things fun and bold. The hearts writing the stories you are about to read have much to say about this as well. And of course, the "if only's" are all too real for them.

Even if you are fortunate to never have suffered the loss of a parent, don't miss this opportunity to hear what other teens are feeling because they are, as so many refer to it, "missing a piece." Your life will be richer for it. What a wonderful time in your life to think deeply about the importance of having—and appreciating—your own parents.

Perhaps you already have a "missing piece"—perhaps you've never had one or both parents present in your life. Or, maybe you were adopted and there is a small voice within that wants to give a "real" face to the mystery of who "Mom" or "Dad" were. Or perhaps you are living with one parent and the other lives far away, and you feel alienated or disconnected from that parent. Maybe you've suffered physical or emotional abuse at the hands of your parents and you are understandably angry for not being regarded as precious in their eyes. Maybe your situation is entirely different from any of these descriptions. Regardless, read these stories with an open heart. When you come upon those who are making their way through personal loss, send love and light their way. This can ease the pain—and burden—they carry. Be gracious and understanding. Remember, as with most all situations in life, when you don't know what else to do, simply say with sincere meaning, "How are you doing?" and then grant that person moments of undivided attention. It will do their—and your—heart good. Such is the spirit behind the meaning of the *taste berry* used as a metaphor in the *Taste Berries for Teens* series.

That being said, it can be helpful to understand a little of the psychology of loss. What follows is a thumbnail sketch of the "journey" through grief. Please understand that this information is not intended to take the place of a trained professional who can best help you (or a friend or family member) cope with loss. It is offered simply as a way to gain a better understanding of the range of emotions that are real for someone who has suffered the loss of a loved one.

Some of the Natural Feelings When We Are Grieving

Denial: The death of a loved one is a shattering experience. Understandably, it's difficult to accept the finality of death. Denial is about needing—and taking—the time to absorb the shock of what has happened. Distancing yourself from memories—both good and bad—of that person is a way to say, "I still can't believe this has happened—and I'm still not yet ready to." And yet, sharing one's feelings helps in moving beyond this pushing away of reality—and so helps you to move to better times. The goal is to heal oneself through the creative struggle of accepting the reality of the loss.

Anger: Understandably, you are angry at the unfairness and finality of death—and what it all means for you (life without the person you love). It's okay to be angry—but important that it not be misplaced (taken out on others, or keep you from attending to your daily needs). It's important to find safe ways to let out or "spend" your feelings, such as going for a run, a long walk or playing sports. Talking with others helps as well. When you reach out and receive the support you need, eventually you'll become less angry.

Guilt: Maybe you did or said things that you wished you hadn't and now there is no way to make amends. Maybe you were mean-spirited or said cruel things. This can make you feel guilty for having your last words and actions not be loving. Counseling (whether your school counselor, clergy or peer-support groups) can help you cope with unresolved issues and help you find ways to forgive yourself (or the person you lost). As time goes on you will remember new things, and so it is possible that feelings of guilt will come and go for a long time.

Depression: In the first weeks of facing your loss, you may have an overwhelming feeling that you "can't go on." You may want to be alone. You may not sleep well, or you may feel like you want to get into bed and not get out. You may lose interest in the things that you are most excited about. You may not feel like going about your daily activities. Your moods may run hot and cold. In time, all this will pass. If you are having a really rough time returning to your "old self" and being interested again in the things that once made you happy, tell someone. Depression can be a stage, but it can develop into something more serious as well. The important thing to remember is that you don't have to go it alone. You don't have to sort things out for yourself. Turn to someone you trust, and allow that person to help you get the help and support you need.

Loneliness: Understandably, you're going to feel lonely. This is only natural. Here again it can be incredibly important to talk to others about how you are feeling. Do not isolate yourself from others. Let others be your taste berry, especially at this time of heartache.

Resolve/Acceptance: Resolve is about acceptance, a "place" in which you've come to the realization that life goes on regardless of your circumstance. It's knowing that even though this shattering experience has happened to you, you must still get out of bed, care for your pet(s), brush your teeth, get to school, pay attention to your grades and get back to your goals. You must, once again, be there for others, just as they are there for you. It's time to do more than cope with the reality of the situation; it's time to adapt to the times that lie ahead.

Forgiveness and Beyond: You've resolved to "get on with life" now, making the choice to remember the good in the person you've lost and to shine the light of the love you've been blessed to have known. You are better able to look toward the future now and embrace it.

You are not the same, but you are able to say, "I'm back!" You may very well have days when the feelings just mentioned overtake your day, but they're short-lived. Now as you revisit the memories and lapse back into one or more of the previous stages of grieving, you know from experience "this too shall pass."

Welcome to these very special stories. Know that you are entering hallowed ground.

❤ *Taste berries to you, Bettie and Jennifer Youngs*

"Not Even a Star Can Outdo the Moon!"

When you lose someone, you revisit your last moments together and play them over and over and over again. It makes me realize how important it is that all of our moments be kind and loving toward each other.

—Mandy Martinez, 18

One evening several years ago Mom and I were watching an episode of *The Wonder Years.* "Life spins like a dime and cuts like a knife," someone on the show remarked. "What's that mean, Mom?" I asked. "It means life goes by quickly and hurts when it's over," she replied, matter-of-factly. "Oh," I said, dismissing it because I couldn't relate. Today I can relate. I know exactly what the phrase means. I've just lost my mother in a car crash, and the pain is so deep it cuts to the bone.

It's only been months since my mother died, but already it feels like she's been gone a lifetime. There are days I think I can't make it through. We were so close, and we loved each other so much. The hole in my heart is bigger than the planet. And everything that happens is a gigantic reminder of just how tragic the loss is. Mom died three days before my eighteenth birthday and only a week before my older brother Robert's birthday. Two months after Mom died, my sister got married—without her own mother to see her on this momentous day. My sister also celebrated her birthday recently—without our mother. My little brother, Dylan, entered his freshman year without his mother and played his first varsity football game without his mother in the stands to proudly watch her freshman son play on a varsity team! Dylan, too, just recently celebrated a birthday—his fifteenth—without his mother. My older brother had his twenty-sixth birthday without her. She missed my first and only prom. And I graduated from high school without her cheering me on, without her ever seeing me reach this great accomplishment, something that was so important to her.

Graduation was especially tough without her. I wore a button with her picture on it so that I could feel she was there with me. I remember standing on stage waiting for my name to be called so I could come forward and get my diploma. The moment I did, I instinctively looked into the audience, searching for her face. Getting a grip on the fact that she wouldn't be there, of course, I soothed myself by saying over and over again, "Good job, Moon!" "Good job, Moon!"—which is exactly what she would have told me—a thousand times!—that day. I touched her button before walking across and I thought, *She's proud, she's proud.* She would have been soooooo proud.

Every family member tried to make up for the loss of her not being there. My sister had given me a handbag and a charm with a heart that had a cross inside. She also wrote me a nice letter, saying how sorry she was Mom couldn't be there to see this, but how I should believe Mom was there watching it all, anyway. The charm had been her last Christmas gift from Mom. She wanted me to wear it as I took my walk across the graduation stage that day. In fact, I was wearing three things pinned to me that day! All held memories of life and times with a young mother we dearly loved.

Memories. So many memories. What I've discovered is that when you lose someone, you revisit your last moments together and play them over and over and over again. In my case, Mom had just picked me up from school. We'd stopped for food, and then she'd said, "I've got to go pick up your brother. Want to come along or be dropped at home?"

"I want to go home," I told her. "I'd like to go get online."

"Okay," she said, cheerfully. We took things into the house from the car. Turning to leave, she said, "Lock the door, Moon." (My mother was fond of telling the story that as a baby, my eyes were as big as a full moon. Then, because my baby brother pronounced my name [Mandy] as "Moondee," the nickname Moon stuck.)

"As if a robber is going to come out and get me!" I replied, laughing. Mom laughed at that comeback. And in the next moment, our baby kitten, seeing the open door, decided to seize an opportunity to sneak outside. The mother cat lay nearby and lazily opened only one eye, watching her wild and bratty little kitten lower his head and belly to the floor (perhaps thinking he then wouldn't be seen), and then, like a bolt of lightning, streak to the door in an attempt to escape. It was a cute and sinister moment from the little creature, and Mom and I caught it. Instinctively, we looked at each other and then broke out laughing. Mom hurriedly pushed the door shut and said, "Look at her watch her kitten! She knew the little creep wouldn't make it past us! She's probably busting up inside laughing!" Again we laughed together. "Well, lock up then, honey. I'll be right back, Moon. Love you," she said. "Love you," I told her. I waved good-bye. Those were our last moments together. It was to be the last time I'd see my mother alive. Five minutes later, she was dead.

I loved her laugh. I miss it so much. I am so happy our last moments were those in which we were so happy, laughing and most of all, moments in which we told each other of our love for each other. It makes me realize how important it is that all of our moments be kind and loving toward each other.

Those first moments I learned of her death were insane. I didn't know what to do with myself. My mother was dead (she was only forty-six)! I was inconsolable. I cried and screamed because the rage I felt for her loss was larger than the air around me. I yelled and screamed at God for taking her, and at the same time begged Him to soothe the searing ache in my heart. I walked to the kitchen, where Mom had set down the remains of the fast food we had stopped to get. I remember putting my hand inside the bag to touch the hamburgers—still warm. I touched her raspberry drink—still cold. I thought, *The hamburgers haven't even gotten cold; her drink hasn't become room temperature, but she had time enough to lose her life. It can't be possible.*

Mom was killed turning onto the highway, a path she'd taken day after day, year after year. But as fate would have it, this would be her last time to ever make that turn. She was hit by an eighteen-wheel truck that had crossed into her lane. She must have been so terrified to see death coming upon her like that.

Her life was over. Our lives together were over.

The viewing, one day after my eighteenth birthday, was filled with stark moments. They were especially painful for me because this was my mother. But they were awful because I felt the pain and anguish of my little brother facing this terrible reality as well. I found myself unable to walk up to see her without my little brother by my side. My little brother didn't want to either. "I won't go if you don't," I told him. As though we each were doing it for the other, the two of us managed to make it to the side of our mother's casket. She looked asleep in the casket. Seeing Mom, little Dylan stood there and repeated over and over again, "That's not Momma. That's not my momma." He was dazed—as was I. All I could say was, "Her neck hurts when she sleeps like that." Lost in grief, I was totally disoriented. I just looked at her and thought, *She just bruised her face, she's fine.* But of course, she wouldn't be "just fine"; in the accident, her neck had been broken, causing her death.

Dylan and I put our hands on her shoulder. "She's cold," my little brother said, patting her forehead. I didn't want to touch her: Reality then might become real, and I wasn't ready to accept it. I had brought a couple of things with me I wanted to place in her casket. I had brought my drawing of a picture of Jesus, a picture of us kids, and a "Mother" plaque I bought her just a few short weeks ago.

Finally, I kissed the top of her head, but only at the hairline. Not too close to her forehead because I didn't want to feel that she might be cold. I kissed her and whispered, "Good night, Mom." I didn't plan on saying anything at all. It just came out. It was as if my own mind was in the ozone somewhere. I kept thinking of all the times I'd come home late from being with my friends, and there she was, sitting in her recliner waiting up for me. I so wanted to go back to that place. I looked at the flowers surrounding the casket, and then became aware of everyone crying.

I broke down then, too. The pain was just so awful.

Her memorial service was two days later, three days after my eighteenth birthday. My aunt was one of the people who stood up and talked. She told people how my mom was—in a very real way, a mother to her, too. Then it was my turn to say something, and I started to cry before I even spoke. I wanted what I was going to say to be clear. But it wasn't. "I'm going to read a poem I read to Mom on our trip to Missouri," I told everyone. "She told me when she died, she wanted me to read it. So I'm going to read this." I looked out to everyone and they were all a blur. I began reading what I considered my mother's poem, which is really a well-known poem called "A Clown's Prayer." "Dear Lord," I began. "As I stumble through this life, help me to create more laughter than tears, dispense more happiness than gloom, spread more cheer than despair. Never let me become so blasé that I fail to see the wonder in the eyes of a child, or a twinkle in the eyes of the aged. Never let me forget my work is to cheer people, make them happy, and make them laugh. Make them forget at least for a moment the unpleasantness in their life. Never let me acquire success to the point that I discontinue calling on my creator in the hour of need, acknowledging and thanking Him in the hour of plenty. And in my final moment may I hear You whisper, 'When you made My people smile, you made me smile.'"

It was difficult to get through because I was crying so hard. I remember looking out into the crowd at the many who had gathered to send my mother off to heaven, and telling them how I felt she was, somehow, still here with us. Everything from that point on is pretty much a blur. Like her life, the memorial service was over all too quickly.

In all, I believe we've lost more than just a mother. We lost a friend, a sister and a daughter—and more. She was the miracle of inspiration for all we hoped to achieve. Much of making anything of ourselves was to see the joy and happiness in her eyes. "I can't wait to tell Mom" was a line a heard a million times from all of us. She was a positive and strong-willed person who would go the distance for you—and she always supported you in going the distance. My dream was to have her watch me walk across the stage and get my high school diploma. I wanted her to see all that I was to make of life in the future. My little brother's dream was to have her there to watch him play on the "Big Boy's Field" (that's what she called it) for his freshman football games. My sister's dream was to have her be there for her wedding. My older brother's dream was to buy her new glasses for her birthday. All those dreams are history now. Sometimes I make a list of things she's going to miss, so that I can deal with them and get them out of the way. There are, of course, a lot of things I still have to deal with because they're not going to go away soon—like having to drive on the road and the very spot where she was killed. Never do I cross that place without my heart skipping a beat.

Just as my life is different now, I am different now.

I once considered my life as rather typical. Each day came and went. Overall, I was a girl who lived inside my own little world, a world where life inside my imagination was bigger and better than what actually happened. Friends, school life and boys were everything. It was "all about me." But no more. I no longer have the luxury of living life slowly or on a small scale. My mother's death has caused me to stand straight and square my shoulders to the world. I am no longer a girl now. I am a woman. It's time for me to take my mother's place in giving all the love and good she sent into the world.

Once focused on my own little world, I'm now focused on a bigger picture. Once insecure and worried about "little" things, I have no more time for that. It is time for me to step forward and be more. I must "outdo the moon" now. I remember back to all those times when I did feel insecure or unsure of myself, and Mom would playfully cajole: *"Oh, you can do it! Believe in yourself, honey! Not even a star can outdo my Moon!"* To remember these playful words and especially to not hear her say them breaks my heart. To have lost that kind of love and support is a scary feeling. Still, I must go on now. I must believe her words; I must LIVE her words. And so, I can and will do it.

In a sense, I'm writing this story now for her. I am hopeful that it will be published in the *Taste Berries for Teens* series, because that would be an accomplishment that would make her proud. I say this because about four years ago I first read one of the *Taste Berries for Teens* books. I loved it, and I told Mom I wanted to write a story and send it in to see if I could get published. My mother was thrilled that I was doing something "so grand," as she described it. The story did not get published, but the authors wrote me back and encouraged me to rewrite it and try again. My mother picked right up on this and encouraged me. Excited, I rewrote my story, "Ciara's Music Box," reading it to my mother a hundred-and-one times. When finally my mother gave a thumbs-up, I sent it in. Sure enough, the story was accepted.

That I'd been published was thrilling. But it was my mother's reaction that made it all the more exciting. She was so celebratory over it! When word came that my story had made it in the book, we sang and laughed and danced around the room! She could be so crazy—she was so young at heart. I loved that about her. "Stars canNOT even outdo my Moon!" she said, laughing and proud of the fact her daughter had a story accepted for publication. And then, "Do it again, Moon!" she encouraged, "Do it again."

I will. Not only because it will make my mother proud, but

because my heart goes out to any young person who has suffered a loss as great as mine and can take comfort in knowing that giving words to your grief helps—at least a little. And I must also do it because life is short—and I don't want to miss a day of it. I never thought losing anyone would be this hard. But life has given me my reality check; I must "cash" it. I just find a way to go on.

I know from having been published in other books in the *Taste Berries for Teens* series that at the end we're to tell readers something they can take away to apply to their own lives. My "ending" for you would be to leave you with this: If you are so lucky as to have your mom or dad alive, be so thankful. Don't wait for a reason to tell them you appreciate and love them. Show it in all you say and do. Because if one day you should, like me, get that phone call that will change your life forever, you just don't want to regret that you didn't. And with that said, I have words for you, too, Mother. I know you know this, but it helps for me to say it. "I'll never give up; I will strive to be all you wished me to be. I'll try my best to become the awesome and loving woman you are. I'll look out for my little brother, so don't worry about him. And I'll do all I can to see that we kids always love and look out for each other. Thank you for loving me so much, and for being the sort of person who is worthy of the enormously searing hurt I now feel. But I'll see you again, Mom. I know it for real. Love, your Moon."

Mandy "Moon" Martinez, 18

AUTHORS' NOTE: *We first "met" Mandy when she submitted a story for publication in our book,* More Taste Berries for Teens. *Her story did not make it into that book, but we encouraged her efforts, gave her some writing guidelines and then suggested she try again. She did. She submitted a lovely story called "Ciara's Music Box," and we published it in* A Taste Berry Teen's Guide to Managing the Stress and Pressures of Life *(pages 288–290). Buoyed by her success, Mandy once again submitted a story called "To Wear Makeup, Own Cool Clothes . . . and Be a Writer," in which she told of her dreams—and goal—to write and be published. We were impressed, and published it in—you guessed it!* A Teen's Guide to Setting and Achieving Goals *(pages 44–46). Then, just as we were writing* A Teen's Guide to Christian Living: Practical Answers to Tough Questions About God and Faith, *Mandy wrote to tell us that she had tragically lost her mom in a car crash. Mandy shared her feelings in those first days in a most poignant piece entitled, "Her Diary . . . My Diary" (pages 277–280). And so it is a special privilege to now have her share this story, an update on her life and times. Mandy exemplifies, in every spirit of the word, a taste berry. She is, in our estimation, a most cool, caring and courageous young woman. Mandy, we stand heart-to-heart with you in your days now and in those that lie ahead.*

All the Ways He Loved Me

The heart heals faster from surgery than it does from the loss of a loved one.

—told to Kyle Ross, 18

Life for me was normal until April 24, 1999, the day my father killed himself.

It's important for me to know that Dad didn't kill himself; the diseases of alcoholism and depression are what killed him. Even with an emphasis on this distinction, his death—and life without him—means my life will never be the same.

Let me first tell you a little about the bright side of my father, a man I loved so much. Dad loved his family and was proud to use the words, "My wife and kids . . ." I am absolutely positive that he loved me, and I'm sure my brothers and sisters would say the same. He had many friends. And he was a very successful businessman. Then, there was that dark side of him, one that felt despondent and hopeless to the point that he used alcohol to drown those feelings out. He drowned himself in the process.

When my father died, my first reaction was relief. I know that sounds shocking, but when you live with an alcoholic, life becomes centered on that person's dysfunction—and the stream of stress it creates. It's a relief, a feeling of freedom, to get out from under the blanket of pain and chaos. I remember when, in the first moments I heard the news that my father was dead, there was an immediate knowing that now our family would no longer be imprisoned by the constant worry about Dad's whereabouts—and worrying whether or not he was alive. As for me personally, now I wouldn't have to experience yet another drinking binge of his, nor worry about when one would occur, or witness and endure his embarrassing behavior in public.

But this sense of relief lasted only for a few moments, when I realized that I'd never see my father again. Never. Not ever. He'd never say, "I love you," again. And I could never tell him to his face that I loved him. Suddenly, there was a deep sadness that my dad would never, ever:

- Smile at me
- Give me a hug
- Help me with homework
- Sit in the bleachers at my sports games
- Gas up my car (for free) as he always did!
- Take pictures of my date and me, or ask me if I needed a clean shirt to wear
- See me graduate from high school—or college
- Attend my wedding
- Be a grandpa to my children
- Be my friend—for life

With these realizations, a deep sadness set in, knowing how much I'd miss him, and he'd be missed forever. And I felt sorry for myself, and for my mom and brothers, Dad's parents and everyone who loved him.

Next came a boiling anger. Wanting to know, "Why did he do this?" filled my head with the fury of a steaming locomotive. When I wasn't centering this question on the disease that he suffered from, I blamed Dad for abandoning his family and, in particular, me (and at a time in my life when I needed him). My father had made a decision, and I thought it a selfish one. But he "couldn't fix what ailed him"—or at least that's what one of his good friends said at the memorial service.

"The heart heals faster from surgery than it does from the loss of a loved one," a friend of his told me at the memorial service. I could relate: My heart had just undergone emotional triple-bypass surgery—without anesthesia. How would I ever heal?

My first attempt was to put on a strong face, even if my

insides were as wobbly as Jell-O. I began the facade the day following the funeral: I'd get up, shower, go to school, and after school, go to baseball practice or hang out with my friends, as usual. Why let my father's inability to handle life stop me from mine? Besides, his death was a thing of the past, now, and I was going forward.

The strategy pretty much worked—except for the fact that my heart wanted nothing more than to withdraw from the world and do nothing but cry. None of my friends could relate to what I was going through. How could they; their fathers were alive. I'm sure some of them thought I was even better off (they had experienced on many occasions my dad's drunkenness).

Then came another wave of self-pity: Life had been unfair to me! And why me? He was the alcoholic! I had been a good son. Why would he want to leave me and miss out on being with me? And why should I get strapped with life without a dad? All my friends had dads. And judging from all the guilt I went through every minute of every day—not to mention the sleepless nights—why should I be suddenly saddled with problems and concerns that none of my friends had to even think about, let alone be the one with the stigma of "the kid whose father committed suicide"?

This was followed by yet another stage of anger, one that collapsed into tears and realization: My dad's gone—no matter what else—Daddy's gone! I cried myself to sleep and awoke knowing that on April 24, 1999, whether I was ready or not, my life was changed. I had to deal with not having a father and the sad circumstances surrounding his death. I had to deal with myself and the pain his death caused me. I had to deal with thinking about my future, without my father in it. I had to deal with a broken heart and put it back together again. I had to take complete responsibility for everything I've done (and will do) and make tough decisions on my own that normally wouldn't have been mine to make until later in life.

I'm doing these things. My father's death totally crushed me, but with the help of my mom, friends and faith, I'm rebuilding my life. My family and I have all been so loving and kind to each other, and that's been helpful. And working with counselors and attending youth group has allowed me to freely talk about my feelings. It helped me let go of the anger and be able to forgive myself for feeling anger toward my father, and to forgive him for the fathering I hadn't received from him (including his not being there in my future). I've come to understand that it was not my father who committed such a desperate act, but rather, the disease from which he suffered. It's been a lot to deal with. Like I said, it's been something that's changed my life.

The result is that now, when I revisit memories of my father, what comes to mind is how much he loved me and all the ways he showed it:

- ❤ The smiles
- ❤ The bear hugs
- ❤ Helping me with homework
- ❤ Being at my sports games
- ❤ Gassing up my car (for free!)
- ❤ Always taking my picture
- ❤ Loaning me his shirts

The list is a long one, and I will always be grateful for his love. And for the years we had together.

Kyle Ross, 18

AUTHORS' NOTE: *We reprint this poignantly beautiful and heartfelt story for you because we receive enormous amounts of mail from teens who not only fell in love with Kyle's heart and sense of family, but because so many shared his plight. Each year, alcohol claims the lives of thousands upon thousands of people. As for Kyle, his heart continues mending, and as a result, he is flourishing: Kyle is now in college, and looking forward. As our readers know, Kyle is a true taste berry, definitely a young man who is most cool, caring and courageous.*

License to Cry

Crying washes away some of the layers of emotions that bind you to pain. Shedding some of this pain can help you move beyond the hurt and transforms guilt into fond memories.

—Sarah Erdmann, 16

I couldn't wait to turn sixteen! There are lots of reasons to want to turn sixteen, and getting a license—translation: DRIVING—is a big one for most teens. Did I want to drive myself to school? Yes. Did I want to drive myself to work rather than being dropped off by a family member, or hitch a ride with friends or anyone else who might give me a ride? Yes. Did I want to go to the mall and to parties and be able to ask whatever friend to go along? Absolutely! Still, the most important reason I was looking forward to getting my license was to drive alone to a certain cemetery.

The thought of a teen being excited about driving to a cemetery may sound a little odd, but for me it was something I had been waiting for since I was ten. That's when my mom died.

I was only six years old when my mother was diagnosed with brain cancer. Even though young, like all adoring kids when their parents are their total life, I loved her and thought she was awesome. But as the cancer took hold, and with each brain surgery—and there were several—Mom began to change dramatically. Radiation treatments were administered, and with each set of treatments, the vibrant and happy person I knew changed even more. There came a time when she was too weak to go on walks with me. Too weak to play with me. Too weak to make dinner and too weak to clean the house.

Then the day came when she was too weak to be "Mother."

My family moved to a bigger house. I had to change schools. Change. Change. Change. Nothing was the same! Mom was moved from the bedroom into the living room. Each day a different family member or friend cleaned the house and cooked meals. Within time, hospice nurses came and went on a regular basis. I felt overwhelmed by all that was going on. I understood what was happening, but it overwhelmed me. I was feeling hundreds of emotions. Crying wasn't one of them.

My mother was slipping away before my eyes, and I was scared. I talked to her the moment I got home from school each day, hoping against hope that this day had been the one in which fate—and health—had taken a turn for the better. Maybe, just maybe, today she felt better. It never happened. Everything was slipping away: Family life as we knew it and my mother as I knew her. Even the "us" was fading. One day as she and I were talking, it dawned on me that for the entire time, she was mistaking me for my brother! It was so upsetting that I cut off the conversations with her and now watched her from a distance.

My mother's health was definitely deteriorating. My confusion and the sense of being overwhelmed grew, as did my broken heart. Though she fought long and hard and tried to be so brave, the tumor controlled her pain, and the pain determined her actions. I just couldn't bear seeing how, while loved ones sat by, there was nothing we could do to change the outcome of what was happening. More angry than confused now, still I could find no tears.

Cancer aims to kill, and like a ruthless thief, one day it stole my mother's life while a friend sat praying with her.

And so more changes followed. Being so young—I was an eight-year-old kid whose mother was so ill—my life didn't look anything remotely close to any of my friends. But after her death, I was even more different—I was an eight-year-old without a mother! Being so young, it took me a long while to accept that she really was gone. Even though by bringing her bed to the center of the house, the living room, where she lay for a full year, still, that she was gone seemed surreal. But still, I did not cry.

Six years passed, years that were mostly a blur. But then came the day I received my license! Not only could I drive myself to school, but afterward I could visit my mom's grave alone for the first time, which I did.

Driving to the cemetery, I was filled with so many emotions. I was more scared than excited, scared that I might cry. And scared that I might not.

When I arrived at the cemetery, I slowly walked to her grave. I kneeled down on the grass and started talking to the gravestone. "Mom," I began, my voice barely audible even to me, "I'm so sorry that I never visit you and that I . . ." It was then that I realized I was looking down at a gravesite. My mom wasn't in there; her skeleton may be, but her spirit had obviously long departed. So I looked heavenward to finish my thought—but the words came out totally different than expected: "I'm sorry that you suffered like you did, and I'm sorry I couldn't make you feel any better." Then I went on to say the one thing that had been weighing down my heart for so many years: "I'm sorry I stopped talking to you when on that day you mistook me for my brother. I'm sorry for being mad at you when you forgot my name. I'm also sorry for being distant, and for not understanding it was your terrible illness, and not you, that took you away from me." With these words, the tears started falling. I thought they'd never end. At least I was crying—that made me feel that my heart hadn't hardened to the point of never feeling again.

In the next moments, a million more words rushed out. I shared with my mother how my life had gone since the day she'd died. This made me laugh, knowing that as an angel now, she probably knew exactly how my life had gone—because she'd been watching me. Maybe she'd even been with me on some occasions. That was a comforting realization. I told her I loved her, and told her how excited I'd been to get my license.

Walking back to the car that day, I knew that a huge burden had been lifted from my shoulders. I felt wiser, kinder and connected to my mother in a new way. I understood more clearly how for all these years I had carried a lot of guilt for having withdrawn in her final months and for pulling away from her when she was so ill. I had been greatly disturbed by my inability to cry over her. Miraculously, the visit to the cemetery that day allowed me to just stop that line of thinking: I was a young child when my mother was ill, a little girl who was naturally frightened by all she saw of death slowly claiming the life of her mother. It would be natural to recoil. I didn't cry and hadn't cried because I didn't know where to start, really. I also came to understand that I didn't have to "wait" to see my mother when my heart needed her: Always, her spirit is within me, and so I need only go to that place within me when I need her. Her love is ever present. I need only believe that. And I do.

All this insight (and more) is mine now. As a result, I am feeling more whole. This is the power of tears and of giving yourself license to cry. Crying, I've discovered, washes away some of the layers of emotions that can bind you to pain. Shedding some of this pain can help you move beyond the hurt and transforms guilt into fond memories.

I am a girl without my mother, and that will never change. But I am a girl who now can recall with love and fondness the memories of her mother who loves her daughter. And so on that day that I got my driver's license, my mom and I held a very important heart-to-heart. We've agreed to meet in heaven, but until then, I need only touch my heart and there she is—still.

Sarah Erdmann, 16

AUTHORS' NOTE: *We first met Sarah when she submitted a story for our* A Taste-Berry Teen's Guide to Setting and Achieving Goals. *In that book we published her story, "The Liver Report" (pages 39–41), as well as included her in the "Best Teen Quotes" in our* 365

Days of Taste-Berry Inspiration for Teens *(page 121). Sarah is also a featured author with the lead story, "The Wind Symphony Audition" (pages 251–254), in our* A Teen's Guide to Christian Living: Practical Answers to Tough Questions About God and Faith. *And she has a beautiful poem, "For You, and You Alone," published in* Living the 10 Commandments in New Times *(page 16). We love Sarah's work, and so it is with much love that we open mail from her. Still, we didn't know that Sarah had suffered the loss of a parent until we put out the call inviting teens to share their stories for this unit. We are so pleased to share her lovely heart with you and all the ways Sarah sees through the eyes of her heart. Sarah is most definitely a taste berry, as well as an amazingly cool, caring and courageous person. We look forward to bringing you more of her amazing wisdom in future books in the* Taste Berries for Teens *series.*

Tell Him . . . I'll Call Back

Don't pass up an opportunity to always "be right" with the people you love. You really never know if this will be your last day to have them in your life.

—Tara Morrill, 18

My parents divorced when I was in fifth grade. I was so angry I didn't even have words to express my feelings. That my parents were going to live in separate places made me mad at the entire world. Going numb was the best way I could cope at that point. To make matters worse, both my mother and father attempted to convey to my siblings and me that each was the "better" parent. Having to deal with the dividing line my parents created through their inability to keep us children out of their own "mess" was emotionally draining. I was so frustrated that I was acting out and saying hurtful things that I didn't truly mean.

Things did get worse: My younger brother and sister and I moved across the country with my mother that very next summer. The good news was that despite living thousands of miles apart, my father called us every day. Still, with the miles came a distance between us. Because my dad wasn't actively involved in my life on a day-to-day basis, talking with him was strained. On the phone with him, I didn't have much to say. As a result, every now and then when Dad called, I would ask my mother to tell him I was at a friend's house, or that I was busy doing homework and that I'd call later. But I seldom returned a call.

Within a year, my father met his future wife. After dating a few years, they decided to marry. My brothers, sisters and I flew to be with them for the wedding. Right around that time, my father had seen several doctors because of a pain in his right shoulder and arm. They all told him it was nothing serious, though they did send him home with a sling for his arm (to relieve the pain he was feeling). Then came the bad news: On the day before the wedding, my father was diagnosed with bone cancer.

Everything after that happened really fast. He'd gotten married in April and by Christmas had become pretty ill. We kids visited him that Christmas. At that point the chemotherapy and medications had left him bald and robbed of his usual liveliness. During our visit he rarely moved from his favorite green recliner and spent most of his time watching movies, just to distract himself from the intense pain, which was becoming more pronounced. I remember watching *The Green Mile* with him on one occasion. As we watched the character who possessed supernatural powers heal a woman suffering from cancer, my father told me that he wished it were that simple. "When it comes down to it," he said, "having your health is all that truly matters in life." To hear these words come out of his mouth was a reality check for me. My father had always been the "macho man" who could fix any problem, be it a broken appliance or a bad day at school. I always admired him for being so strong and for making me feel safe and secure. When he told me all he wanted was his health back—and that it was all that mattered—I realized that the cancer had become the one problem he couldn't fix. That was very unsettling.

That Christmas was the last time I saw my father. The cancer had spread throughout his body, leaving him with no other option but to surrender to the disease. On January 20, 2001, we received a phone call from my stepmother informing us Dad had died.

The reality of death didn't hit me until we were flying down for the funeral. Suddenly, I found myself angry with God: Why would He allow this to happen? This was followed by immediate feelings of being jealous of those who still had their dads alive—because I didn't! Then I realized that even though my dad and I hadn't lived close to one another, at least I'd had him in my life. He was but a phone call or a plane ride away. But no more. Death had ended my options of ever hearing his voice or being hugged in the way he always did. No longer would he be there for advice, or simply as someone who was always more than ready to listen to me and to the things I was involved in.

Death had been cruel; it changed my life in ways I could not believe. I also found it difficult to look at my friends and others in the same light. Even being young, I've learned, is no guarantee that a father (or mother) cannot be taken away. With this realization came the sudden and acute pain of remembering how many opportunities I had to tell my own father, "I love you," but didn't. This is a very painful feeling for me. I can never make it right because I will never have that chance again. Knowing this, I would tell you to never take your family and friends for granted, because life is completely unpredictable. You just never know. Don't pass up an opportunity to always "be right" with the people you love. You really never know if this will be your last day to have them in your life.

Tara Morrill, 18

My Turn Up to Bat

Part of how I'm healing the hurt of my father's death is through achievement—through setting goals and accomplishing them.

—Thomas L. Watson Jr., 18

My dad was killed, along with his copilot, in a small-plane crash. My dad was piloting the plane. While taxiing down the runaway, the plane hit a patch of sand and skidded out of control, crashing into another plane.

I won't ever forget that day, though I have put much of the grieving behind me. My biggest goal now is to be focused. I want my father to be proud of me. And I want others to see and know me, and to think that my dad must have been a really great father to raise someone as strong and successful as me.

My dad was a great man. He was a good father and a good husband. He was an attorney with a very successful practice. I carry his name: Thomas L. Watson Jr. For that, I am proud and thankful. This is another reason that I want to fulfill his legacy. I don't feel that I am forgoing my life in completing his. Being an attorney is something I genuinely want to do, but reaching the goal is especially important since it was something my father was excited about as well. He and I often talked about how the sign on our office would be Watson & Watson—Attorneys at Law. Always, I told him that I wasn't sure if I was smart enough to make it through so much school. "You can do it, son," he'd always say to me. "The most important part is making the decision to pick up the bat and step up to the plate. After that, it's all pretty easy."

I miss him so much, but it is exactly at those times that I remind myself to "pick up the bat and step up to the plate." Especially when I'm hurting or missing Dad, I try to make sure that I'm on track with my plans. Not that I'm overlooking taking the time to grieve his death. But a good part of how I'm healing the hurt of my father's death is through achievement—through setting goals and accomplishing them. All this will help make the future happen. For example, getting into a good college is important. I'm going to have to pay for college myself, so I'm a serious student because I need decent grades to win a scholarship. But knowing what I'm aiming for at least makes me work for grades without complaining. I go the extra mile because it's important that I do.

Mom is a big help, too. I'm really good with her, and I try not to cause her to worry about me. She says to me, "You're so like your father. You even have his values." I love it when she says that. And I think she's right. My dad and mom were really in love, so I want to be married someday. I'd like to be married to someone as loving and kind as my mother. I want to have the kind of supportive marriage the two of them had. I have one sister, and I think Mom and Dad would have had more kids. Mom says they wanted more. I want kids, and I want to marry someone with family values. I really can't talk about these things with others my age because these sorts of goals seem so "grown-up" to many my age. And why not; they would be to me, too, if it weren't for the fact that having lost my dad means that I've had to grow up faster. But I'm okay with that, too. I feel a little alone, but I stay focused. Dad would want that. I want that. I want to become as much like my father as I can.

I'd say that my father has had a really good influence on me. For sure, his death has shaped my goals, or in the least, caused me to feel that, yes, I can "pick up the bat and step up to the plate." As a result, I don't see doing drugs or placing a party-scene sort of life above my desire for accomplishment and achievement. That is the route I'll take in my life. I intend to do all I can to carry on the legacy of being a great guy just like my father.

Thomas L. Watson Jr., 18

"IMP: SAVE"

Thinking of my mother as a young woman with a newborn made me love her in a way I had never imagined.

—Amanda Boyd, 14

Until several weeks ago, I had some vague idea of what had happened to my mother, but I didn't quite know the whole story. Then, in the back of a storage closet I came upon a box labeled "IMP: SAVE." Curious, I retrieved the box, opened it and found that it was filled with papers—medical papers and other mail and documents covering the last five years of my mother's life. I took the box to my room and read each piece of paper carefully, learning the truth—the real story—of my mother's journey through cancer and the last months of her life.

As it turns out, two years before I was born she was diagnosed with a cancerous tumor on her right lung. She received twelve weeks of chemotherapy (once a week) and twenty-four treatments of radiation. The doctors said the radiation had made the cancer disappear and that if it didn't return within a five-year period, then she would be free of cancer forever.

Then the question arose about if she would ever be able to have children. She was only given a 40 percent chance of ever conceiving, and even if she did, the baby would be abnormal or deformed. She wanted a child and was willing to take this incredible chance. She did get pregnant and had a normal pregnancy. On January 4, 1989, her baby was born. That would be me! I weighed six pounds, fifteen-and-one-half ounces. I was twenty-one inches long. Thinking of my mother as a young woman with a newborn made me love her in a way I had never imagined.

And yet, just six months after my mother had given birth to a healthy baby, the doctors discovered another tumor, this one behind her heart. So then my mother went through an operation that is pretty similar to open-heart surgery. After seven-and-a-half hours, the team of doctors determined that the tumor was too big to be removed. They stitched Mom back up, telling her that her only hope of living was to undergo chemotherapy. But her oncologist said that it was the chemotherapy that had caused the tumor in the first place! So surgery was attempted one more time—and the results were dire, as well. Her liver and lungs almost failed, and she went into a coma. The doctors said that her chances of coming out of it were very slim. So Dad called the entire family (even my aunt who lived in Panama) to come to see her in case it was the last time.

Then, after being in the coma for six days, my mother miraculously came out of it. She was put on a dialysis machine to remove the toxins from her body. Only five dialysis treatments later, her health showed signs of improving, and she was moved from the intensive care unit and told she could go home! For a while it appeared that with each and every day, my mother got stronger. Obviously, it was only "borrowed" time, because within a few days my mother passed away—on the day of my parent's seventh wedding anniversary.

At the time of her death, my mother was only twenty-nine years old.

Much of the information was revealed in a long, long letter my mother had written to a man thought to be the inventor of a medicine to cure cancer. She was pleading with him to provide her with this miracle-working wonder drug. I don't know if she ever got the medicine or not, but it makes me wonder "what if."

Reading through the papers and documents I discovered has been helpful. I'm putting together each new little piece of the puzzle. For sure, learning about what was going on with her was startling. And it was really "up close and personal" to read things in her own handwriting. But I have all kinds of unfinished business. For one, it really bothers me that no one ever talks about my mother anymore. Just because she is dead doesn't mean that I don't think about her, or that I no longer need her. She had a life. I am living proof of that. I've been trying to get Dad to open up more about Mom and to tell me things. But talking with him is not very helpful. He's erased almost all memory of his first wife and my mother. He is remarried and has "moved on."

I have a lot of questions and do hope Dad will open up about things. Surely, he knows the answers to the questions I have. I do believe that everything happens for a reason. So I'm trying to believe that my mom was taken away from me for a reason. I have yet to find that reason, but I intend to. But in the meantime, I refuse to let my mother's life come and go without a legacy. This is all the more reason that I have to learn more about her. I want to know what she liked and didn't. I want to know what her dreams and aspirations were. I want to know what her hopes and dreams were for me, her daughter. I plan to investigate all this. I want to, in some way, give her life the IMP: SAVE label that was on all of the written and stored documents. Not that I know for sure what it means. No one will tell me, so I've decided IMP means, "important." And that's the way I feel about her life. She is important. Her life was important. And it still is.

Writing this story has been helpful. It's the first time I've ever told anyone the whole story about my mother. It's not going to be the last time.

Amanda Boyd, 14

Urn on the Mantle

There are times when I'll be walking along and a certain memory will come up. Or I'll be doing something, and I'll get just an overwhelming feeling of sadness. It's like a sinking feeling, kind of like the feeling you get when you're traveling fast over a bump in the road and the car "drops" down.

—Lou Gartland, 16

My grandma is in poor health and now living in an assisted-care home for the elderly. Dad and his dad—Grandpa—had just visited Grandpa's wife. Dad and Grandpa were on the freeway just two miles from home when a car traveling in the opposite direction crossed the median and, making an illegal U-turn, pulled onto the freeway, colliding with Dad and Grandpa. Two cars, five people, a drunk driver, and one minute later, two people had been killed and one person seriously injured. My father was one of the two who died that night. (My grandpa broke his right leg but is fine now.)

They tell me my father died instantly. That doesn't make me feel any better. It's been a full year now, and still there are some things I really can't talk about. I mean, when someone asks about my father, I can say the words, "My dad's dead" or "I lost my father a year ago," but I can't bring myself to say, ". . . in a car accident." That his death is the result of a drunk driver seems so unjust. If it hadn't been for the unconscionable fact that someone had been drinking to the point of inebriation and therefore should not have been behind the wheel of a two-ton machine—a car—then my dad would be alive. Am I still mad? You bet. Do I think I'll forgive the drunk driver? Probably not in the near future. Yes, I know I need to forgive him, and I am working with a counselor to help me deal with my angry feelings. Still, I'm not ready to move on just yet.

While there are lots of things I'm not ready to move on with just yet, what to do with my father's ashes isn't one of them. The accident was so bad that they could hardly find body parts. The decision was made to have my father's remains cremated. You still have to bury the remains. Right now, my dad's ashes are in an urn at my aunt's house. I'm not sure how I feel about this. I've heard that a lot of times people will scatter the ashes over an ocean or lake. We don't live near water, and my father couldn't swim and so didn't like the water. He didn't even like to go fishing. But he liked to go pheasant hunting and especially liked to hunt in a certain wooded area about twenty-five miles from where we live. Personally, I think the ashes should be scattered over that wooden area. I believe that while he liked to hunt pheasants there, he mostly liked the peace, serenity and beauty of that particular wooded area.

I've talked with my mother about this. She says to leave things as they are, "for now." I think, like me, the ashes are simply too painful—a surreal reminder that we have lost my dad. I know that in the beginning she thought keeping the ashes at our house would be a good idea, but I think now it's all a little too much for her. Whenever I tell my aunt we should have given dad a "proper burial," she says, "He's where he's supposed to be: here with us." Maybe when I have an apartment of my own I'll ask my aunt if I can keep Dad's ashes at my place, and then I'll give Dad his freedom.

I still think about Dad all the time. Sometimes a week will go by and I don't think about him at all. But then there are times when I'll be walking along and a certain memory will come up. Like how we always used to go to the batting cages on Saturday morning and then to breakfast, just the two of us. I still miss that. Or I'll be doing something, and I'll get just an overwhelming feeling of sadness. It's like a sinking feeling, kind of like when you're traveling fast over a bump in the road and when the car "drops" down, your body goes down before your stomach does.

Only that's a good, "swooning" feeling. The one I'm left with is more of a frightening feeling.

Right after Dad was killed, I started getting in a lot of fights at school. I even got arrested for shoplifting. Both are unlike me. I'm not someone who goes around getting in fights, and I'm not a thief. But one day, while I was standing at the cash register waiting to pay for some candy and chips, I stole a pair of workmen gloves that were hanging nearby. I still don't have an explanation for stealing the gloves; it's not like I was ever going to wear them. That's when Mom said I needed to go to counseling. The judge thought so, too, so I was told I had to go for six months. At first I hated the idea, but I know it's the right thing.

Attending the sessions will mean that I don't have a permanent record for the theft, and it is helping me deal with issues. For example, the counselor told me I had "unfinished business"—that I was angry mainly because I hadn't "come to terms" with my dad's death. So with the counselor's help, I'm learning how to do that. It's really surprising to see how my anger affects me. Like a month ago when I was playing varsity football, one of my teammates made a really great play. He looked up into the bleachers and waved at his dad. His dad was standing, cheering and grabbing everyone around him saying, "That's my son! That's my son!" I don't know why, but I just walked off the field. Am I mad that I don't have a dad to do that for me? Well, yeah, I am. But who am I mad at—the driver of the car that killed my dad? Well, geez, that doesn't resolve things, right? I mean, my dad is not coming back! So I need help to just not be angry.

The counselor I'm seeing now told me that when I'm feeling really bummed, it can be helpful to do a little ceremony to let go of some of the heartache within me. One of his suggestions that I find helpful is that when I'm going through a mood, I write Dad a letter and tell him about things, and how I wish he were here. Mostly, I tear these letters up, because in them I just pour my heart out, and I wouldn't want anyone else reading them—ever. But sometimes I'll reread the letter and then attach it to a helium balloon, and I'll go to some place that has special meaning to Dad and me and let the balloon go.

So in all, I'm making my way. At least I'm finding ways to not let the anger I have over his death cause me to do drastic things—like stealing! Or walking off the football field in the middle of a great game! As for scattering Dad's ashes in the wooded area, well, who knows, someday I may just want Dad's ashes on a mantle of my own. And feel really okay with that. We'll see.

Lou Gartland, 16

Missing You

I'm only fifteen. But having lost my mother, I'm a lot older than that now. I've matured more than someone my age has to. I'm more aware and conscious of people's feelings. And I've become a stronger person and more moral.

—Erin Ruder, 15

My mother, a nurse anesthetist at a Los Angeles hospital, was on duty in the surgery room with a patient when suddenly she couldn't remember how to conduct the procedure. Alarmed at what might have caused my mother's sudden disorientation, the doctors in the room saw to it that she be taken to the emergency room for examination. My father, a physician at a nearby hospital, was called. All kinds of tests were done. The results were devastating beyond belief: Mom was diagnosed with cancer—which had already spread to her lungs, brain and liver. She was only forty-nine years old! She was also the mother of three young children: me, who was twelve at the time, and five-year-old twins!

As usual, my mother confronted this dreaded disease in the same way she lived life: head on! I loved that about her. She was an awesome woman, strong and independent, a person with fortitude and big dreams for her life. Born of Mexican descent to a poor but hardworking family, this was a woman who, from those humble beginnings, made a decision to go to college and did—paying for it herself. She became an anesthetist and married a doctor (my father). They had me and then, after years of trying to conceive, my brother and sister (twins) were born. As I'm writing this, the twins are only eight (I'm fifteen). Her dreams were all in place, she had her children, a husband she loved and her career. At the time, our family was also building a new family home. But then came news of the disastrous cancer.

When the results came in, my dad called me. I could tell from his voice that something was wrong—if only he'd get around to it! My mother simply grabbed the phone from my dad and told me flat out that she had cancer. I so loved her head-on approach to life! And of course, she never thought the cancer would claim her life. In her usual style, she intended to do everything possible to rid of herself of it. From the day she learned about it, she did everything medically possible to stay alive.

Well-laid plans to beat the cancer and her positive attitude in hand, I was still worried. I guess it would be fair to say that I simply didn't want to believe that she was sick. So sometimes, I'd intentionally pick a fight to see if she was strong enough to fight back. I didn't do this to be mean as much as to see if she was still the feisty person I knew. It was like I was testing her endurance. I guess I needed to be reassured that she was strong enough to beat cancer.

Mom was a strong person. She was, in fact, the strongest person I've ever known. Fighting cancer is a long and tough battle, a real struggle of enduring pain and endless rounds of medical testing and procedures. Still, Mom never cried or complained. But as time went by, her health did worsen. Because of the swelling on her brain, things eventually progressed to the point where Mom couldn't write or walk. Eventually, she had to be admitted to the hospital. She stayed for three months.

This was a new phase of even tougher times for the twins and me. I would dread visiting her, because it was so terrible to see my mother in such pain. And it was frightening to see her hooked up to all kinds of tubes and things. But she was still my mother, and I needed her. Sometimes I'd lie right beside her and just hold her close. But no amount of loving her and needing her could stop the cancer from spreading. In time, her words turned to mumbles, and sometimes she couldn't even express how she felt.

Wanting to live, wanting and needing to be there for her family, Mom continued to fight to try to overcome the cancer.

And though she was by now in agony from the growing pain, still she never complained. And then came some progress. For a moment, it seemed like she was in remission, though in looking back, I think she was just putting up a good front for us all. Still, she truly believed she was going to overcome the cancer. For a while, even the doctors thought it might just be possible. So looking forward to seeing the new home we were building, Mom came home for a week. But she couldn't walk up the stairs to the master bedroom. She had to sleep in a bedroom downstairs.

The cancer was persistent. And one September day, I shared my last day with my mother. I helped her walked outside, sat with her, and we talked. She was concerned about us kids and she was concerned about her husband as well. "Take care of your little brother and sister," she said. "And do all you can to get along with your dad." Perhaps this is when it struck me that there really would be a time that I would no longer have my mother in my life. It was a really terrible realization. The second my dad got home, I left the house. I left and went to see my horses—one of my great passions—just to be alone and to watch them run around in their paddock. I so needed this distraction from all that was going on.

When I returned home, my mother was asleep. I kissed her good night. Later that night my mother had a seizure. She was taken to the hospital, where she went into a coma. The next day, I visited her. I told her I wanted to be like her when I grew up. I placed my hand in hers; she squeezed my hand while she was in the coma. I still play that back in my mind: amazing how such tender moments can rip your heart out. The next day my brother kissed her good-bye. Right after my brother, my sister, my dad and I said good-bye to her, my mother died.

Life will never be the same. I know this is an understatement, of course, but every day I'm learning new ways in which this statement is true. One at a time, I sift through the memories. One of the best of these is just to remember what an awesome woman she was. I know that I would like to develop the qualities of a bold and great personality, and the tenacious way she plunged into life. And always I keep in mind how she handled the obstacles in life and how strong she was, and how she always chose to overcome problems. I know that like my mother, I want to be an emotionally powerful and personally competent person. Because I've seen her model this, I think I will be, too. My mother was also a good mother. Because of her example, I've learned how to take care of a family. Someday, when the time is right, I want to be a mother myself. I hope to be as nurturing and optimistic as my mother was.

And every day, I keep discovering just how important one's mother is to your life. I miss my mother. I miss her love and her being there to tell me how much she loved me. But I also miss the small stuff, her daily involvement in my life. I'd give anything to hear her say, "You're wearing that to school?" or to remind me of my curfew. I didn't want to hear it then, but now I'd give anything to hear her being a mom, offering up her guidance and direction and showing me how to be a woman.

I also miss what the future might have been for us. There is the big stuff, like her being there for high school and college graduation, and to see me get married. Seriously big things like that. But I so miss the little things that might have been as well. You cannot imagine how much I'd love to have her to just go sit down to lunch, or to talk to about "boy problems" or to take me on a huge shopping spree! I so wish I could just talk to her and tell her everything on my mind.

I just wish she were alive.

All this has been an experience that I would give anything to not have been a part of my life. But it is. So now I have to figure out a way to let all these emotions be in me but not take me away from being a loving person—or to sidetrack me from my goals of going on to school. And to figure out my life, a career and all. I know I've changed. I'm only fifteen. But I'm a lot older than that now. I've matured, probably more than someone my age has to. And I've become a stronger person and more moral. I've also learned a lot about people and tolerance. I'm more aware and conscious of people's feelings. I'm better able to listen to others express themselves without judging them. And I don't get involved in petty issues, such as getting caught up in the rumor mill at school. And when I do hear something, I'm more likely to feel empathy for the person involved. Other people's feelings—and my own—are more important to me than simply who is dating whom, or how much money someone spends on clothing. So in terms of what is important to me, my priorities have changed. I try to be a really good big sister to my little brother and sister, who at such a young age have lost the most important person in their lives. Things like this are what really are important now.

I'm angry that Mom has been taken away from me; still, I'm learning to let go of some of the frustration I feel for having lost her. I try to imagine that she is watching over me and looking over how I live my life. While I try not to give advice, I'd tell you to cherish the time you have with your parents. I know it seems a little preachy, but do all you can to accept your parents for who they are. Forgive them for not being perfect, and for sure, thank them for the love they do give you. Take the time to just be with them. Decide that you want to create positive memories, ones that the two of you will never forget. Go ahead, sit down and just listen to the stories from their past, those of their boy- or girlfriends, and of the struggles and arguments they had with their own parents. Know that time is precious, and life is not guaranteed. Bother to ask your mom or dad how his or her day went—and listen to what is said. And let them be human. As much as you don't want to believe it, they're looking out for your best interests. Granted, when they say that you have to be home early and that you can't date until you are married, that is annoying. Still, they probably aren't trying to ruin your life as much as trying to protect you.

As I write this, I think how much I'd give to have my mother alive to express these things to me. Which brings me to the point of needing to say, "Mom, thank you for my life and for all the days we did have together. It is because of your love and guidance that I am becoming a quality person with a great outlook on life. I treasure all the great moments we shared, good and bad. Know that I'm trying to be a nurturing sister to the twins. Every day, I help them with their homework and I talk with them about the problems they come across. And you'd be so proud to know how much Daddy and I are improving in the ways we communicate. We are affectionate with each other, and we talk about our feelings with each other—it's all good. I love you with all my heart, Mom. I will never forget your love and your strong will—and all the ways you were such an awesome woman. I will be, too, you know. Love, Your Daughter."

Erin Ruder, 15

Teen Talk: Helping Each Other Cope . . .

Ethan Leffer, 17: My best friend's father died last year. Ethan and his dad were really close. In the beginning, I was pretty freaked out by the whole thing, because I can't really imagine having my father get killed in the tragic way his father was. I knew it had to be really hard on my friend. When my friend came back to school after the funeral, some of the girls told him things like, "I'm sorry about your father." But most of us guy friends just kind of pretended that nothing had happened. I thought that probably was not such a good way to handle things—even though I'm sure we did this because we didn't know what to do or say for fear of creating more pain for him. It seemed weird to be walking along and talking about things, but not bring up something that was as major in his life as having his dad get killed. So finally, I went to the school counselor and asked how someone is supposed to act or what you're supposed to say to a good friend who has lost his father. I mean, you can't pretend it didn't happen, and I didn't want to act like I'm emotionally illiterate or anything.

Talking with the counselor was a big help. She told me to just be as supportive as I could, like when I noticed that my friend seemed down or especially sad, that it was okay to say, "Do you want to talk about it?" Or even just to listen, and then to say things like, "I'm here for you if you need me." She also said not to say things like, "I know what you're going through," because no one can know that unless you've lost a parent, and even then we really can't know completely, except for the fact that that person is facing a big loss. The counselor also told me that sometimes after the loss of someone you love, the person could go into depression. She told me what to look for and said that if I thought my friend seemed like he was getting depressed, then I should encourage him to talk to a counselor so he could get professional help to work through his feelings.

So that's what I'm doing. Just being a good friend and not putting any pressure on my friend. I just try to be as kind and sensitive as I can be. It must be working, because I notice my friend calls me when he's down. And the other day he asked if I wanted to share a locker with him for the upcoming football season. So I think we've grown closer. And I'd say the main reason is that he knows that I'm aware that there is a part of him that is hurting. He knows that I care. And he appreciates that.

Diane Sierras, 15: One of my best friend's mother died two months ago. She had been sick for about a year. Of course, my friend is devastated. It's so hard to know what to do to help her. Because we're so close, she talks to me about how she feels. She always says she just wants the pain to go away. The first few weeks following her mother's funeral were especially difficult for her. I'd see her in the hall, and she'd have tears in her eyes. Sometimes I'd pass by the counselor's office and there she would be, sitting on the couch with Kleenex tissues held to her face. In those first days, I didn't really know what to say or how to best help her. I just wished I could give her some advice or some magic words to make her feel better. But nothing I could think to say sounded right.

Then one day when she was talking about an experience she and her mother had, I asked if she had a picture of her mother with her. She smiled, her eyes lit up, and she opened her purse and took out a really great picture of the two of them standing on a bridge and waving to the camera. This memory was a fun one and a very special one for her. So then my friend went on and on about what a great person her mother was and what fun that day had been for them. A couple minutes later she put the picture away, and reached out and gave me the biggest hug. Then she told me I was the greatest friend ever!

So helping someone can be just to let them talk about the good stuff, because surely those memories help them through all they're going through. I think that was true for my friend that day. I do know that it has moved our friendship from one of good friends to being really close. Just last night she called me and said she'd just gotten into bed, and she was thinking about her mom and her sadness was "huge." So she called me because she felt she could do that, and that I'd be okay with it. She cried a little and then said she felt better, and thanked me for listening. So I think just being a good friend and letting the person go through the feelings that come up, and being there when they do come up, can be a really helpful thing.

Cammie Oden, 14: When I was five years old, my mom and dad divorced. Right after that, my father moved to another state. My mother had to work full-time. So it was my grandmother who came to pick me up at the bus stop every day after school. Every day after school, I went to my grandmother's house and stayed there until my mother got off work. I spent a lot of time with my grandma. So we became very close. She was "mother number two."

When I got older I could be on my own after school. I saw my grandma on weekends sometimes and holidays. I was so busy. And I guess I thought my grandma would always be there. She always seemed so strong to me—kind of ageless. Well, my grandmother died a couple of months ago. At first I was dealing with it all just fine, but then we had to go through and clean out Grandma's things. That was the worst thing. While we were doing all this, I kept thinking of all the good times between Grandma and me. When it came time to give some things away, like the big old chair that was her favorite, I wasn't ready to part with the memory of always seeing her in the chair. Even parting with some of her favorite clothing and things—it was so hard.

I still think of Grandma. I feel really bad that in the final months of her life I didn't go visit her more often. When I turn on my computer, there is an ad that always comes up where a teenager says, "Mom, Grandma is calling. I'll just tell her we'll call back later." When I first saw that I didn't think anything. Now when I see it I'm disgusted by it, because I know that it can be really easy to think grandparents don't carry the same weight as talking to your friends. Having lost my grandma, now if a friend was on the line and my grandmother called, I'd have no problem telling my friend I'd call her back because Grandma was on the line.

Brad Charett, 16: I lost my dad to bone cancer. He was only forty-nine years old. In the last two years of his life, he was pretty sick, so we did spend a lot of time together. Still, when he died, I was so beside myself that all I wanted to do was eat and sleep. In the first two months after his death, I gained fourteen pounds. That's not good. I was late to school a number of times, and I stopped going to choir practice on Thursday nights at my church. All these things made me feel even worse. I think I was in a depression. Finally, Mom said I had to go to group counseling. In this group, we were able to talk about not only how to get past painful memories, but how to take care of ourselves now and go forward.

Just getting out again and talking about things with other teens, who themselves had experienced loss, was good. Taking extra good care of yourself when you're grieving is important. You have to be patient with yourself, because some days are better, and worse, than others. I'm coping the best I can. My feelings aren't as intense as they were in the beginning. Life is getting better. Which is good, because when you lose a parent, life as you once knew it is gone. You have to rethink your life, because nothing is the same. Friends are really important in helping you get whole again.

Heather McHale, 17: I had a friend whose father was diagnosed with lung cancer. In the early days, she didn't really talk about it. But then her father died. My heart felt for her. I know how much she loved him. I attended the services with her. The family chose to celebrate his passing in a really terrific way. Sitting in the church auditorium, we all watched on a giant projector the "life and times" of her father. I thought this was a really special way for the family to celebrate his life—remembering him through some of their favorite memories. Everyone enjoyed this, but it was sad, too. I sat clutching a tissue, wiping away my tears. I hadn't known him well, but I knew that losing a father must be a terrible, terrible thing. After the ceremony, I saw my friend walking out of the auditorium composed. I reached out to embrace her—causing her tears to break loose. All I could do between sobs was tell her how sorry I was. Having had a friend go through the experience of losing a parent, I am better able to appreciate and understand the importance of parents everywhere—especially my own.

Part 5

Courage: We're All Heroes in the Making

Courage is the first and foremost of all qualities,
because it is the one upon which all others depend.

—Winston Churchill

Character is like a tree, and reputation like its shadow.
The shadow is what we think of it;
the tree is the real thing.

—Anonymous

Commitment isn't the time you spend. It's the difference
between sitting on an angry bull and
having your hand roped to his back.

—Ty Murray, World Champion Bull Rider

Courage is not the absence of fear. Courage is doing
what needs to be done in spite of the fear.

—Bettie B. Youngs

If not now, when?

—The Talmud

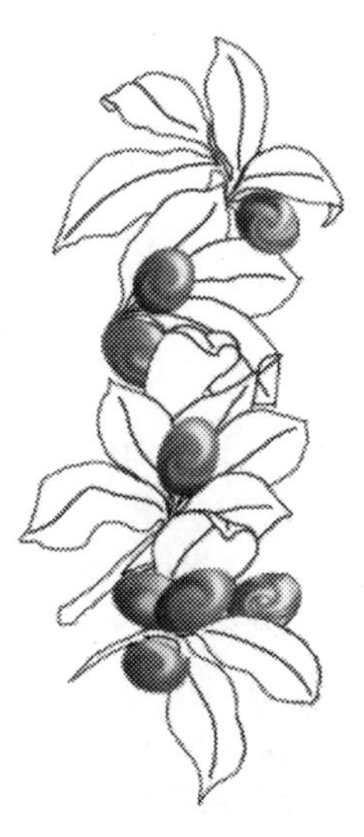

A Word from the Authors

From the French word *coeur,* meaning heart, courage is, as Winston Churchill (England's courageous leader during World War II) once said, *"The first and foremost of all qualities, because it is the one upon which all others depend."* He's right about that: All emotions, all behavior, all the strength of character for that matter, require great heart. Courage is the first and most important "ingredient" determining our willingness and ability—our readiness—to act in positive, loving and responsible ways.

Courage: What a wonderfully powerful word; saying it, even just hearing it, evokes such a sense of "goodness." But what is courage, and what does it take to be considered as someone who is courageous? When you think of five people you consider courageous, who comes to mind? Take a moment and make that list.

Who made your list of "Five Most Courageous"? Was your mother or father on the list? How about a certain best friend, or a particular aunt, uncle, grandma or grandpa? Did a principal, teacher, coach or the leader of a particular country or nation make your list? Does your "Top Five" include someone battling an illness or a terminal disease? How about a particular group known for their bravery, such as soldiers, firefighters or others who often put their lives on the line in helping others? Are you on your list—do you consider yourself to be one of the most courageous people you know?

What does it take to be a hero, in your eyes? To help you answer that question, take a moment now and describe the traits or reasons that each person (or group) on your list is courageous. The value in doing this exercise is because all too often courage is thought of as a wonderfully positive quality, but one in which only a chosen few attain. This is not the case: Courage is not an elusive quality. Nor is it out of reach to anyone. We all need it, and we all can develop it. We are all heroes in the making!

It's been said that courage is a "muscle"—and that the more you use it, the more you develop it. Do you believe that? Do you think courage is innate—that we are born with various degrees of it—which then would explain why some people seem to be more "courageous" than others? Or is courage a trait that can readily be developed—and so those who act in courageous ways become "people of courage"? Interesting questions, aren't they? In this unit you'll get a chance to see how teens such as yourself have answered these questions for themselves.

Regardless of the road each of us takes to become courageous, we learn that courage is needed if we are to experience "full" lives. For example, do you want to experience love? If so, then you have to also risk heartbreak. What about friendship? Yes, that too means that just as you put yourself out there to make friends, you also have to risk rejection—and maybe even betrayal. How about success itself? Yes, again. Just as you "go for it," you also open yourself up to the possibility of not reaching your goals. Yes, courage is needed in all that we do. Does that mean that it comes without fear? No. You see, courage is not the absence of fear. Courage is doing what needs to be done in spite of the fear. We all experience fear. But those who live life with great heart—courage—make the decision to not let their fears stop them. A great basketball player for the Boston Celtics, Bill Russell, once said that he became so nervous before basketball games that he threw up! His fear didn't stop him from becoming a world champion eight times and one of the greatest centers to ever play the game.

Fear is a pretty useful emotion in its own right. It warns us of danger. It says, "There is a risk here, so be careful or turn back." This can save us from a lot of trouble, even save our lives. So fear is a useful emotion. The problem is that sometimes we have too much fear and it holds us back from doing things we should be doing. Of course, sometimes we have too little fear, and we foolishly rush into situations that we should avoid. That's why it's important to use our minds to evaluate the messages that our emotions give us. We want to ask ourselves, *What is the risk here and what is my purpose in taking this risk?* Without knowing the risks and the potential rewards, we can't be courageous, only reckless. For example, the kids who do drugs for a momentary thrill are often unaware of the real risks or their own hidden purposes. So they aren't being courageous, only reckless.

Courage means that you listen to your emotions. Then you decide whether it's worth taking the risk or not. If it is, you take a deep breath and go for it! If it isn't worth the risk, then you breathe a deep sigh and pass. Each, by the way, requires courage because, after all, passing on opportunities that carry too great a risk takes the courage to be willing to live without getting everything that you want. And in our "you can have it all" culture, that takes courage, too.

Many times we think of courage as having risen to the challenge of an extraordinary feat that takes a great deal of physical stamina or emotional fortitude. An example of this would be to risk pain or injury for the sake of rescuing a victim or standing up to a would-be attacker. But courage is often a subtle taste berry. There are many times when courage comes into play that we may not even be aware of. Here are eight of the most common:

Emotional courage. It is easy to see how we need courage when dealing with physical challenges, but handling our emotions can take just as much courage. As fifteen-year-old Cecily explained, *"When Aaron dumped me, I was crushed. I just never even saw it coming. We had been dating almost a whole year, and I really loved him a lot. When he announced that he 'had feelings' for someone else, I thought I would be sick. I felt like never going back to the same school again. And I was down on love: I just knew I never wanted to ever get that close to someone again."*

Risking emotional pain does take courage. When we allow ourselves to be vulnerable to others, when we let them inside, we open ourselves up to the joy of love and friendship. But those opportunities also carry with them the risk of rejection, loss and the pain they can cause. Having the emotional courage to rebound from pain, such as Cecily shared after her breakup, and to risk being vulnerable again does not come easily. When we have been burned, our fear of fire grows stronger. But we need the warmth and energy fire can give us, so we learn what the experience has to teach us about others, and ourselves. Then we gather the courage to approach the heat once again.

Love isn't the only emotion that requires courage. The fear of embarrassment and humiliation is extremely powerful. But giving in to this fear often leads to many missed opportunities and much regret. Courage is also required when a negative emotional pattern is getting in the way of success. For example, many people have trouble overcoming shyness, anger and depression. These patterns may have worked at one time to protect the person from pain, but over time they usually create many more problems than they solve. Tackling them requires courage and sometimes the help of a qualified professional, as well as other strategies. Why courage? Because when we give up familiar patterns, even ones that no longer work, we risk the unknown. What will happen to me if I stop being shy and take more chances? How will I get what I want if I don't use anger to intimidate others? What will become of me if I stop being depressed and start spending more time with others? Change does carry risk, and courage is needed to even begin making those changes that can improve our lives.

The courage to risk failure. A willingness to try, knowing that you may fail, takes a courage that comes hard for many people. But without this courage, such people fail to try new things and lose the chance to grow in the process. As thirteen-year-old Erica explained, *"I really wanted a part in the school play, but there were so many girls trying out that I didn't think I had a chance, even though everybody told me I had a really good voice and all. So I just kept making up excuses so I didn't have to deal with it. Then when this girl got the lead—someone who really wasn't much better than me—I guess I realized I could have gotten a pretty good part even if I didn't get the lead. Besides, all my friends who just got into the chorus seemed to have a great time just being in the play. I wish I wasn't so afraid of trying sometimes."*

Teens like Erica live life like it is better not to try than to try and fail. By not trying they protect their self-esteem from having to deal with failure. But they really have it backward. Every successful person who has ever lived has experienced failure. They have learned the important lesson that you get some of what you try for, but you don't get any of what you don't try for. They also know that they can learn from their failures how to be better next time, so they keep improving.

The courage to be imperfect. Many people in our competitive society have come to believe that they have to be perfect in order to be okay. To a lesser extent we all need the courage to accept that it is acceptable to make mistakes and even fail. We can learn from those experiences how to do better next time. Without this courage, we cause others and ourselves endless misery in a vain attempt to be what is impossible to be: perfect. It takes much courage to accept ourselves, flaws and all. As Rebecca Lane tells it, *"I am a big-boned girl. My mother is nearly six feet tall, and my father is six-feet-four. I'm fifteen and stand five-eleven. I'm not a skinny-minny: I weigh 150 pounds. Because I tower over many of the boys in my school and could pick most up with one arm (no joking), others take a lot of potshots at me. It takes a great deal of courage for me to stand tall and take their ridiculing in a good-natured way—as opposed to being really upset and even rude in return. But I've made that choice to say basically, 'Hey, this is me, and I like it.' I've decided to accept myself, and not fall for their taunts."* Knowing the discrimination teens often face over "body perfection," it's clear that Rebecca has opted for courage: to stand tall even in the face of taunts from her classmates.

The courage to persevere. This is the courage to keep going when the going gets tough, whether in school, with friends, on the job or in sports. Inertia is a powerful force that drags us down and tries to get us to give up. When we give in to this force prematurely—in other words, when we could have succeeded if we had only stuck with it—we limit our chances of success in many ways. Many successful people have said that the reason they succeeded when others failed was that they stuck with it when others gave up. Simply put, they had to "keep on truckin.'"

Did you know that one of the most famous presidents of all time, Abraham Lincoln, lost something like sixteen elections before becoming president? And Steve Smith, a most well-respected astronaut—veteran of two space flights, more than three hundred Earth orbits, and three space walks (his story is profiled in the first book in the Taste-Berry series: *Taste Berries for Teens: Inspirational Short Stories and Encouragement on Life, Love, Friendships and Tough Issues*)—tried out a total of five times before he succeeded in earning his coveted spot as an American astronaut. And Julie Mayor failed to make the cut for the U.S. Olympic Soccer Team three times, but that didn't stop her from trying yet a fourth time. Today, Julie Mayor can lay claim to being an Olympic gold medalist. What if Lincoln, Steve and Julie had given up the first (or second or third!) time they failed in their attempts to reach their respective goals? The lesson is simple—if you want to succeed, you must have the courage to persevere.

The courage to change. People tend to trust and be comfortable with what is familiar, even if what is familiar isn't all that pleasant or successful. It takes courage to change, because change carries the risk that things will become even worse. Change also requires work, and work can be difficult and tiring. The courage to change our approach, our attitudes, even ourselves can pay dividends when we dig deep and accept that sometimes change is necessary. Certainly, such is the case for McKenzy Jean's friend (whose ordeal is profiled in the story, "The Deepest Cut," found in this unit). McKenzy's friend will, no doubt, find her journey to be a long and arduous road "back."

The courage to delay gratification. The slogan of a two-year-old is "I want what I want when I want it." Part of maturing is learning that some of the things that are most worthwhile in life don't come instantly. People without the courage to delay their wants for real satisfaction often find themselves settling for instant gratification.

It takes courage to deprive yourself of instant gratification—whether it's drugs, alcohol or premarital sex. We all want to have fun, become gratified and enjoy life, and when opportunities to do so come along, it is natural to want to say "yes." But sometimes the cost is too high. The cost of using drugs can be addiction, even death. The cost of cheating or lying is the loss of integrity and character, and often the trust of others. The cost of overeating, smoking and doing other unhealthful activities can be severe down the road. Oscar Wilde once joked, "I can resist anything but temptation." Yet, resisting temptation and being willing to delay gratification are hallmarks of courageous people.

The courage of your convictions. This means doing what you believe is right, even when it is not always easy or convenient to do so. For example, if you believe that people shouldn't pick on other kids, do you have the courage to stand up to those who are teasing someone even though they may put you down as well? If you believe that cheating is wrong, do you have the courage to avoid cheating when many of the other kids are doing so? It is easy to say you have a conviction that is honorable and just, but having the character to put those convictions into action takes courage.

The courage to march to your own drummer. There are times when the majority is going in a direction that you know in your heart is wrong, or at least wrong for you. The peer pressure to go with the flow of the crowd can be overwhelming, but following your own moral compass and sense of what is right for you is often of profound importance. Of course, you want to be sure that you aren't just following a reckless or rebellious urge that can backfire on you. This means taking the time to talk with trusted people and look into your heart before jumping to a hasty decision. But when you have tested the merit of your beliefs and feel reasonably confident in your decision, it takes a lot of courage to stand up and go your own way. That courage has a heartbeat all its own.

Are you convinced that life is a journey filled with lessons in developing courage? Probably so! Hopefully, you see yourself as a hero (or heroine) in the making. By recognizing that all of living takes great heart and great courage, we can cut ourselves some slack when life seems not to go as we hoped it might. When that happens, we vow to get back on our feet, dust ourselves off and try again. If we can do that for ourselves, then we can also be a taste berry to others in helping and encouraging them in their doing the same.

In this unit we asked teens to share an experience in which they recognized courage in the making. As you'll see, many times this meant overcoming a hurdle or a discouraging time. This is a most important revelation. Have you ever been discouraged? Most all of us have. It's important to know that we can all learn how to turn that around—and it's important that we do. You see, negative thinking just makes you feel more discouraged. Discouragement leads to behavior that is unproductive or even destructive. This creates more failure, more negative thinking and more discouragement. Those who get caught in this discouragement cycle find it very difficult to break out. Of course, the opposite is also true. Positive thinking helps generate the courage to improve life and make things work. These successes generate more positive thinking and more courage. You become *encouraged.* There is a saying that "nothing succeeds like success." This means that when we start having successes in our lives, we often have more successes. The reason is that we become encouraged to try harder, and handle mistakes and setbacks in stride without giving up.

How do you break out of a failure cycle and into a success cycle? How do you keep a success cycle going? How do you stay encouraged and not discouraged? As the many teens we heard from in doing this unit will tell you, the first step is to stop discouraging yourself. Next, encourage yourself. When we discourage ourselves (or others), we are actually removing courage and disrespecting who we are. So half the process of building courage is to use discouraging moments as opportunities for creating encouragement—which is precisely the definition of a taste berry!

❤ *Taste berries to you, Bettie and Jennifer Youngs*

An Acrophobic's "Plunge"

From here on out, I'm going to "go for it!" I was put on this planet to live, not just breathe.

—Mike Siciliano, 17

"Go ahead, jump!" a buddy of mine taunted, and then dared, "Bet you won't!" I looked into the water from where I was standing and knew he was probably right. Standing practically on top of the world—at least it felt that way to me—and thinking of plunging into the depths of an endless ocean below, I was scared to death! I'm an acrophobic (I have a fear of heights), so you can imagine the chill that went down my spine as I considered the possibilities of taking up the dare. I moved closer to the edge of the three-thousand-feet-high platform to take a better look at the distance "down" and began thinking—which is probably the worst thing I could have done.

"You can do it!" one voice coaxed.

"No, you fool! You'll kill yourself!" warned another.

"Oh, go on! Do it!" the first one prodded.

"But I've never done this before!" pleaded the more sane voice.

"That's because you always play it safe," mocked the first.

"I can't," assured the second voice.

"C'mon! Don't wimp out—jump!" taunted the first. (I hate losing to that voice.)

So I jumped!

The good news is, I'm alive to tell the story!

Okay, let me tell you that I didn't jump three thousand feet. It was more like three hundred feet. Well, in truth it was actually thirty feet—but it most definitely felt like three thousand to me. And since I'm setting the record straight, the jump wasn't from the top of the world, but rather from a yacht on which I was a guest. But just so you can empathize, you should know that a crowd of nearly fifty pretty cool kids from various teen organizations stood watching—many of whom were friends and classmates (and one who was a very special girl—if you get what I mean) from my own school! All were looking to see if I'd take the bait of jumping off the yacht and into the water. What could I do?

Even though I didn't want to jump, how does one say "no" when everyone in the whole world is watching? I mean, if I hadn't proven myself as "I can do this, no sweat!" I'd never live it down. I'm sure you know the feeling. As I stood there looking down into the water, I cannot describe the fear I felt knowing I just had to do it. It seemed more like suicide than heroics to me. I mean, I can swim, so it's not like jumping meant automatic death by drowning, but I really am terrified of heights. I looked down—which momentarily snapped me to my senses—and I backed away. But then I remembered that voice saying, "You always play it safe . . . ," and something in me just let loose. In a split second, I whirled around, took a ten-feet running start and vaulted into the air!

Here's the thing: The jump was a moment I will never, ever forget. It was absolutely, positively and completely exhilarating. Sailing through midair on my way into a bottomless ocean, it occurred to me that my entire life had been lived with reservation, a holding back. Everything was structured; the clock ruled my life. I lived a boring schedule of predictable activity. Why did I always play it safe? Living life that way was as useless as using a flashlight in broad daylight. No more. Sailing through the air on my jump that day, I vowed that from here on out, I was going to "go for it!" I was put on this planet to live, not just breathe. As the ocean grew closer to my face, I realized the difference.

I hit the water.

It was baptizing. I am a changed person. I emerged from the water a different person, and not just because I'd found the courage to jump, but also because in the seconds it took for me to go from the top of the yacht to the water, I discovered how liberating it is to feel that one is courageous. And in that moment, I understood I must live bravely from here on out. Now when I hear a voice inside my head trying to hold me back or limit me—by causing me to doubt myself, or by reminding me of times when I failed at something and so may fail at this attempt, too—I recall the voice that said, "C'mon! Don't wimp out—jump!" I don't mean to say that I take dumb risks, but that I have made the decision to be a courageous person. I have decided to "go for it." And that has made all the difference.

I'm happy to report that I'm not as afraid of heights as I once was (even though I probably won't ever be a skydiver or anything else that involves great heights). I like the way I feel now. All because of that one jump!

Mike Siciliano, 17

Curlicue on the Mountain

As a rock climber, there are always certain moments when you're terrified. But when you reach deep down for courage, you move from fear to action, and that's when you discover that Sir Edmund Hillary was right: "It's not just the mountain we conquer, but ourselves."

—Emily Manning, 15

Looking up the mountain, I surveyed the huge cliffs: one enormous boulder overlapping another. All I could manage to say was, "Whoa!" A feeling of sheer terror overcame me, and I quickly ran through my "safety net" check: Whistle, water, phone, flares, patting my pockets to actually feel these things. I'd come to climb this mountain. Terrified or not, I was going to give it my all. *Okay, let's go,* I told myself realizing it was now or never!

I just love this sport, and being outdoors in nature is one of the many reasons. Most always Mother Nature is "speaking" at the top of her lungs. Today I see vibrant bluebells with their delicate little heads bobbing in the wind; water droplets glittering like jewels on their velvety blue and purple petals; Indian paintbrush bursting with their elaborate fiery red blooms; birds soaring the skies. I scan the panorama, taking in the grandeur. "Grandeur": it's such a great word, one that really describes the view of nature—most especially for me when I'm hanging from a mountain midway up!

I also love rock climbing because it fills me with power. Nature is so awesome, and "playing in it" makes me feel so honored. Here, in the middle of the mountain, all this beauty is mine for the gazing. I own the sunshine. I own all the sounds around me. In fact, I pretty much own the world! It's a really great feeling! Always, I sort of feel like the mountain is happy that I want to climb up on top of its shoulders, knowing that from a certain height and angle I can appreciate Mother Nature even more than by standing amidst it on the ground.

While the surroundings are serene, the sport itself is not what I would describe as tranquil or peaceful. You need all your wits about you when you're doing a climb. But I wouldn't call it nerve-wracking, either. "Exhilarating" best describes it. A little of this has to do with the fact that you are literally hanging off a mountain, and so you literally hold your very life in your own hands. On the mountain, I'm competing with me—and only me. It's a one-on-one challenge: Me taking on ME! Can I do it—well, I'd better, right? There is no sloughing off when you're rock climbing! On the mountain, you'd better be ready to dig deep for courage, because there are times when you need every ounce you can find! Every moment is about looking out for your safety. You are, after all, hanging on a rock cliff!

I also like the feeling of self-reliance. In this sport, even when you go with a group, in the actual climb most moments are spent alone. This is a time when the "It's all about me!" slogan really fits. It is all about me—and not falling! With each step, I learn a lot about myself. I had to learn to trust myself in ways I'd never done before. And I had to develop the confidence in myself so that I actually could trust myself. But once I did, then the world opened up to me on a whole new level. And that's when I knew I could do anything! I love that feeling.

On the mountain, I own myself.

Rock climbing also tests your endurance. You have to "endure" the climb. In the beginning of it you feel good. Even great. But then a couple of hours later your fingertips are tortured. Your legs are aching and cramped. Your dreams of getting to the top turn to questions of "how." Your confidence turns from "when" to "if." And there is no shortcut. It's a long way up and a longer way down. No point in sitting around. It's up or down, and there's a price to pay, either way.

Now in the middle part of my climb, I look up, knowing I still have a long and steep climb ahead. "Let's go!" I said, urging myself onward and up. Yes, once again I'd accepted the challenge: I would climb Mt. Crested Butte. And so I continued. One step, and then another. And another. Yet another. Gasping to take in the thinning air. Another step. And another. My water jug tugging at my waist, pleading with me to rest. On I went, taking care not to crush too many cow parsnips or mule's ears, all flowers blooming along the trails. Finally, I saw the boulders, and I knew the steep part of the climb was over. Still, the most treacherous part of the climb was yet to come. A new thrill, a new "high" and more exhilaration.

Looking down for a foothold among the rocky crevices flipped the world for a moment, but it righted itself when I looked up again. The wind pulling through my hair, I felt like an eagle soaring high with the wind. Suddenly, my handhold slipped and I almost fell, but I grasped a rock just in time. I moved my hand from the unstable rock to a solid handhold and, catching my breath, gazed upward. I had come so far! Only a little more to go. Handhold, foothold, handhold, foothold. It was drilled into my head. Handhold, foothold. Don't fall! Handhold, handhold, handhold. Handhold—where is the handhold? No time for doubts, no room for mistakes. Concentrate. Search for the handhold. Concentrate. Search for the handhold . . . Don't you just love it when an experience brings out the best in you? In this sport we call it "peak performance." Peak performance creates a natural high all its own.

Always, when I get to the top, I feel as though I've conquered the world! Standing here now, I peek downward and swoon, feeling more than a little dizzy with the height. I look at the town that lay out before me. Rolling hills and streams riddle the landscape. From this view, it looks like a map. Above the town are beautiful mountain peaks, snowcapped peaks with lush green bases. And then I did what I always do when at this point in my climb: I pulled the cap off my Sharpie, and, swelling with pride, signed the log, feeling that with my signature, Mother Nature had just given the mountain to me!

And now for the relaxation part. Lying on the rock, I watched as clouds rolled past and spotted a mountain climber, an elephant, a water jug and a cougar. Interesting mix. Finally, the afternoon sun shone brightly, reminding me that it was time to go home. Enough courage development for today! In the solitude, a single bird chirped, and as it did, I added a final curlicue to my name. It was time to head back down the mountain. *My mountain.* Sir Edmund Hillary was right: *"It's not just the mountain we conquer, but ourselves."* Yes, it is during rock climbing that I most understand the nature of courage. For sure, it is when I feel the most courageous.

Emily Manning, 15

Three Phone Calls

It's easy to think of courage as people like firefighters. But because my mother is so sick and we kids are doing all we can to help her and to keep our family together, I think our little family is what courage is all about.

—Carolina Christopher, 14

My mother has diabetes. It's hard for her to keep her insulin balanced, so sometimes she falls into a deep sleep and it's really hard to wake her. That happened about two months ago. She wasn't feeling well, so she took a nap. When I tried to wake her up for dinner, I couldn't. I called 911, and she was taken by ambulance to the hospital. We were told that she was in a coma—and that she might not ever come out of it.

My two younger brothers and I were really scared. I was scared for my mother. And I was scared for us kids. My dad hasn't lived with us for many years. We never hear from him, so if something happened to our mother, I didn't know what would happen to us.

My brothers and I had to stay with a family from my church while my mother was in the hospital. For almost a week, my brothers and I were not allowed to see her. I think people thought it would be too disturbing for us to see my mother lying in a hospital bed with tubes running in and out of her body. But we wanted to see her, and when we were told we couldn't, all three of us cried.

A week later the doctors told the family we were staying with to bring my brothers and me to the hospital. My mother wasn't doing well, and they weren't sure if she would make it through the night. I tried not to cry. I wanted to be brave for my little brothers. We went into the room and talked to her quietly. We held her hands and kissed her forehead. I told her I loved her and wanted her to come home. I asked God to make her better. I begged Him to make her wake up from the coma—at least for a little while so we could talk to her. My littlest brother just didn't understand what a coma was, so all this was very confusing to him. It was sad to watch him.

When I left the hospital that day, I truly felt like it would be the last time we kids would ever see our mother. I wasn't sure how she could get better when even the doctors thought she was going to die. Then at two o'clock in the morning the phone rang, so I knew that couldn't be good. I hurried out of bed and ran to the stairwell to hear what was being said. It was the hospital. My mother's blood sugar had stabilized and she was responding well to the medication the doctors were trying to give her. She wasn't awake yet, but she was slowly improving. Mom needed lots and lots of rest. I was so thankful she was alive.

The next morning, every time the phone rang my heart stopped. I eavesdropped on every phone call, to see if someone was calling about my mom. I asked God to help my mother. We were warned that even should she come out of the coma, there was no guarantee she would be "normal" again. I didn't care. I just wanted to be able to return to my own home with my mother and brothers, and have life return to normal. Before lunch that day, the phone rang again. It was the hospital, once again giving an update on my mother's condition. They said her condition had not changed. The next day, the hospital called again. The woman we were staying with smiled and did a thumbs-up! When she hung up the phone she announced, "Hallelujah! Your mother has come out of the coma!" I ran screaming to find my little brothers to let them know, and also that we could now go see her.

I was so anxious for the day to be over so I could go visit Mom that I could hardly eat my lunch. At the hospital, the doctors told us that my mother could talk, but only a little. She still had lots of tubes down her throat, so that made her talking difficult, but she could squeeze our hands to let us know that she heard us. I was so relieved to be able to tell her I loved her and to know she actually heard me. When my little brothers patted her hand and kissed her forehead, a tear trickled down her cheek. I could tell she wanted to say something but couldn't. It didn't matter. Her tears said it all. She squeezed our hands and then drifted back to sleep.

The doctors said that we had to let her rest, and that her coming out of the coma was a miracle. This whole thing has been pretty scary. I was really so afraid my mother was going to die. We kids are so young. I just turned fourteen, so if my mother died, I worried that we three kids might have to split up, that we'd be put in foster care. If that happened, then maybe we wouldn't see each other ever again. My father didn't even come and see my mother in the hospital, nor did he call to see how we kids were either. So I knew it wasn't like we could go be a family with him.

So this has been a really frightening time. I think we've all been brave—and courageous. I know that when people think of courage, they think of people like firefighters and all. But I watched my little brothers on so many occasions be extra good, like doing their homework or even going to bed without being asked to because they didn't want to cause trouble. Sometimes when they would leave the house in the morning I could see they missed having their mother send them off with a hug and a kiss. I knew they were as scared about Mom as I was. Having watched all this, I believe that our little family is what courage is all about. We clung together and hung together. Luckily, we are now back together.

Our mother is home now and doing better. We three kids take really good care of her. We try not to cause her any trouble or stress. We want her to stay well. We need and love her. We're so scared of what our lives might be like without her.

Carolina Christopher, 14

Marching Orders from the Heart

How do you find fault with someone for telling you that he needs to break up with you because his heart has made a choice—and it didn't choose you?

—Elizabeth Moria, 17

We should never have fallen in love, but we did. Now I stood trembling, looking up at the love of my life. Searching for words, with tears in his eyes he looked away. Neither of us could find words. And so we stepped into each other's arms and held on. *Be cool. And brave,* I told myself. I had hoped this day would never come. But it had. That the two of us were here in this heart-defying moment meant Nick was madly in love with Alison—STILL.

Our love just happened; it wasn't a planned thing. Alison, my best friend since first grade, dated Nick. He lived nearly two hours away. So that we could double-date, she'd set me up with Nick's best friend, Chris. Though I saw Chris a couple of times, we didn't hit it off, and so we didn't go out again. But Nick and I had feelings for each other right off the bat. We had so much in common. We both had a passion for music, loved to write, and he made me think about things. Conversation between us was easy.

He's just a friend, I'd tell myself. But that didn't stop us from driving the two hours to see each other. And when we couldn't do that, we'd talk on the phone for hours on end. I was falling for him.

One day when Nick drove down to see Alison, before he visited her he came to see me. We went to the park. We were walking when he suddenly stopped, took my hands in his and told me he thought he was falling in love with me. I was stunned. But happy, too. He told me that since the first day he met me he thought I was special. He said it hurt him to think that I could be with any boy other than him. Hearing his words, I couldn't move. This is what I had been waiting for: to have a boy feel this way about me and tell me these beautiful words. He said it was difficult to "live a lie" but next to impossible to ignore his feelings for me. I looked him in the eye and told him that I felt the same way about him. The words just poured out. I told him that he was the guy I saw when I closed my eyes. That he was the guy I wanted to take me to the winter ball. I was about to tell him a million more things, but before I could say another word, he leaned down and kissed me. The kiss was filled with so much grace and beauty. It left me dreaming for weeks.

So that was how things started. Nick and Alison then broke up. For the next month Nick drove to visit me every week. Week by week, our relationship grew. It was awesome. But then one week Nick didn't show up in the place we'd always met—the coffeehouse. I sat in the coffee shop for three hours waiting for him, but he never showed. I eventually went home. There was a message waiting for me from Nick asking me to call him.

I grabbed the phone and dialed his number. He apologized for keeping me waiting in the coffee shop and then told me that on the way to meet me, he'd run into Alison. They had talked and were now back together. He said he was sorry that we couldn't continue to see each other. He told me that what we had was "wonderful" and "just great." He told me how sorry he was that he had to give me up. But he had to: He was STILL in love with Alison. He said he was driving over on Saturday, and he wanted to tell me in person.

So here I stood, my heart dying. But how do you not feel for someone when he is telling you that he needs to break up with you because his heart has made a choice—and it didn't choose you? How do you find fault with someone saying, "I've got to follow my heart"?

If it took courage for him to follow the orders of his heart, then I'd have to tell my heart to "march on" as well. March on out of his life. Hurt and devastated, but having heard the pain in his voice, all I could do was say, "I understand." Too stunned to cry, and too proud and brave to go crazy, I gathered my courage and sweetly said good-bye.

Holding each other, I could feel his heart racing in his chest. Finally, I broke the silence by whispering, "I'll never forget you." Nick just shook his head, and with tears falling, told me how sorry he was. "I know," was all I could say, giving him one last kiss. With that, he turned and walked to his car.

In that moment, my heart grew a full size. I think it takes real courage to end a relationship with someone you love. I do know that Nick was someone who found himself in love with two people. And that he had to make a choice. He could have been callous and played the two of us. Or he could have allowed the relationship between us to come to light and to let us two girls be the ones who shed tears—or worse, to "fight" over him. But Nick had found his courage to ask his heart to sort things out—and then to tell me in person. As difficult as it must have been, he'd found the courage to let me down—to walk away from me—as gently as he could. Even if he had to hold his heart in his hands in doing so.

As I watched him walk away, I understood what it means to truly love someone. Yes, I felt really sorry that I was the one who had lost Nick. But Alison loved him, too. And he loved her. What a lucky girl.

Though Nick and I make a point of never being in the same place at the same time, every once in a while we are. Every single time I see him, all those feelings I have for him come rushing back. Still, I see him with Alison and how happy they are together.

It takes courage not to call Nick and to go running after him pleading my undying love. It takes great courage to simply cry alone, and to not call, write or e-mail him. Most of all, it takes courage to put this love behind me. In time, I'm hoping my heart will let me do just that.

Elizabeth Moria, 17

Alison's Wig

Sometimes someone can be in your life for even a brief time and affect you more profoundly than someone you've known all your life.

—Angelica Maxwell, 13

When the teacher first told our class about Alison, I figured she had to be really mad about the way her life turned out. She was sick with leukemia and so had been in and out of the hospital for the last year. Now she was going to be coming to our school. The teacher assigned her to sit at my table. I thought it was cool that she would be my table partner. The teacher also told us not to be shocked when we saw her. Because of the "treatments" she'd had, apparently Alison had lost some of her hair, but she had been "fitted for a new wig" and would be wearing it to her first day of school. Even though it was October, we were going to welcome Alison like it really was the first day of school.

I thought I was prepared to see her, but I was totally shocked when Alison came into class. I didn't realize she would be so strange-looking as well as so frail. She walked with crutches. She told me she had a wheelchair to use sometimes too.

Alison was so proud of her wig. She was so thin that it hardly fit her head, but she wore it proudly anyway. She said it kept her head really warm. Contrary to my thinking she'd be mad about being so sick, she was a really happy person. She had the best smile, and she laughed all the time. I was sure she was mostly happy to be back at school and out of the hospital. I wanted to ask her a lot of questions but decided to wait until she got a little better. I didn't want to make her feel bad or anything. I do think it's really amazing what she's doing. I would be really afraid to be that sick. I wonder if she thinks she's going to die? I know that would frighten me, especially if I looked in the mirror and looked as sick as she does. I saw a picture today of Alison in the fifth grade. She looked like a completely different person. She was wearing a soccer uniform. It's hard for me to understand how someone so young (she's fourteen) can have such a terrible disease. She has to be one of the most courageous people I know. She is really sick but tries to act normal. She says every day is a "new day," so she wants every day to be a good one.

Alison was at school for a couple of weeks, and things seemed to be going pretty well. Then, just a few weeks later, our class was told we were getting out of school early on that day so we could visit Alison in the hospital. She was sick again and had been in the hospital for over two weeks. We made her cards and sent her get-well messages, but she hadn't been strong enough to come back to school. The teacher prepared us for what we were going to see. We talked about cancer and hospitals, and some of the treatments Alison had gone through. I was a little nervous, but I couldn't wait to see her. She is really nice. I wondered if she was still wearing her wig.

At the hospital, the nurses took us on a tour. We saw the new babies through the window of the nursery and passed through some of the other areas of the hospital. I saw labs where they draw your blood, and I even got to practice giving a shot to a dummy! It was a nice tour and made me feel like a hospital must be a wonderful place to work—until I saw Alison. She looked terrible.

Alison was so happy to see all of us, though! The nurses hadn't told her we were coming, so she was completely surprised! She started to cry. I started to cry, too, but only because I felt so sorry for her. I thought she would look better, but she didn't. She wasn't wearing her wig. That was the first time I'd ever seen her without it. She didn't have any hair at all—or eyebrows. I really thought she might be dying. What if she would never be strong enough to leave this place?

Alison died during the night after our visit.

I can't stop crying. The teacher says Alison was so happy about our visit. She says the chemotherapy had weakened her body too much and that's why she died. I wonder if Alison knows how sad we are for her? I wonder if she's in a place where she's happy and not in pain anymore? I think about the empty seat next to me, and I can't stop crying.

I think Alison is by far the most courageous person I've ever known, because she could have quit fighting her cancer a long time ago. But she didn't. She kept fighting—and with a smile on her face. She was friendly and pleasant to everyone. The rest of my year will not be the same. But I do know that even having known Alison for the short time I did, I learned more this year than some people learn in a lifetime. Sometimes someone can be in your life for even a brief time and affect you more profoundly than someone you've known all your life.

Angelica Maxwell, 13

Life . . . Beyond the Love of My Life

The only way to make pain go away is to go all the way through it.

— Kara Ryan, 19

Jason and I belonged together, and we knew it. Even when we'd get upset with each other and break up, we'd always work things out and get right back together. We'd dated for three years. We knew we'd always be together, forever.

We were wrong about the "forever" part: Near the end of our junior year, Jason was killed in a car accident.

When I first heard news of the accident—and how it happened—I didn't believe it. They said Jason had fallen asleep at the wheel. I knew that couldn't be, since anytime he was tired he would pull over and sleep it off. Or, he would turn his hat backward, turn the radio up and start singing along—his method of staying alert to get home safely. Always, he was so safety-conscious.

As news from the investigation came to light, I learned that, in fact, Jason hadn't been driving that night. Because he was tired, he'd let his friend drive. His friend had fallen asleep at the wheel. The two friends were just a mile away from Jason's house.

Regardless of who had been driving, Jason—the love of my life—was dead. He was seventeen.

For the next months, my life was a total blur of tears. My heart was broken, and nothing could put it back together. Day in and day out I was a walking zombie, just going through the motions. All I wanted to do was crawl into bed and sleep—yet nights were often sleepless. My sleep wasn't the only thing that suffered; so did my grades. I just wanted to run away—from this school, this town, everyone. I needed to get away from the memories of Jason and me—memories that lived in everything I did every day and every place I went. My family and friends just couldn't understand how deep this loss was to me. Nor could they understand why I never could get over him. "You've got to move on," they'd say. But all I could do was scream, "No!"

I did move. Eventually, everyone thought I needed "a change of scenery"—feeling it would help me forget the past. And so I went to stay with family friends who lived about an hour away. Throughout the next year, I kept to myself and tried to stay busy by going to school and getting good grades. I also worked as many hours as I could. But no matter how many miles away I was from the place where Jason and I had created so many memories, still I mourned. Months passed. I graduated from school and started college. I got my own apartment.

Living on my own was the best and the worst thing that ever happened to me. It was good because it was a new start. It was bad because living alone made it easy to isolate myself from others even more than I had before. Then I started drinking. I told myself it would help me forget. Because the grieving was so intense, and because I knew how wrong it was that I was drinking and then justifying why I was, I decided to get some counseling. "Moving on isn't happening," I told the therapist. "Nor has moving to a new town helped. A part of me is missing—and no one understands how much I loved Jason. Will it always be this way? Will I hurt this way forever?"

The counselor has helped me learn that memories live within us, which is why pain—and love, too, for that matter—follow wherever you go. Getting through the pain, I've learned, takes a great deal of courage, because the only way to make the pain go away is to go all the way through it. So this is what I'm doing now. I'm going through it—as opposed to running away. And I stopped drinking. Drinking kept me from dealing with my real emotions in honest, straightforward ways. It also made me moody, and I'd go into crying jags.

I've also moved back to my old town to face the past I had tried so hard to leave behind. I'm working my way through things one person and one memory at a time. It is so hard. I'm never going to be the same person as when Jason and I were in love and looking forward to a life of being together forever. Still, I am finding courage day by day to go forward. I'm learning to adjust. Some days are better than others, which is why I'm staying in counseling. With the help of a therapist I'm learning to grow strong without being bitter. I'm learning to face the future without Jason with the hope that one day thoughts of him will make me smile instead of cry.

Kara Ryan, 19

The Deepest Cut

"Cutting" sounds disgusting, even offensive, but we should talk about it because it happens a lot. Maybe we can help others before they reach such a place of despair.

—McKenzy Jean, 17

One evening as I was watching a six-hour marathon of *Saved by the Bell,* my phone rang. I rolled over to pick it up, only to hear sobs of a friend on the other end. "Hello?" I said, but the caller hung up. I knew who it was from caller ID. I decided to just wait and see if she would call back. She did. But all she did was sob. I knew she was really going through a hard time, and I also knew her as someone who was into some pretty dark things.

"Stay where you are," I instructed. "I'm coming over." I rushed over to her house, fearful of what to expect because this was not the first call of this kind she'd made to me. The house was dark; no one else was home. I checked the door and found it open.

The moment I walked in I could hear her sobs. There sat my friend, huddled in a corner of the dining room. I went to her, put my arms around her and wiped her tears with the sleeve of my sweatshirt. "Everything's going to be fine, okay?" I said, trying to reassure her. Helping her up, I noticed the marks on her forearms. She had done it again. Seeing that I had noticed, she apologized. "You don't have to apologize to me," I told her. "But you've got to get help. You can't continue this." I found some Band-Aids and Neosporin in the bathroom, and dabbed the two red and swollen wounds. I'm not sure how long my friend had been cutting on herself, but I did see other thin lines, scars that would stain her skin for years to come. I put Scooby-Doo Band-Aids on her torn skin. "Thanks," she said, still crying. I wrote her parents a note saying she was at my house and then told her to come with me.

Though I put on a brave front as we were going to my house, I was really scared for her. Cutting oneself sounded like a really deep, dark place, and I didn't know if just being at my house would mean she could be trusted to not hurt herself some more. I worried that maybe she needed to be hospitalized. I mean, I really couldn't relate to why someone would deliberately slash herself.

The next day, I talked to the school counselor in private, who told me that teens who suffer from depression, or feel as though they can't talk to anyone, sometimes deliberately hurt themselves. Then she told me something that I found frightening: She said that "cutting" is something that happens a lot! So I've been doing a little research on it and discovered some unbelievable news. As an example, one teenager out of ten deliberately harms him- or herself! Is that frightening or what? I also read an article where Princess Diana was quoted as cutting herself, and some other well-known people, movie stars included, also admitted they suffered from this. So obviously, self-mutilation is a bigger problem than many would like to believe. I know self-injuring sounds disgusting, even offensive, but even so, I think people need to talk about it. Then maybe we can help others before they reach such a place of despair. I know my friend felt really awful about herself, especially after she cut herself. Maybe bringing the problem out of the closet would mean that others wouldn't have to feel so alone and suffer alone.

As for my friend, she is now receiving the help she needs to stop hurting herself. I can tell she is getting better. Just last week as I was entering my house, I saw a handmade envelope on the doormat. On the front it read, *"For McKenzy, ONLY!"* I opened it and read it: *"To my dearest friend in all the world. You sat with me in the dark, caring enough about me to calm my feelings of panic. Thank you for being the most dependable and faithful person I know. Thank you for having the courage to be my friend when so many others couldn't. And thank you for helping me get help! Love always, ME."*

While she had thanked me for having the courage to be her friend, I believe it is my friend who is the courageous one. She is working hard to confront the "dark and ugly." That can't be easy. But she very much wants to get beyond this and to get on with her life. I'm confident she will.

McKenzy Jean, 17

The Long Way Home

It takes a lot of courage to be a "good kid." It's not always easy or convenient to take the high road and do the right thing. And putting up with the pressure you get from your friends isn't always easy either.

—Kelbi Perkins, 16

I once saw a TV commercial where a young boy takes a really long and out-of-the-way route home from school. He does this because if he were to take a shortcut, he'd have to go through an area where a gang is busy "turfing" the streets. It's a "don't do drugs" commercial. The point is that staying free from drugs won't always be easy or convenient. I feel that way about being a good kid. I think it takes a lot of courage to be a "good kid." It's not always easy or convenient to take the high road and do the right thing. Putting up with the pressure you get from your friends isn't always easy either. It's no fun being labeled a Goody Two-shoes. I should know, because I was.

Most all of my friends think it's cool to break rules—and as often as you can get away with it. I guess things change from "it's cool to be good" to "it's cool to break the rules" around eighth grade. I'm not sure why this is, but it is. Things weren't always this way. I grew up in a pretty big town, but I was still going to school with the same kids I'd known and gone to school with from kindergarten on. In eighth grade I moved to a really small town. The small town had only 7,145 people living there. I made lots of friends and was considered to be one of the most popular girls at school. I didn't have to work for it; everyone just sort of thought of me as cool. I was cool with that. But then I discovered that there's a lot of pressure being popular, because I had to keep up with everyone. It's expected. But I did the best I could, and everything was cool.

The next year I tried out for cheerleading squad. Then I moved up to varsity halfway through the season. Being as visible as I was, I was invited to a lot of things. The more parties and socials I attended, the more I noticed how much my friends worked really hard at being as bad as they could. As an example, I was invited to a Halloween costume party. The invitation said we'd have some food and then all go trick-or-treating. Well, it's not exactly what happened. I got there on time, but the party was already going strong. There were no adults around, and six-packs of beer were sitting everywhere, and lots of kids were holding a beer as they danced. That wasn't the only thing that was there; chew was there also. Some kids were smoking cigarettes, and I could have sworn I smelled pot in the air. All this put me in a bind because as a cheerleader, the school lets you know that you are "ALWAYS representing your school—whether in uniform or not." So my being at a place where there was alcohol and drugs was against school rules. I could get kicked off the squad. But I didn't want to be there for another reason: I didn't want any part of being around alcohol and drugs.

I knew I had to get out of there as soon as possible. I changed quickly out of my costume, grabbed my bag and left without saying good-bye to anyone. I went to my aunt's house and called my mom to have her come pick me up. As we drove home, I felt dumbfounded that my friends were drinking and smoking. I felt proud of myself for having made the decision to leave. The next day at school I learned that the principal and teachers had found out about the party. I was told that some of the kids who attended the party had gone around boasting about themselves. Like drinking some beer makes you cool—what's up with that? Many athletes were suspended from games, and some were even kicked off the teams. You can imagine how proud I was of my decision. It was like, "Whoo-hoo! Thank goodness I made the right choice!" Because the penalties were stiff for those who had broken the rules—and I was not among them—my decision to leave the party actually made me look like the smart one! So that was good!

Not too long after that, however, another incident happened that threatened my "smart decision/good kid" status. I'd been invited to a friend's house—a guy—to hang out. He invited some other friends over, and I was cool with that. In time, out came the liquor, cigarettes—and the pot. I was offered some. I said no. Well, no one wanted to hear it. My father was the athletic director at school, and they knew it was really important that he not find out what they were doing. They knew that if I joined in on the drinking and smoking, for sure I wouldn't say anything. But I stood my ground, so then they were in a bind. They flat out told me that if I told on them, they'd not only be mad at me but would make sure no one in school ever talked to me again. So I knew my being there wasn't going to be pleasant.

I found a phone in one of the back bedrooms and called my parents. No one was home. So then I walked to the local pizza place where many of my friends hung out. Two friends were there. Knowing they wouldn't tell a soul, I told them what had happened. I then called my aunt, and she came to pick me up. While once again proud of my decision, I knew that the next day at school, I would no longer be seen as "smart/good/cool kid" but rather, Goody Two-shoes. Probably the only thing that saved me from that fate was that because my father was the athletic director, they couldn't be too mean to me. If they were, it would probably come back to bite them—like maybe they'd think they wouldn't make the team or something. But from that point on, things were never the same for me.

I'm a junior now and still making smart choices. Lots of my friends have made some pretty dumb mistakes. Luckily, my best friend Megan is also someone who can be counted on to make smart decisions. So at least I have someone to hang out with. Still, it's really hard for me to go through high school with the peer pressure and all the jokes that are made because of my "good/better/best" choices. I try not to let it bother me, but it's not easy. It's hard to tell your friends that you're trying to do the right thing, not because you're a "Goody Two-shoes," but because you don't want to mess up your life. I want to make the choices that are likely to help me reach my goals—which are more than just getting through school without being grounded for life, or jailed! So I'm prepared to sometimes take the long way home.

Kelbi Perkins, 16

Bulletproof Faith

Don't think of yourself as a coward because you're scared. The difference between a hero and a coward is not fear, but what you do with the fear.

—Sergeant Jeff Struecker, Eighty-Second Airborne

The incident in Mogadishu, Somalia, made famous by the book and movie *Black Hawk Down,* changed my life. It all began after high school when I visited an army recruiter. I asked, "What do you consider the toughest job in the army?"

"Being an airborne ranger," was his quick reply.

"That's what I want to be."

I joined the army—and went to war. In the 1989 invasion of Panama, Operation Just Cause, and later in Kuwait, Operation Desert Storm, I was shot at and placed in many dangerous situations. But I never thought I was in danger of losing my life. All this changed in 1993 in Mogadishu, Somalia. The United Nations had been handing out food to the starving people in this East African country. There were several warlords in Somalia, and most of them had no problems with the United Nations. One, Mohamed Farrah Aidid, saw the United Nations as a threat to his power. He began to ambush and kill U.N. workers. In one raid he killed and mutilated twenty Pakistanis. The goal of my unit, Task Force Ranger, was to capture Aidid and bring his key men to justice for the death of those Pakistani workers.

Prior to our final mission on October 3 and 4, Task Force Ranger had conducted six successful operations. Everything had gone exactly as planned. But on that seventh mission, generally referred to as Black Hawk Down, things changed. I was a twenty-four-year-old squad leader and placed my nine men in two Humvees. We led a ten-vehicle ground convoy into the city. The job of the convoy was to retrieve the Rangers and Special

Operations Forces who had been dropped by helicopter onto the roof and in the surrounding alleys of the target building. We were to return them and their prisoners to our base.

The operation went exactly as planned, with one exception: A Ranger, Todd Blackburn, in a Black Hawk helicopter, missed the slide rope and fell seventy feet to the ground. He hit headfirst, and our medics felt he would not survive unless he received immediate special medical care. As soon as I arrived at the target building, my commander called and told me to take Todd back to our base at the airport. We loaded him into a Humvee, and with my two vehicles around him, we began to make our way back to the airfield. Mogadishu is about seven-by-two miles in size, and 1.5 million people had gathered there from all over Somalia to be fed.

When we turned the corner onto Hawlwadig Road heading for the airfield, it seemed that all 1.5 million people were on every rooftop, doorway and window shooting at us. I placed a Ranger on each side of my vehicle to defend us. Sergeant Dominick Pilla, the best machine gunner I've ever seen, was sitting behind me shooting at targets on the right side of my Humvee. As we drove through the hail of enemy bullets and grenades, a Somali gunman pointed his AK-47 at Dominick. Both fired and both were killed at the same moment. Pilla was shot in his forehead and died immediately, slumping into Ranger Tim Moynihan's lap.

Tim began to panic and lose control. He screamed, "Sergeant Struecker, Dominick Pilla has been shot! He's been hit! He's been killed." I looked back and saw the entire back of my vehicle painted red with Pilla's blood. For a minute I felt panic along with everyone in my Humvee. The only thing I could think to say to Moynihan was, "Tim, take Dominick's place. You need to keep us alive."

We made it back to the airfield. As doctors were taking Todd Blackburn off and removing Dominick's body, my platoon leader said, "There's been a Black Hawk helicopter shot down. Get your men and go back into the city." I thought to myself, *There is NO way I can go back out there.* But knowing I had to, I sent my men for more ammunition and fuel, and began to clean Dominick Pilla's blood off my vehicle. As I was doing this, I remember asking God, "Am I going to die tonight?" I believed beyond a shadow of a doubt there was no way to survive this situation. I didn't know what to do or say, so I did what any Christian would do in this situation, I prayed. I didn't negotiate with God; I simply said, "God, I need your help; I'm in over my head!" Then I pictured in my mind Jesus in the Garden of Gethsemane. I could see Him bowing His knee before God and praying before He went to the cross. I could hear Him say, as if He were right next to me, "God, if there is any way possible, let this cup pass from me." I prayed those same words. Then I remembered what Jesus said next. "Not my will, but Yours be done."

At that moment, I realized something I had known since I became a Christian at the age of thirteen. As a Christian, no matter what happens to me in this life, if I live or die, I am firmly in God's hands. My wife, Dawn, had just written to tell me she was pregnant. I thought I'd never see her again or hold my child. If by some miracle of God I survived this situation, I would go home to my family. As a Christian I also knew if I died I'd go home to heaven and be with my Savior. *So no matter what happens to me tonight, I'm going home. I'm going to be safe,* I thought. From that moment on, I felt no fear. It didn't matter if I lived or died. Still, I did believe that none of us would survive. I just prayed, "God, don't let another one of my soldiers die."

As we loaded up our vehicle to go back into the city, one of my men, Brad Thomas, came to me. He said, "Sergeant, I can't go out there. I've a wife and family back home. I can't go. I know I'll die." I said, "Brad, I know you're scared. I'm scared. We're all afraid. In fact, if you're not afraid, there's something psychologically wrong. But Brad, don't think of yourself as a coward because you're scared. The difference between a hero and a coward is not fear, but what you do with the fear. I won't make you go, but I need you." With these words, I left him alone and got into my vehicle. In the rearview mirror, I watched Brad pick up his weapon. He got back into his vehicle fully expecting to die. He was willing to give his life for the mission. I felt my heart swell with pride as I drove out the gate.

We drove out of our base a second time. The Somalis were setting up roadblocks and burning tires at every intersection. They fired their weapons and grenade launchers not ten feet away. Miraculously, none of my men were killed. Soon we met a group of Rangers whose vehicles were badly shot up. Several had been killed, others wounded. Their vehicles were nonoperational, so we loaded the Rangers on ours and took them back to the base. I thought, *We're safe; we've gotten everybody out. We're okay!*

Then my commander told us half of our men were still in the city, and he sent us back a third time! More help was needed, and the UN forces stationed close by were asked to assist with their tanks and armored cars. A huge convoy was assembled, including two Pakistani tanks and Malaysian armored cars, to rescue our men. I thought, *Surely the Somalis will not fight armored vehicles.* But as soon as the tank turned down the main street, every Somali weapon began to fire. For the next twelve hours, the convoy fought its way into the city. It was eight the next morning before we were able to recover our men. My Humvee was ordered to follow the last tank out. I said to myself, *The tank is leaving before us?* I told my machine gunner, Brad Paulson, "We'll be the last vehicle out, so face your gun backward, because everyone behind us is a bad guy."

We had driven about a mile when Brad said, "Sergeant, there are men running down the road after us." I looked and saw 145 American soldiers looking scared to death, running down the road shooting at targets to the left and right. We had left 15 men in the city! My platoon leader was in his vehicle ahead of me, and I decided to let the convoy go. We backed up, loaded those men and drove them to security.

I'll never forget what I saw at the stadium. It wasn't the bullets or the blood that made such an impression on me. It was the men I had served with for so long. I had let them know I was a Christian long before we went to Somalia, and I had tried to share my faith with them. Then, they had wanted nothing to do with it. Now they were all ears. On October 4, those battle-hardened Rangers came to me with tears in their eyes and a lot of questions. "How could this happen to us? We're supposed to be the best in the world. Why would God allow it to happen? What happened to my friend who just died? What's going to happen to me if we go back into that city and I die?"

I didn't have all the answers, but there was one question to which I did know the answer: "What will happen if you die tomorrow?" For the next several days I told as many people who would listen what happens when you die. "The answer," I said, "is in the Bible [Hebrews 9:27]. I don't know when you will die, but everyone will die, and a moment later stand before the judgment seat of God. Two kinds of people will stand before the judgment of God. The first are those who have never put their trust in Him. These people will suffer eternal separation from God. The second are those who have said, 'I have placed my trust and faith in Him.' They will spend eternity with God the Father in Heaven. Can you say if you died right now you would know for certain that you have eternal life? I know for sure if I die this very moment I will spend eternity with God in heaven. I hope you will make a commitment to God and settle forever your relationship with Him."

Yes, going to battle takes courage. There is no doubt about the fact that the possibility of death in war in real. But it takes courage to confront the truth of life as well. And the truth is that we are God's children. And we must have the courage to confront what that means.

Are you struggling with finding the courage to live your faith? If you want, write to me at the address below. Be sure to mention that you read this story in *Taste Berries for Teens #4*.

Sergeant Jeff Struecker, Eighty-Second Airborne

AUTHORS' NOTE: *Chaplain Jeff Struecker invites you to write him at Military Ministry, 6060 Jefferson Avenue, Suite 6012, Newport News, VA 23605.*

Teen Talk: My Take on Courage

Publicly Speaking . . .

I like to think of myself as courageous. I mean, I have no qualms about charging into the spotlight and dribbling through a zone press on the basketball court—everyone watching, and with "need to win this game" written on their faces. I can hold my own when standing up to someone flirting with my girl, or square off with a would-be bully just looking to pick a fight. But the thought of standing up in front of the entire class and making an oral report, now that is another matter! I mean to tell you, before I even get to the front of the room, my heart starts beating and I swear it sounds as loud as thunder in a mountain storm. Scared is not the worst of it. Always, I think, *Oh, man, what if I get up there and can't remember what I'm supposed to say?* I can see myself standing there, shaking, dry-mouthed, everyone staring at me in stone-cold silence while even my friends tried vainly to suppress their giggles. I sometimes actually wonder if a person could die from embarrassment. Sometimes I think I could! But I do know that I have to overcome this fear—and the sooner the better, because if I don't it's going to follow me into college and maybe even when I go to work for some big company. I know that if I don't learn to overcome this fear it will slow me down in life. After all, even corporate presidents have to give speeches to their board of directors and when appearing on camera for some charity or special event. What I most want to work on is developing the courage to speak in front of others.

Brad Tannen, 17

"And the Grammy for Best New Group Goes to . . ."

I think it takes courage to dream a big dream and then go for that dream. It's been my experience that sometimes people feel free to put down your goal. Maybe they do this because they can't imagine going for such a big goal themselves. Or maybe they're jealous that you've dreamed the dream and made a plan to make things happen. Or maybe they don't believe in you personally and don't think you can accomplish your dream. I know that in telling people my goal—which is to have my own band and to also be a recording star—some people look at me and say, "Oh, how nice to have such big plans." You can hear it in their voices that they're patronizing you. They don't believe you can do it. Others will immediately tell you that your chances for success with such a goal rests somewhere between zero and zilch. Others will warn you of the dire consequences of life on the road, or the perils of fame and fortune. So I guess my point is that it can take a lot of courage to be up front with others about your goals. I think that's unfortunate. Why shouldn't you be able to share your goals and plans for your life—especially if they are of the stature and magnitude such as mine? But I'm not worried. I've lots of courage.

You might say I've earned the courage! When I gathered a couple of buddies to start a band, in the beginning we were just awful. But that's to be expected. We were just learning to play, and our singing, well, let's just say we were rough and off-key. So as not to scare the people and pets in the neighborhood, we hung carpet on the walls of the garage as a sound barrier. Disorganized was our middle name, though in those early days, it would have been a good name for our band as well. When we got tired of practicing—or couldn't take anymore, whichever came first—we'd walk out, leaving guitars, drums and drumsticks scattered everywhere. We knew "good" and "a shot at the big time" were awhile off! We now look back with laughter.

But even with others criticizing us and not believing in what we were doing, we kept to our music. Always we reminded ourselves of the goal: We were going to be musicians—outstanding ones. And we were going to write and record popular songs.

And yes, we were going to be famous. We stayed true to our goal even though in the early days of our band it was hard to get anyone to hire us—even if we agreed to play for free! Now we're getting really good. We still come into contact with people who do not believe in us, which brings this back to courage. In this business, while we get asked to play more and more, rejection is still high. But then again, we're going after some pretty impressive billings these days. And with that, the possibility of rejection often gets larger. So when it comes to courage, we know we need it. We've learned that others might not always believe in us, but we can always believe in ourselves.

I'm happy to report that we're finally at the stage where we've mastered our instruments, fine-tuned our voices and can admit that we're talented. I'm also pleased to report that now we're at the stage of looking to get a major label interested in us. We're hoping Sony will sign us, but there are three other good labels we're interested in as well. We have an agent, and we've recently cut a demo. When we heard it for the first time, we were thrilled. I don't know if it will be a breakthrough for us, but we're hopeful. So I'd say to you, have the courage to dream a big dream and head in that direction, no matter how many trials you must go through. I've found the courage to stay true to my goal. I'm not out to sell 120 albums. I'm out to sell 120 million albums. So I'm going to experience rejection. And success! I've got the courage to handle both!

Bow Morris, 17

Megaphone Messages . . .

One of the greatest insights into courage I've ever had was in trying to understand C. S. Lewis's famous quote: *"God whispers to us in our pleasures, speaks in our conscience, but shouts in our pain. It is His megaphone to rouse a deaf world."* At first, I found myself asking how it applied to life, especially to the crisis times in life, because I think it's natural to ask, *Why would God allow such a terrible thing to happen?* I have come to some conclusions: While I don't think God is "shouting" at us in our pain, I do believe that our pain can snap us into reality—especially from the distractions of daily routine, and get us to refocus on what is meaningful. I do think that in chaos and pain—when we are in desperate need—God has our attention, and so it's an opportune time to draw closer to Him. Personally, I think He uses our pain to open our minds to see His greater purpose and plan.

I also found myself asking, "Why is God's voice a *whisper* when we are in pleasure—why does He feel so distant when we are in 'happy times' in our lives?" I mean, are we so selfishly focused on what we are enjoying and what makes us feel good that the pleasure or self-focus overshadows what God is trying to give us? For example, when you are enjoying a good time with your friends at a football game or watching your favorite movie, is it possible to hear God's voice, and is it louder than a whisper? What does it take to be able to hear God's voice during times of pleasure? I think I'm coming to terms with these questions. I believe that the only way to hear God "shout" or "whisper" is to have the courage to live your life centered on your faith. God must be the first and foremost priority in your life. If we don't, then exactly how can we hear His plan for our lives?

So when I think about courage, I start with me. I hope always to stand up in my faith and live it.

Eric Bishop, 17

Look Before You Leap Is What I Say . . .

I was always the gung-ho guy willing to try anything, no matter how stupid it was. Once, I jumped off a thirty-foot cliff into a river without even checking to see how deep the water was. Talk about stupid! I heard about a guy who got paralyzed like that when he hit a tree under the water he couldn't see. I guess I was more lucky than smart sometimes. But all that changed when I enlisted and got my first taste of a real war. I was still pretty gung-ho, but the rules kept me pretty well in check. Then, when a guy in my platoon stepped on a land mine and had to have both legs amputated, boy, that sobered me up in a hurry. I still have the guts to get the job done, but I'm more cautious now. I look before I leap these days, because I've learned the delicate balance of courage over fear.

Randy Caldwell, 19

Missing Factor 8 . . .

If I've learned anything about courage, it's from my brother Conrad. He is the bravest, the most courageous person I know. When Conrad was six months old, we noticed that he bruised easily. We didn't know why. On one particular day, my baby brother was so bruised that Mom and Dad were actually worried that if they sought medical attention, the doctors might actually think he had been a victim of child abuse. Mom and Dad did take him to the hospital, of course, and after extensive tests, it was discovered that little Conrad suffered from hemophilia VIII. What this means is that should a normal, healthy person suffer an injury, certain factors combine to form a clot to stop that person from bleeding to death.

Conrad is missing "Factor 8." This means that should he bump himself to the point of splitting his skin, he could bleed to death. Fortunately for those suffering from Factor 8, the moment they suffer an injury, they can be injected with a synthetic factor that stops the bleeding within minutes.

One evening about four years ago, Conrad got a gash on his head the size of a BB. It wouldn't quit bleeding. From just that one injury, in a three-day period of time, he was taken to the hospital three times! Finally, on the third day, they admitted him for tests. That's when it was discovered that his body wasn't responding to the injected Factor 8. Thinking it was a virus, Conrad's body was rejecting the injected synthetic Factor 8. A couple of months later, Conrad was admitted to the hospital again, this time for surgery to implant a Broviac, which is a plastic tubing line inserted into a major artery. The idea was to give him some Factor 8 every day, and that, hopefully, his body would learn how to use it again.

My poor brother. Complication after complication after complication. It wasn't long after all this that he began getting infections in the Broviac line, and the poor little guy had to be treated immediately for a new dilemma. One year, he was in the hospital around fifteen times, often one week at a time! Once, when we didn't know that he even had an infection, Conrad almost died. In fact, the nurse said that if we'd brought him into the hospital even one hour later, we might have lost him. Luckily, the little guy pulled through. He's getting better, but still has one ordeal after another.

If you were to see him, he pretty much looks like a typical little boy. He likes to play ball and loves to ride his bike (always wearing his helmet). Though he's improving, this will be a lifelong battle, one that can cost millions of dollars. At the moment, Conrad's medical costs are well over a million dollars a year. Amazing, isn't it?

Because we almost lost him and miraculously didn't, Conrad got showered with loads of attention from friends and relatives. He's even been on the front page of the newspaper several times. And, he's had his picture in magazines and has even been asked to appear on television. For his birthday, we went to the zoo, and the restaurant of his choice—McDonald's, of course!

I can't help but admire him. I do think he is one courageous little boy. I know that he's going to need real courage for a long time to come. He's had so many medical complications. Hospitals and doctors and nurses and needles and tubes and machines are a part of his life. I wonder what that must be like personally knowing and living so self-consciously. I get up, head out the door without so much as a thought about my body functioning right, doing everything it's supposed to and when it's supposed to. But not Conrad. He can't even ride his bike without a special helmet! So his life is not going to be business as usual. I worry about when he gets to be a teenager, knowing how cruel teens often are with one another. I know that stage, too, will take great courage. Luckily for Conrad, by then he'll simply ooze with it, because for this little boy, courage is something he's had to learn each day he gets out of bed.

Glenda Slabaugh, 15

Freedom Fighters Rank High on the Courage Scale

When I think of courage, for certain those who serve in the military come to mind. And for good reason! I have many family members who have been in the service—and some still are. My father, Dean Trask, was in the marine corps and served in Desert Storm (also known as the Gulf War). My great-grandfather, Everett Burres, served two terms in World War II, as did my other great-grandfather, Lawrence Derrig. During the Vietnam War, my grandfather, Orval Kinne, was in the National Guard. During that same time, two great-uncles, Mark Burres and Kevin Burres, were in the service, too. I also have a step-great-grandfather, Charlie Wagner, who was in the Coast Guard. And Chaplain Jeff Struecker, who is my step-uncle (and whose incredible story—"Bulletproof Faith"—is in this unit), was also in the military and served in a number of war conflicts.

Having seen so many members of my family proudly serve their country, putting their lives on the line for our freedom, I have a real respect for them both as courageous people and as American soldiers. And because our family shares this legacy, I know from hearing their many conversations how courageous the many others who serve in the military are as well. To me, those who serve in the many branches of the military—and freedom fighters everywhere—are brave and courageous beyond words. Whether it's the marines, army, navy, air force, National Guard or Coast Guard, all who serve their country are heroes to me. All freedom fighters rank really high on the courage scale in my book!

Hali Trask, 13

AUTHORS' NOTE: *Hali, a most cool, caring and courageous taste berry, is also Bettie's niece and Jennifer's cousin!* ❤

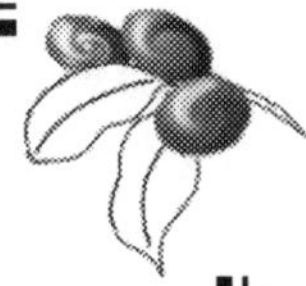

Part 6

Dying for Attention: A Candid Look at the Importance of Teen Self-Worth

He who knows others is learned;
but he who knows himself is wise.

—Lao Tzu

The longest journey is the journey inward.

—Dag Hammarskjold

You can be pleased with nothing
when you are not pleased with yourself.

—Lady Mary Wortley Montagu

The worst loneliness is not
to be comfortable with yourself.

—Mark Twain

Personal growth can be painful, because it
can make us feel ashamed to face our own darkness.
But our spiritual goal is the journey
out of fear-based, painful mental habit patterns,
to those of love and peace.

—Marianne Williamson

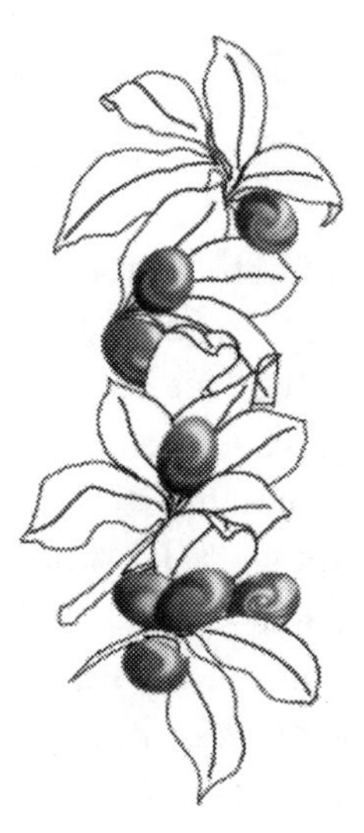

A Word from the Authors

In our *Taste Berries for Teens* series, which are inspirational short stories and encouragement on life, love and relationships, quite often we come across teens who find themselves face-to-face with health-oriented issues. Accounts such as Alana Ballen's "My Bipolar Disorder" (in *Taste Berries for Teens*); Amy Manning's "Would You Ask Me Out If You Knew?" (in *More Taste Berries for Teens*); Katie Phillipsen's "Alopecia Areata, a.k.a. Aunt Fester" (in *Taste Berries for Teens #3*); and Gina Rivera's "A Secret Too Big to Keep" (in *A Taste-Berry Teen's Guide to Managing the Stress and Pressures of Life*) are extremely popular with our readers and always generate enormous amounts of mail. Again and again we hear from teens who after reading such stories say, "Me, too. I'm coping with that as well," or "That teen describes what I'm going through. . . ."

So, when we put out the word to teens that we were starting a new book in our series and were interested in doing a unit on "mind/body issues," it wasn't a surprise to us that we received a huge response discussing their personal struggle with body-image issues. Still, we couldn't overlook the fact that a great many teens wrote about the perils they faced with their attempts to control weight—many of whom came dangerously close to an eating disorder. And many, we discovered, were already in the throes of an eating disorder, primarily anorexia, though incidence of bulimia was common, too. We also took note of the fact that the letters and e-mails were not just from girls, but guys as well.

Anorexia, like bulimia, is an eating disorder—one that experts believe starts by having a "distorted body image." In other words, when a person looks in the mirror, he or she believes that if only his or her body were different, then he or she would be better liked and accepted. So the size and shape of one's body is seen as both the problem ("Others don't like and accept me because of the way I look.") as well as the cure ("When I look different, others will like me more."). Seeing one's body as the way to being better liked and accepted, this person sets about changing his or her body. But just as drinking or using drugs can impair your health and lead to addiction (a physical and psychological dependence on chemicals), using extreme methods to lose or gain body weight can put your health at risk—and can lead to an eating disorder.

While you'll find more information in the boxed section at the end of this chapter, in a nutshell, anorexia is about limiting the amount of food you eat, whereas bulimia is about eating but then purging (throwing up) that food. If these methods sound drastic, it's because they are. But no one sets out to deliberately become a victim of anorexia or bulimia. An eating disorder may start out as a relatively simple desire to maintain or lose weight, but when the practice continues, it can morph into a disease. Both anorexia and bulimia are dangerous because both prevent the body from getting the nutrition it needs to function properly, as well as to sustain good health. Robbing the body of nutrients essential to growth and good health has dire consequences: It can lead to poor health and, potentially, death—due to malnutrition.

Anorexia is classified as a disease, because (like bulimia) it has specific symptoms that can be identified, diagnosed and treated. The different stages meet certain criteria, such as:

- Progressive: without treatment, things get worse;
- Predictable: you can predict the progression of symptoms and stages;
- Chronic: it is treatable, but "recovery" is ongoing; and
- Terminal—without treatment, you could die from this condition.

The degree to which we are accepting of ourselves—warts, flaws and all—is an important contribution to our own self-worth. That our bodies are undergoing such rapid and dramatic change in adolescence, and because our peers are all too quick to judge us on the size and shape of our bodies, teens are especially vulnerable to resorting to drastic measures to lose weight. Because eating disorders are dangerous, and so prevalent among teens, we've chosen to include this subject in our book.

As you can see, we've opened this unit with Vanessa Vega's moving account of a ten-year (and misguided) search for self-worth. Like so many teens, Vanessa felt that others didn't like her "enough," but would "if only" she were as "skinny" as some of the popular girls in her school. This distorted view in tow, Vanessa set out to transform herself—doing those things that, in turn, led to an eating disorder. As with most eating disorders, hers, too, became a monster of a habit that took control of her life. Excerpted from a journal she started in the seventh grade, Vanessa brings her message to you by way of journal entries, ones that chronicle her way into—as well as out of—the jaws of anorexia. Vanessa's journal section is then followed by accounts and comments from other teens who are coping with body-image issues, have friends or family who are, or simply want to voice their opinions about the importance of not allowing someone else's opinion to be more important than taking good care of yourself.

What do we learn from these teens about the importance of self-worth? For one, we learn that many teens sincerely believe that body image (the size and shape of their bodies) is the primary criteria for being seen as "cool" and for being accepted by others. We also learn that while an eating disorder is not a "glamorous" thing to talk about, we must. It is a serious problem and one that affects many teens.

We also learn that eating disorders are NOT "just a girl thing." Statistics show that one in eight of those diagnosed with eating disorders are male. What has been particularly good about publishing stories like those mentioned at the beginning of this unit is that it has resulted in our hearing from a good number of the guys who themselves are coping with issues related to body image. Whether because they wished to maintain or shed pounds to make the cut for a certain weight category for sports—wrestling being the biggest one; shed pounds (calling it "getting lean") in order to "build muscle mass"—saw it as a way to gain better acceptance or popularity with peers; or to gain the attention—if not affection—of a certain special girl, the fact is that guys have body-image issues just like girls do.

That body size and shape is viewed by teens as key to acceptance is not surprising. Most any teenager will tell you that if you weigh too much (or too little), there's going to be some form of discrimination coming your way. Sad, but true. Probably moms and dads everywhere can relate: Who wants to be the skinniest—or heaviest—boy or girl at the beach? So no matter how much parents, teachers or self-esteem experts may tell you to love yourself and not be concerned about what others think of the size and shape of your body, you know that if that person was standing in your shoes—if he or she was walking down the halls in your school—then he or she would know what you know: How your body looks is grounds for acceptance—or not. For membership in most cliques, especially the "cool crowd," rules apply. Those whose bodies carry pounds beyond the point of "cool" may find themselves left out.

Of course, it's not just your peers sending this message; so is much of the media. Luckily, even the movie industry—often cited as a part of the problem for setting the standard of "beauty" as synonymous with "being thin"—is trying to be a part of setting the record straight. Stars such as Kate Hudson, Halle Berry, Nicole Kidman and Julianne Moore (see *www.facetheissue.com*) are among the many industry professionals who are working to help young people gain a more realistic attitude concerning their bodies and the "thin myth."

So how do teens, as Jennifer Youngs says in her book, *Feeling Great, Looking Hot and Loving Yourself: Health, Fitness and Beauty for Teens,* "value health first, stay fit and still look 'hot' without falling prey to health-destroying tactics"? We hope this unit provides insight into finding answers to that. It is our fervent hope that this unit will help you gain a truer understanding of the importance of caring for your health. And we hope that it will cause you to examine the significance (value) you place on gaining approval from others at the risk of your own health and emotional well-being.

As important, we hope you will take the time to understand what it takes to be—and feel—"whole." For example, all young people need to learn to:

- *Self-validate:* Your sense of self-worth should not be based solely on how others think, feel or behave toward you, but rather, it should be more "internally" derived. You have to talk to yourself and believe what you say. Self-validation is important to your being able to resist peer pressure.
- *Self-soothe:* You must be able to "self-soothe"—which means to have a talk with yourself when life heaps itself upon your head. You must learn to manage your emotions and emotional discomforts in healthful and effective ways. When you're hurting, you must be one of the people who is able to "comfort" you.
- *Tolerate discomfort:* You must also be willing to tolerate

discomfort. Life often involves conflict, anxiety, disappointment, rejection, failure and other uncomfortable experiences. Increasing your tolerance for these kinds of discomforts helps you manage the stress and duress of life.

- *Express feelings:* You must be able to express what you think, what you feel and what you want. And, you must be able to communicate in ways that others will hear what you are saying—and want to.
- *Go for integrity:* You must be willing to not sacrifice your integrity, or engage in destructive behaviors such as addictions, deceit or impulsiveness (which are all unhealthful forms of self-soothing). You must be willing to stick up for your values.

There are others, too, but we provide these as an example. And by the way, growing a solid sense of self is a lifelong process. Still, as a teen you should be well on your way to learning these important avenues to self-worth.

Having said that, if you are struggling with an eating disorder, do not hide your secret. Get the help and support you need as quickly as you can. Bringing your problem to light and getting treatment and the support you need to stay healthy is a sign of strength. All are indications that you're becoming your own taste berry, willing and able to honor your health. In short, take care of yourself. Getting out of the jaws of an eating disorder is not easy; still, with treatment there is hope for recovery. The important thing is that you get the care—treatment—you need. Here are some ways to begin that:

- Reach out. Talk with your mom or dad, school counselor or family doctor—who can refer you to someone trained in the area of eating disorders.
- Come clean about what you're doing with those who are trying to help you. Don't worry about what they may think

of you. Many therapists practice in areas where they themselves have overcome the same or similar issues, or have a great deal of experience in helping others such as yourself. For sure, they have a genuine interest in helping you overcome your personal struggles to get well.

- Keep a journal. Getting your thoughts down on paper helps you see your feelings for what they are. This can prove useful in making decisions for your well-being.
- Get into counseling. Counseling can help you sort yourself out and help you find better ways to deal with the problem times of life. A trained therapist can help you work through difficult feelings such as shame and guilt, as well as help you uncover and deal with any deep dark secrets you are harboring.

If you've never struggled with an eating disorder, know that we each have an obligation to do all we can to help others see their lives in the most positive light. Here are some things you can do to be certain you do not contribute in any way to someone else falling prey to the perils of an eating disorder:

- Do not tease, pick on or poke fun at someone regarding his or her body—whether it's height, weight or anything else that impacts a person's perception of self.
- Do not tolerate or endorse rude comments or insensitive jokes that can contribute to others feeling insecure or inadequate.
- If you believe someone is seriously jeopardizing his or her health (either from using alcohol, drugs—including steroids—or is bingeing and purging), have a talk with your parents, or the school principal, counselor or teacher about your concerns. All will know how to best get your friend or classmate the help and support he or she needs.
- Feeling as though you don't fit in, or that you're not liked,

> is a terribly alienating feeling. Do all you can to help others feel a part of things. Be a taste berry in all that you do to model friendship and goodwill toward others. Remember, life is a journey—and we are all interdependent. Do your part to help others feel comfortable in their own skin.

Eating disorders are heavy issues, aren't they? Our hope is that you will carefully read and think about this unit, and openly discuss it with your family and within your circle of friends. Share it with someone you know who can benefit from the wisdom that "acceptance" begins with a willingness to respect and care for oneself.

Again, do your part. Just as we can all work together to create world peace or to conserve the world's natural resources, we can make the world a kinder, gentler and more accepting place in which to live. Be a taste berry: Help bring this "place" into being. It starts with self-acceptance and then the acceptance of others.

❤ *Taste berries to you, Bettie and Jennifer Youngs*

Below are some facts from the National Association for Eating Disorders and the National Association of Anorexia Nervosa and Associated Disorders.

Characteristics of Anorexia (Nervosa)

- Deliberate self-starvation with weight loss
- Intense, persistent fear of gaining weight
- Refusal to eat, except tiny portions
- Continuous dieting
- Compulsive exercise
- Abnormal weight loss
- Sensitive to cold
- Absent or irregular menstruation
- Hair loss—because of inadequate protein in the diet

Characteristics of Bulimia (Nervosa)

- Preoccupation with food
- Binge eating, usually in secret
- Vomiting after bingeing
- Abuse of laxatives, diuretics, diet pills
- Denial of hunger or drugs to induce vomiting
- Compulsive exercise
- Swollen salivary glands
- Broken blood vessels in the eyes

Physical Repercussions from Both Diseases

- Malnutrition
- Intestinal ulcers
- Dehydration
- Ruptured stomach
- Serious heart, kidney and liver damage
- Tooth/gum erosion
- Tears of the esophagus

Psychological Repercussions from Both Diseases

- Depression
- Low self-esteem
- Shame and guilt
- Impaired family and social relationships
- Mood swings
- Perfectionism
- "All or nothing" thinking

Who Is at Risk: Ages eleven through seventeen are vulnerable because in adolescence there is fat in "all the wrong places." There is also the issue of what culture tells us about having an "attractive body," which is all too often described as a thin body. About 30 percent of anorexics are male. There are as many bulimic men as there are anorexic women.

Typical Length of Illness:

- 77 percent duration from one to fifteen years
- 30 percent duration from one to five years
- 31 percent duration from six to ten years
- 16 percent duration from eleven to fifteen years
- It is estimated that 6 percent die
- Only 50 percent get "cured"

What Causes Eating Disorders:

There are so many avenues to developing an eating disorder. There is no one single cause but rather a complex interaction between the biological issues such as dieting, genetics, and psychological issues such as control, personality factors, family issues and a culture that promotes thinness as an ideal.

Medical Complications:

More individuals die (either from cardiac arrest or suicide) of eating disorders and substance abuse than any other psychiatric illness. It is estimated that 75 percent of Americans practice some form of self-mutilation. Ninety percent of self-abusers begin cutting as teenagers. Fifty percent of people who self-mutilate will attempt suicide at least once in their lives.

You may also find more information by writing or calling these national organizations:

American Anorexia and Bulimia Association
165 W. 46th Street, Suite 1108
New York, New York 10036
212-501-8351

National Eating Disorders Association
603 Stewart Street, Suite 803
Seattle, WA 98101
206-382-3587

American Psychiatric Association
1400 K Street, NW
Washington, DC 20005
(202) 682-6220. *http://www.psych.org*

Focus Adolescent Services
(877) 362-8727. *http//www.focusas.com*

National Institute of Mental Health
5600 Fishers Lane, Rockville, MD 20857
(301) 443-4513. Fax: (301) 443-4513
http://www.nimh.nih.gov

1-800-DONTCUT—SAFE Alternatives Information Line

SAFE Alternative Program (Self-Abuse Finally Ends)
www.selfinjury.com

"Thinner Is the Winner": Not "Just a Girl Thing"

The phrase "dying for acceptance" is loaded with truth.

Vanessa Vega

As a teenager, I never felt really good about myself. I never considered myself "good enough" to be friends with those who were seen as being more intelligent, more athletic or more outgoing than I was. I never believed I could be popular. In my mind, others didn't want to pal around with me—or want me to pal around with them. I wasn't cool enough to be popular or invited to parties, or to hang out at the movies, the mall or wherever.

I'm not exactly sure when, where or how my sense of low self-worth came into being, though I do remember that even as a young girl, I needed the approval of others in order to feel good about myself. To me, acceptance meant that *others* liked and approved of me. So that was what I worked for: *approval from others.* When my parents were proud of me, or if I got the highest grade in a class, then I was "good enough." It never dawned on me that others already saw me as "okay as is." Nor did it dawn on me that acceptance was also something I should be giving myself. Being "good enough" had to come from others.

Being "good enough" was easier *before* I became a teenager. Then things really changed. Being a teenager meant NEVER feeling good enough. In fact, in adolescence, nothing much went according to how I thought it might. I had great expectations that everything would fall into place: Everyone would like me and think I was a really cool girl, and would want to be my friend.

But it wasn't like that at all. In fact, everything was really out of sync: My body was growing really fast, some parts changing shape in ways I wasn't sure if I liked. I felt "big" and clumsy. My emotions were erratic—really up or really down. My moods ran hot and cold as well. My brothers were getting more annoying and getting on my nerves—as were my parents. The picture at school wasn't that much better: My classmates made fun of my curly hair, my glasses, my braces, my big feet and even my being "too smart." Without questioning it, I just agreed with their assessment.

So I strapped on my "not good enough" ball and chain of an attitude and drug it everywhere I went. I applied low self-worth to every situation and to every experience imaginable. When my parents divorced, I felt that maybe if I had been a better, smarter or more "popular" daughter, then maybe the divorce wouldn't have happened. When no one asked me to a dance or when a particular someone didn't choose me for a friend, it was because I didn't measure up. That I viewed life from the lens of feeling "unworthy" was really crippling. I felt that everyone was better than me. I often had a "poor me" attitude. This left me frustrated. Being frustrated made me upset; being angry made everything seem overwhelming. Life just "happened," and I had no say in it or control over it. Looking in the mirror one day, I decided that if I were thin, I could change my circumstance. So that's what I set out to do: Get thin. Yes, I'd show the world, and in particular the classmates who made fun of me—most especially those boys who ignored me—how "perfect" I could become. So that was my plan: GET THIN! Then I'd be "good enough." Then others would accept me. Then others would want me to be a part of their groups and invite me to join them in all the things going on at school and on the weekend. They'd want to be with ME. Then I'd be happy.

I pursued my new goal with a vengeance! I was more disciplined than even I thought I could be. I dieted, and I ate practically nothing. Little did I know I was starting a dangerous habit that would get completely out of control, one that would take on a life of its own—and almost cost me mine! At only thirteen years of age I found myself sitting in the doctor's office crying. When he asked what was wrong, I told him my life was awful because I was fat—

which in my mind represented all that was wrong with my life. The doctor took my hand and explained that I was not fat, and that if anything, my weight was dangerously low. So my sense of being "fat" was just that: It was in my head.

Starving myself for so long had become not only a habit for me, but it forced my body into developing a condition called anorexia. While I didn't know my "condition" had a name, I did know I was in the grip of something powerful—powerful enough to basically "own" me. I say this because my not eating became a total obsession for me. Every waking day was centered on food and weight, even though I was thin! But even though I was already thin, I didn't intend to stop my now daily habit of consuming practically no food. I was dying for acceptance, and committed to the one goal I had decided was the ticket to getting it. But with dieting came strange sensations—and not only from food deprivation, but also from the methods and tactics I was using to lose weight. This "feeling strange," feeling "out of sync" led to my writing about it. While I started to keep a diary in the fifth grade (writing mostly about school, friends and family, and about my dreams), in the seventh grade I started writing about what was happening to me. By eighth grade, my goal to get thin was in full bloom, and so my writing turned into a running account (a journal) of how I was going about that.

Little did I know then that my journal would go on and on for years—almost ten years! Keeping the journal was good for me, if for no other reason than because it gave me "someone" to talk to. An eating disorder, even if you don't know that's what you have, is an isolating—"alone" and lonely—experience. It is a head game—your own. You feel like you have a "top secret" and you cannot, and must not, tell anyone. For sure I didn't feel I could tell my parents that I was desperate to get skinny. And for sure I couldn't tell them what I was doing to achieve it. It's not like I could go to them and say, "Mom and Dad, I'd like you to know that I'm starving myself to death in hopes that the kids at school will like me better." And of course, you really can't tell any of your friends either. So, as is true for anorexics, I kept "my little secret" to myself. Days passed, as did weeks and months—and years. All the while, my body grew weary and depleted. The sicker I became, the less rational I was and therefore less able to recognize the extent of my self-destruction. I was moving closer and closer toward the very real possibility of literally starving myself to death.

Looking back over my journal, I can now see the long and painful struggle I faced on a day-to-day basis. What follows in the next section are excerpts from my journal over the years. As you'll see, below each entry I've made comments basically reflecting back on that time in my life. I've called this part, "In hindsight." I've added these notations just recently—and specifically for you, the reader—as a way to shed a little more light on the steady progression of what started out as wanting to lose pounds and then grew into a disease—in my case, anorexia. I didn't set out to develop an eating disorder. It's not like I knew that what I was doing would lead me into a disease mode. But again, distorted thinking is just that. When I was in the throes of my disease, I didn't know that I was being as self-destructive as I was. It is my hope that by sharing these most personal entries with you, you might recognize some of the things you're doing and question if it's healthful for you or not. Should you believe that you (or a friend or family member) suffer from anorexia (or bulimia), then I hope you will be encouraged to get help. If you or no one you know is suffering from an eating disorder, then I hope that by reading this unit you will be more able to talk openly about the very real issue of how easy it is for teens to have a distorted view of their bodies—and why.

An eating disorder is more powerful than you can imagine. The belief that I wasn't good enough, and then trying to prove my worthiness through becoming "thin," nearly cost me my life. I am not proud of some of the things I have done. But by getting help, I've restored my emotional and physical health. Now I am a healthy young woman living a full and productive life. You can, too.

If you are in the throes of an eating disorder, I want you to know that you are not alone. Thousands and thousands of teens—boys included—start what may seem innocent enough—the desire to not gain weight or to lose some, and then a habit develops and turns into a disorder. If you have an eating disorder or are on the way to developing one, get help so you don't suffer the damage that starving your body of the nutrients it needs is sure to cause. I can only tell you that in looking back, anorexia was for me a long, long, long time of deep and dark despair. Luckily, with help, I did manage to break out and escape the powerful grip it had on me. This is what I wish for you, too. I still see a therapist, because every now and then, especially when I'm really stressed or facing a really tough situation, I still have a tendency to resort to the old habit of being really hard on myself. I'm all too quick to be really down on myself or work out to the point of exhaustion. These are not healthful or loving ways to treat yourself. When I catch myself doing that, I immediately call my counselor. Reaching out for help and support helps me return to more effective ways to handle life's problems. It's true: You must be your own taste berry.

Here, then, are some of my journal entries. As you can see, they reveal distorted thinking about the way I saw my body (as both reason and "cure" for acceptance). Though there is not enough space to print my entire journal, from the entries I've selected you can see how my distorted body image grew into my becoming anorexic—as well as my struggle over the many years to get out. Oh yes, the phrase "dying for acceptance" is loaded with truth!

Vanessa Vega

P.S. At the end of the journal entries section, I've given you an update on my life today! V. V.

Pages from the Diary of a Teen

November (eighth grade)

Dear Journal,

I hate this school. I wish I could run away. Gail and I were supposed to be best friends, but I found out she's been talking about me behind my back. I wish I could tell her off, but then she'd really say mean things! Everybody hates me! In gym class a group of girls cornered me in the shower and started to make fun of me! When I got out, my clothes were missing. The bell was about to ring and I knew I'd be late, so I started to cry. Seeing me crying, the same girls who had ridiculed me in the shower started laughing. Just as they did when I looked everywhere for my clothes—in the lockers, under benches, in the bath area and the bathroom, too. Finally I found them way up on top of the locker bins. I hate when people are that mean! I know they pick on me because I have weird hair and wear these stupid glasses! Just wait, one day I'll be beautiful and then even the snobs will wish they could be my friends. If I were as thin as Jessica and Tammy, everybody would be sucking up to me.

In hindsight: Middle school was the first time I saw other girls my own age naked. We all had to take showers in gym class, so the comparison was on: Some of the girls had rounded hips and breasts, while others hadn't developed very much at all. I was somewhere in the middle—which should have made me feel okay about myself, but it didn't. Seeing that "same age" bodies could vary so greatly only added to the "distorting" view I had of my own body. If I had been more accepting of my own body, seeing it as being in a "normal" stage of development—still growing and changing—then I would have been less critical of my body and not so down on myself. If this had been the case, then comments from others, while mean-spirited, wouldn't have hurt so much. If I'd been on friendly terms with myself, perhaps I would have even laughed and joked along with them—at least up to a point. If that had happened, perhaps I would have felt more kinship with them—which in turn would have made me less not liked.

As for my being singled out, I wasn't the only girl who was picked on. While it was the so-called cool girls who did the mocking, everyone was made fun of for something, whether it was for having small breasts or big ones, for being too tall or too short, too skinny or too "fat," for not wearing the latest hairstyle or trend in clothes, or for wearing glasses or having acne, or whatever. Again, because I was not accepting of myself, I didn't get it that *everyone* got picked on. Instead, I was angry with myself that others could make me feel bad about myself, and that I wasn't strong enough to confront them and make them stop. It was all about "everything is wrong with ME" (which I then decided was because of the way I looked). But rather than stick up for myself (accept myself), I decided "thin" was the name of the game: If I were thinner, then I'd be better liked. So already at this young age, I associated "thin" with being liked and accepted. I placed a really big importance on what others thought of me—and made that the basis of my happiness. This is very sad, because this sort of thinking leads to what is called "disassociating" with yourself. In other words, you stand apart from yourself—like there are two of you. One of you stands there, while the second ridicules, judges and is critical of you. How sad is that?

February (eighth grade)

Dear Journal,

There is a school dance coming up soon. Most everyone's already found somebody to go with or at least to meet up with once there. I just hope that somebody will ask me, but I don't think it's going to happen. As gross as this sounds, at this point I'd go with anyone who asked me. Does that suck, or what! NO ONE wants me for a girlfriend. They would if I were prettier. And skinny! All the "It Girls" are skinny. That must be why they all get asked by the boys to dance. Because some of these girls aren't even nice—and the most popular ones are really, really snobby. They're even mean to the boys who ask them to the dance. But the boys ask them anyway. Just because they're skinny. I wish I were skinny.

In hindsight: Though it seemed to me that everyone but me had a date, the truth is, I only knew one girl who had a "date." But of course she'd have a date: She and the boy were "an item"—they were "going steady." Everyone else—at least in seventh and eighth grades—was pretty much in my shoes: "dateless." But again, it was eighth grade! While some of the boys and girls may have wanted to be paired up as a "couple," at the same time, most would be embarrassed to be. In eighth grade at my school, we were just turning our attention to the opposite sex. While all we talked about was "love," the truth is, even a kiss on the forehead was a big deal. Walking down the hall holding hands was just something no one was ready to handle. Many of us were still in the stage of playfully slapping or punching someone we liked (anything for physical contact). Even a written note took the route of being passed from best friend to best friend, to a brother or sister of a special someone—because most of us were too shy to simply hand it over to the "special someone." A love note was even riskier business: If it fell into the wrong hands, it was sure to turn up in the form of a serious rumor, and you could count on snickers coming your way for a long time to come. So again, that I was unduly critical of myself for not having a date, being that down on myself, was unrealistic. It was also too self-punishing, because it wasn't like anyone was considered an outcast for not having a date BEFORE the dance. Now, not being asked to dance once there, well, that was an entirely different matter! If no one even bothered to ask you to dance, that was a bad sign! And of course, who likes feeling like a wallflower? No one!

So here I am, an average eighth grader with the same issues as everyone else, but in my head, I saw myself as being the only unfortunate soul in the entire universe to be in my predicament. Once again, I took this to mean that I wasn't liked—but would be "if only" I were thinner. But get this: I didn't have a weight problem! That perception was all in MY head! Self-worth has largely to do with your own perception of you! How do you see yourself? Whatever it is, your self-picture is very important! And by the way, it's YOUR perception that counts the most. You get to decide: You can be "okay" or see yourself as lower than the worth of a rock by the side of the road. You might as well decide you're a human, someone who is learning, changing and growing. Sometimes, most especially when you're going through a tough time, it's all too easy to feel really down on yourself. Don't. Cut yourself a little slack and get on with your day.

April (eighth grade)

Dear Journal,

Well, geez, what a surprise: No one asked me to the dance! Worse, NO ONE even asked me to dance once there. Not even that geek Lance Martin. I'm such a loser. I sort of expected it, but still, it made me sad. I thought someone would ask me. I even wore my new skirt. The moment I got home Mom asked me if I had a nice time and I had to say "yeah" because she bought me the new skirt especially for the dance. I really don't know why no one likes me. Mom says they're just jealous because I get good grades, but it's not my fault that I do. Sometimes I don't even try and I still get good grades. I really hate being called "four-eyes" too. But Mom says I can't get contacts for a long time. To try to make me feel better, she took me to get my hair styled in a new way. Now it looks really awful—like I have a bush on top of my head. I want so badly to be cool. At the dance Kristin and everybody was talking about how cool Jessica is, and how all the boys think she's the coolest girl at school. Kristin said everyone thinks Jessica is cool because she's so skinny. "Thinner is the winner," she said. So then we started talking about who else in school is skinny and concluded that all the cheerleaders were, and so was everyone who had made Pep Squad. It must be nice to be skinny. I wish I were. Then everyone would want me to sit with THEM in the cafeteria and at Pep Assemblies. Everyone would be saving ME a seat on the bus, hoping that I'll want to sit with her. And at dances EVERY guy would line up and just pray that I'd even consider dancing with him—which maybe

I would, and maybe I wouldn't. But I get to be the one to decide. I just wish that day would get here. Everybody says girls get really cool between the eighth and ninth grade. They'd better be right, because next year, I want to be soooooo cool!!!!

In hindsight: The rejection I felt by not being asked by anyone to dance was painful. I really wanted to do something to turn things around. So I began to make some changes. Looking back, I'm not sure if the new hairstyle really did look like a "bush on my head!" I mean, I did get a lot of compliments about how nice it looked. I may have been the only one who was "down" on the way it looked. Because I didn't root for myself, I couldn't take refuge (comfort) in my mother's acceptance of me: She was quite tuned in to my feelings. Think about how important that is: How many times—when the world is down on you—do you turn to your mom or dad or someone who cares about you, and at least for a brief time, their love and acceptance of you makes everything okay? You see, you're likely to take less comfort in how those around you support and root for you if you've made the decision you're not worth their love and attention. That's a problem. As for my mother, her getting me a new hairstyle and a new skirt for the dance—all efforts to make me feel better about myself—didn't do much to help me feel better about myself; the reason being that I didn't much like myself. So then, how could I value that my mother did?

As you can see from this journal entry, as an eighth grader, I was intense about acceptance. Unfortunately, I concluded that it was all about being thin ("skinny"). Deciding that I didn't like myself as I was, I started spending a lot of time daydreaming about the new me—the skinny me. I was convinced that a skinny me would mean I'd be accepted, even sought after. Having heard the rumor that a girl's body changes "between the eighth and ninth grade," I was pretty excited. Becoming a "new

Vanessa" was going to happen very soon: Summertime was going to come and wave its magic wand, transforming me into Cinderella (or even better, a clone of classmate Jessica Walters). Well, you can't hurry nature. Nothing much changed during the summer before ninth grade. I was still a normal-sized, glasses-wearing and naturally curly-haired smart girl. I couldn't have been more disappointed!

July (before ninth grade)

Dear Journal,

"Thinner is the winner" so I need to start watching my weight. For sure I need to stop eating fattening foods. I've heard that school food is really fattening. Some girls I know smoke because they say it cuts their appetite. Smoking is not for me! I can't even stand the smell of it. I'll have to just not eat so much food. I should also go out for sports, because exercise is a good way to lose weight, too. I have a good idea: I'll go out for tennis. I don't know how to play, but it can't be that difficult. Samantha Jacobs plays and she's about as coordinated as a duck on ice. So if she can do it, I can. Athletes are never fat. They're mostly thin—it has to be from the exercise and because it burns calories. I've noticed that the athletes are really popular, too. Especially when they win something. When I win a match, it will be announced over the PA, posted on the bulletin board in the student center and published in the school paper, so everyone will know who I am. That's cool. Going out for tennis will help me burn calories and I'll be noticed. Great. I'll finally be

thin, and everyone will think I'm cool and want to hang out with me. Yup. Good idea. I'm going to sign up for tennis the moment school starts.

In hindsight: There is a bright spot here in that I decided that one way to gain acceptance was to be noticed for achieving in a competitive sport (tennis). Also good is that I did see exercise as a way to lose weight—which if you need to trim pounds, this is one good way of doing that. (But, keep in mind that I DID NOT need to lose weight!) It's unfortunate that I saw sports from the vantage point of doing something to rid myself of my present body weight—as opposed to enjoying the sport as well as the rewards of learning how to play well, and to enjoy the camaraderie of my teammates. And certainly, sports can be a great way to achieve a cardiovascular workout—always important to maintaining good health. But that I saw sports as a way to remedy my "something's wrong with Vanessa" complex was purely distorted thinking. Down on myself, and sure that being thinner was the way to get others to like me more, I'd do whatever I had to do to get thin; I'd even give sports a try. Even more bad news was my focus on my weight, and looking for ways to get thin was becoming an obsession. Obsessed with my body, food was also emerging as an enemy. (My distorted thinking of myself as the first enemy!)

August (before ninth grade)

Dear Journal,

I have the chicken pox and the flu! My brothers have it, too. I can't stand it! I'm so itchy I can't stand it! I'm not supposed to scratch myself because if I do, I'll get scars, but it's so hard not to scratch. To stop the itching I have to take baths in oatmeal. It's really a nasty feeling—covered in oatmeal. Yuk! The good news is that because of all the sores in my mouth, I can barely eat—which means that I'm not gaining any weight. I even have sores on my eyelids and in my hair. It's driving me totally crazy! Who knows what I'll look like when school starts? So much for the new Vanessa—though what's great is that I lost weight because I was sick and couldn't eat. I can actually see my ribs and feel my bones. It's great. I'm not quite as skinny as Samantha and Jessica, but close. I'm not going to eat for the next two weeks—then maybe I will be as skinny as they are. Now for hoping these ugly sores go away so when school starts next week, I don't look so freaky or else everyone will think of me as a total geek.

In hindsight: Because I hadn't eaten much (due to being sick), I'd lost a great deal of weight during this two-week period of time. One day when I was looking at myself in the mirror, I could see and feel my bones, and I was very happy about this. A light-bulb went on in my head: If I stopped eating, I could be thin. Suddenly, it wasn't just a matter of wishing my body would do it on its own (for sure, the "magic" of summer didn't produce the results everyone said would happen), or that I had to wait around for a really bad case of the flu (or chicken pox). I could get thin by pushing my plate away. That seemed reasonable to me, so I pledged from that time forward to limit the amount of food I put into my mouth. Because I was eating so little, my stomach was constantly begging for food. Because I wasn't getting the calories and nutrients I needed to keep my body happy and healthy (I was after all, an adolescent—so still growing), I was sometimes dizzy and often had a headache. My stomach growled constantly, of course, and coping with the constant hunger pangs was a problem.

So this is a time when I began a serious attempt at dieting. No longer "wishing, wanting and waiting" for my body to magically transform into "perfect," I cut back on the portions of food I put into my mouth. The bigger problem is that no matter how "thin" or "heavy" we are, the human body needs a certain amount of nutrition on a daily basis. Yes, cutting calories is an effective way to not gain weight. Still—and most especially in the teen years—our bodies need essential nutrients and minerals to support growth and development, and to sustain health. Any teenager who diets should do so knowing the importance of how to limit calories without neglecting his or her body's need for important essential nutrients. In short, a diet is never a matter of "whatever"; it should be done with great care, meaning under the watchful eye of a health professional—such as a nutritionist or family doctor. If you feel you need to lose weight, please, please do so only with the care of someone trained in nutrition and care of the body.

November (ninth grade)

Dear Journal,

I was an idiot for thinking high school would be any different than middle school! The same kids are here, so how can things be different? Everybody still runs out with the same old crowd they did last year, and everyone thinks of everybody just as they did last year. Worse, I've gained back all the weight I lost while being sick, and I'm really upset about it. And I didn't make the tennis team; I didn't make honor choir; and, everyone still thinks of me as a "teacher's pet." Mom says everyone's just jealous, but I don't know why they should be. It's not like anyone knows me; in French class, we had to make these stupid Christmas cards and give one to everybody in the class. I'm sure the only reason I got any was because we were required to give one to everyone. Four idiots in the class didn't even know my last name, and two stupid people had to ask me how to spell my first name! About the only person who even talks to me is this really weird girl in my English class, and she's a total outcast. She dresses in black and never talks to anyone. Still, everyone knows who she is—and I'll bet they know her last name and how to spell it, too. Around school, she's talked about almost as much as the popular girls—even if what they say about her isn't all that flattering. She's super, super skinny. I asked her how she stays that way, because no one could be that skinny naturally! She says she eats whatever she wants (even meat). She smokes, too. Gothic Girl told me something interesting—that she eats and then she makes herself throw up so then she can't gain any weight. Gross! I could never do that. I hate throwing up—just the thought of doing that is disgusting!!! But it would be nice to eat anything and not get fat from it. I'll go to the library and see if I can find any books about how to lose weight.

In hindsight: In reading the tone of this journal entry, I can just hear the anger! The Vanessa (me) in ninth grade was really feeling "left out" from being seen as "everybody's friend." And because I was so down on myself, because I had so disowned any sort of kindness and compassion for myself, I saw my being "left out" as a function of my weight. I was also feeling really frustrated that I'd so easily gained back the weight I'd lost due to being sick. When I learned from "Gothic Girl" that she'd found a way to eat and not gain weight, I was interested in knowing what I could do that would help me get and stay thin. While the throwing-up method (bulimia) of weight loss wasn't for me, I was willing to find something I could do.

So during this time, the focus of all that is wrong with me and wrong with my life remains on my body. Therefore, my body was an enemy. Feeling "mad" at my body for putting on weight allowed me to feel abusive toward it. Because I had disassociated with my body—me against it—I was treating it like an entity separate and apart from me. Rather than treating my body kindly, I was willing to punish it for gaining weight (growing)—and I would do this by not giving it any food. Being thin—really thin—remained the goal. And so I continued to control how much food I ate. This means, of course, that I am working myself into the habits that lead to anorexia. This is also the beginning of my exercising as a way to lose weight. Again, since I wasn't on good terms with myself, I would not only exercise but also "work out like a madwoman," pushing my body to an extreme, forcing it to take grueling and punishing workouts.

In hindsight, I feel so sorry for young Vanessa—a young girl who believes that others do not like her very much and doesn't even come to her own defense by at least being her own friend. She, too, is "tough" on Vanessa. How sad. Are you ever too tough on yourself? If you are, you'll learn that it never makes things better.

January (ninth grade)

Dear Journal,

It's not just school that sucks! So does life! My parents took us to Disneyland. In the middle of all the "fun," Dad informed us that he and Mom were divorcing! Though Dad hasn't been around very much lately, I never imagined he'd really leave for good. He did. So much for all the hard work in making grades and all that I did to letter in music. All the babysitting just to show him how responsible I was. Figures. Nothing I do is good enough. Thanks so much, Dad! And I've already lost seven pounds—and you're not around to notice! I was so mad at my dad that I became a machine. I did about a billion push-ups, sit-ups, lunges and dips. I'm really sore today. I cut myself, too. It really hurt—but it made some of the anger go away. I put a Band-Aid on it. I hope Mom doesn't notice the Band-Aid or she'll make me go to the counselor again.

In hindsight: When my father informed us that we would never be together again as a family, I was, understandably, devastated. But the day when I came home from school and saw that furniture had been removed, I knew things were really over between my parents. I felt betrayed. I was mad at him—which is also understandable. Even normal. But consider what distorted thinking it is when a young person believes she could have prevented a divorce between two adults "if only" she had been more "perfect" in some way—if only she had accomplished a certain goal, won an award of some kind or been more kind—or thin. And while I was angry with my parents for getting a divorce, that I use the failure of their marriage as a right to turn on myself—and to the point of self-loathing—is not healthy thinking.

So to take the anger I felt toward my parents out on myself, not only did I limit my eating to next to nothing, but also I intensified exercising to the point of nearly collapsing from exhaustion. How angry is that? What is also true is that I "cut" myself that day. While incredibly sad, it is not uncommon for teens in the throes of an eating disorder to practice some form of self-mutilation. In fact, nearly 65 percent of those who are diagnosed with an eating disorder do this. Yes, it sounds gross, and it is. But it is also emotionally devastating to the person who hurts herself in this way. Imagine putting a gash across your arm or leg because you are angry to the point of loathing (being disgusted to the point of hating) yourself. Imagine how awful you then feel because you hurt yourself. This is another problem with having low self-worth: When you feel bad about yourself, you are not good to yourself. When you are not being good to yourself, you feel bad about yourself for feeling (and doing) that. It is a terribly vicious cycle—one that goes from bad to worse.

Cutting myself was by far the darkest secret I had. No one knew about it for a long, long time. So that you can understand a little bit better why someone would do this to him- or herself more than once, what happens when you cut yourself is this: It momentarily frightens you. It's scary to think you've done this to yourself and that you've caused yourself to bleed. The "fright" causes your brain to release chemicals into your body, ones that are similar to an adrenaline rush (perverted though it is!). For me, the fear and shock of seeing myself bleeding momentarily took away some of my anger (for about ten seconds!). Of course, depending on the nature of the cut, there is also going to be a scar—a simply awful reminder of an awful practice in an awful time in your life.

As for me, a couple of years after I first began to cut on myself, I was found out. The good news is that I got help. I spent a great deal of my time in therapy dealing with this behavior and learning appropriate ways to express my anger. Therapy also helped me learn to love myself, to stop turning "life rage" into "self-rage"—and self-rage into self-inflicted wounds. If any of this is going on for you, don't feel as though you have (or are able) to deal with things alone. Get help immediately. If I had, it would have saved me from many more years of pain and sickness. Are you worried about you or a friend? Get help. You may be saving your or their life.

July (before tenth grade)

Dear Journal,

Well, just great! I'm finally at summer camp, and wouldn't you know it: A parasite has cut me out of what could have been a cool time. Here I am, in "camp hospital"—what rotten luck. I've waited all year to get to summer camp and here's where I end up. There's something in the water here that totally gave me diarrhea. The camp director came and got me this morning and took me to the nurse and she said, "Get in bed, now." So now I'm in a room all by myself trying not to cry. This was supposed to be my big chance to show how "mature" I am, all ready to learn how to be a real camp counselor so that when I come back next summer I can have my own group of kids. The only good thing about being this messed up is I'm not gaining any weight and, hopefully, I'll lose some. What's bad is that there are some really cute guys here learning to be counselors and I'm quarantined. They'd better not send me home. I'm hoping to check out a cute guy by the name of "Eric-something."

In hindsight: While I had been placed in the camp's infirmary for diarrhea (which was caught innocently enough), the truth is, because for well over a year I had been severely limiting the amount I was eating, my body was pretty run-down. By starving it so much, my body wasn't getting all the nutrients it needed and was so depleted it could barely fend off anything, including whatever it was that was in the water at the camp. So already at this stage, my body was showing signs of being really run-down. For a teenager, I was sickly and exhausted easily. This was also the first time I had ever been sick away from home—which to me was a horrible feeling. Mom was always so attentive when any of us kids were sick, and I so wanted to have her take care of me now. I was lonely, sick and frustrated, and shut away in a strange room far away from home. It was not a good feeling. That I was interested in the boys at camp was a good sign! Luckily, it made me want to get back to this camp experience—especially checking out the guys (mostly "Eric-something").

October (tenth grade)

Dear Journal,

I feel so depressed, like I am in a pit so deep I will never be able to crawl out. I'm tired all the time. And I'm sick and tired of being sick and tired! There are just so many pressures. I'm sick of all the expectations—even my own. I'm STILL a nobody at school, basically. I have two friends and that's it. Mom says I'm just depressed and need to see my counselor more often. Yeah, right! Like seeing a counselor is going to improve my life. I seriously doubt if talking to a counselor is going to help me get a date to the prom! Being thin is the only way that's going to happen. Food. Food. Food. It's all about food. Food is the enemy. I'm practically starving myself, and I'm still fat. But I'm going to be thinner, that's all there is to it. Thinner is the winner. Think winner. Think thinner! Thinner, thinner, thinner. I weigh a hundred pounds. My goal is to weigh ninety-two pounds. I'm close. I should be able to meet my goal in less than two weeks. When I sit down and put my legs together, my thighs touch. I need liposuction. That ought to be good for at least five pounds. Or I think it should. I don't know anybody who's had it but I've heard about it. But Mom would say no. She says no to everything these days.

In hindsight: At this point, I met the clinical definition of being anorexic. I was dangerously thin. I was five-feet-five and weighed only a hundred pounds. I was, as someone said, "skin and bones." I hadn't yet started my period, because my body fat was too low. Still, I still saw my body as "too fat." I was in counseling, but had not yet fessed up to my extreme dieting, nor to anything else I was doing to get thin (such as exercising to an extreme). Intensely focused on weight loss, I was willing to put this "goal" even above the way I was feeling. Dehydrated and malnourished, I was tired, moody, argumentative and was having a difficult time focusing and concentrating. I continued to believe that my luck—and life—would get better if I would just stay true to my dieting and exercise regime—even if the methods I was using were extreme—and often painful. But I continued my punishing habits of doing more: I did extra homework, extra chores around the house, repetition after repetition of push-ups and sit-ups.

None of this was easy. Starving myself—literally and figuratively—was hard because, of course, my body needed food and so I was hungry. The discipline it took to not eat was one thing, but an even larger problem was controlling my hunger pangs. So I looked for ways to do that. To trick my taste buds into thinking I'd eaten something, I'd brush my teeth, again and yet again. At home I'd make a production of cooking. When I served everyone, I made sure there was none left for me. When I cooked, I purposely set out certain ingredients to "gross me out"—to turn off my appetite. As an example, I'd open the can of Crisco, scoop a large mound of it onto a plate, and tell myself that if I ate food, it would sit on my thighs like that pile of lard on the plate. I found this an effective way to kill my appetite.

As you can see, at this point I was an emotionally, as well as physically, sick girl. My distorted sense of self had led to habits that by this point had grown into a disease known as anorexia. It was the disease, and not me, who was in charge of me. In other words, even if I had looked at a plate of french fries and said, "Oh yes!" my brain would have said, "Oh, no!" Or it would have punished me by demanding a quad-zillion push-ups, sit-ups and who knows what else! And I would have complied—regardless of the pain. In looking back, what strikes me is how often many of us are together in group situations and still don't help each other. Certainly, I was rail thin and looked sick. But no one said a word.

March (tenth grade)

Dear Journal,

All this work and still my body is flabby—I look like a cow! It's no wonder that I still don't have friends or a boyfriend—I'm fat! This morning I passed Jessica and she didn't say anything to me.

I hate being invisible. I don't know why Jessica and Mandy wouldn't think of me as their friend. I'm almost as thin as they are. And we're in three classes together so it's not like they shouldn't notice me. But they don't. Well, four more pounds and they will. I know the rules: "Thinner is the winner"; only the thin girls get the guys. I've been dieting so long, but I still weigh too much. I got on the scale this morning and I was one hundred pounds! How could anyone like me this way? Too much! I'm going to do better! I had rice three times this week—that's way too many carbs. I've got to do something else to get rid of this flab. I'm sleeping too much. That has to be why I'm gaining weight. Tonight, I'll exercise more. I look at girls in the magazines and wonder why I don't look like they do. Mom always tells me how beautiful I am, but I think she only says that because she is my mom. How can I feel like I'm beautiful when I still don't look like the girls in the magazines? All the boys are always saying how beautiful the girls in the magazines are. They even cut out pictures from the magazines and tape them on the insides of their lockers. Even my little brothers look at girls and magazines and think they're really cute. So I know what to do. I've just got a ways to go. Yesterday in gym class one of the girls called me "Gorilla Legs." I've seen gorilla legs, and they aren't skinny! Just wait, there will be a day when even Jessica will look at me and say, "Wow, Vanessa! Look at you! You are so skinny. You look great." Then all the other girls will wish they looked like me. And the only way I'll ever hear those things is to lose more weight. I can never forget that the thinner is the winner! I'll do twenty-five jumping jacks, and maybe twenty-five push-ups, too. At least that many sit-ups. I think I can use my mom's free weights if I'm quiet and put them back before morning. She has such a fit when she knows I use them. She says I'm thin enough without exercising—which is not true, because I still haven't lost as much as I want to. It seems to me that the harder I work at being perfect, the less perfect I become: Is that possible?

In hindsight: If there is any one thing that characterizes this entry (and time), it is that I was not only unhealthy, but emotionally "sick" as well. My body and brain were not getting the nutrition they needed to function properly, and so I was beginning to fail at a lot of things. I was really unhappy. Though I blamed this on my mother because she spent so much time working to support our family—which meant I had to look after my younger brothers—my unhappiness was deeper than about the responsibilities I had at home. The fact that I didn't have many friends, or a boyfriend—and it seemed like everyone else in the entire universe did—didn't help. The angrier I got, the more intensely I dieted and exercised—even though I was physically, emotionally and spiritually exhausted. At times I prayed to God to "take my life." When my counselor asked if maybe I should ask God for comfort and to protect me (from myself!), I told him I couldn't find one reason God would love me enough to do that. I was so down on myself that when my therapist remarked, "God doesn't make trash," I tried to convince him he was wrong. I honestly believed that I was a failure. I felt totally alone and was sure I was. I'd decided that not even God could love me. That's feeling pretty unlovable, don't you think? You would think that at this point the light would have come on in my head saying, "Geez, Vanessa. You're pretty depressed. You'd better start eating!" But no, I was still convinced that I'd feel better and that life would feel better when others thought of me as thin enough to be "good enough." Sad, but true.

Again, this is the importance of not standing apart from yourself—to not "divorce" yourself. If you sincerely believe that other classmates do not want to be around you, this is no time to sign out on yourself as well. I did, and you can see how detrimental that was. In the least, go have a talk with the counselor. He or she understands the importance of feeling you belong and are a part of things. Your counselor, even a favorite teacher, will help you understand more about how you can be better liked and accepted. Do not believe the answer is all about your body. If you need to lose weight for health reasons, again, like the advice I gave earlier, do that under the care of your family doctor. In the least, turn to your mother and ask her to help you out. If she says something like, "Oh, you're perfect as is," and you know that's not so, ask her if she will take you more seriously. Try it. You will see that your mother (dad, too) is not insensitive to the way you feel about your body, or how you see your body in relation to being liked and accepted by your friends and classmates.

July (summer before eleventh grade)

Dear Journal,

Finally summer camp is here! I'm an "official" counselor and get to have twelve girls assigned to me! Yeah! And hey, a guy, "Calvin," watched me all day! Better yet, I got kissed! What a surprise, but I liked it! It happened as we were going around to the cabins, making sure all the kids were in and the lights were off. So romantic. It was dark out so we had to use flashlights to make sure we didn't trip on any tree roots. Calvin stopped walking, so I did. He pulled me to him—man, it was the best kiss ever! I started laughing because I got so nervous! I wanted him to kiss me again, but he didn't. But he held my hand as we walked the rest of our night patrol. I'll remember this night FOREVER! I'm really glad that I've been so strict on my diet because I don't think that Calvin, who is three years older than I am, would've kissed me if I hadn't been as thin as I am now. So it's really important not to gain any weight while I'm here. The food looks fattening. Luckily I brought saltine crackers and bottled water with me. Everyone tells me to eat, so I make sure I talk a lot. I've learned that as long as you talk a lot when you eat, people don't really see what's on your plate. And, if our table runs out of anything, I'm the first one up to get more. My goal is to not gain a single ounce while here. With all the hiking I'm doing, surely I must be burning off the calories I eat. I love the kids and they love me, but I never have a moment to myself. If I leave them for one moment, they ask, "Where are you going?" Part of me is ashamed because the person they love is living a lie. Most of the girls have told me they want to be just like me when they grow up. If they only knew what my "real" life is like, they wouldn't! If they knew how my days go, and if they felt all the pain my body is in, they wouldn't want to be me. Being me is NOT fun.

In hindsight: I'm sure I received my "first kiss" just because two young people liked each other and wanted to kiss. But in my mind, that kiss would NEVER had happened were it not for the fact that I was thin. Thinner is the winner—and I was thin so I had won the kiss. Which meant that I needed to stay thin so that when I returned to school, other guys would find me attractive, too! Getting attention—and affection—was still all about being thin: It never occurred to me that anyone could like me for my personality and sense of humor, or just simply because I was a great gal.

By the time I got home from camp, I was down to eighty-eight pounds! But I had been hoping for eighty-five! Even more telling of my low self-worth is that I didn't think it was much fun being me. And I was in pain—intense pain, because of my being so hungry all the time—but still, I refused to feed my poor, starving body. Unfortunately, my body was already in a serious stage of ruination because of the starvation I was putting myself through. Though my journal entry doesn't reveal it, I was also doing other (ghastly) things to stave off weight: I was taking enemas, using diet pills and pushing my body to the point of extreme muscle strain from all the intense exercise I was doing.

If all this sounds sick—even horrible—it's because it was. But again, doing something long enough forms a habit that seems second nature. Anorexia is a disease because after you've practiced the habits of not eating long enough, your brain demands that you continue acting in this way. Or if your distorted view of yourself tells yourself you are "too fat," then when you look in the mirror, no matter what image is shining back at you, you're going to see yourself as "too fat." Again, this is another reason that we must each be willing to be on good terms with ourselves. We must be willing to not compromise our bodies because we want to be or look like someone else. Which also means we must not compare ourselves to others.

What is also so important is that if we can all read my journal entries and say to ourselves, *What on earth was this girl thinking—why on earth did she put herself through all this?* then we can also make headway into breaking through the secrecy of eating disorders (such as anorexia and bulimia). I knew what I was doing was awful, even disgraceful—so much so that I couldn't and didn't tell anyone. Who can you tell without then feeling awful and disgraceful? At least when you're the only one feeling this way about you—that you loathe yourself to the point of hurting yourself—then there is only one person (yourself) thinking you are the lowest form of life on earth. But if you, the reader, can understand the nature of an eating disorder, how it starts in your mind and then grows into your body taking over—your body thinking it's doing what the mind wants—then you can understand how an eating disorder can happen to me, and to you. And to anyone.

One day later . . .

Dear Journal,

I passed out on the beach last night. Talk about embarrassing. I was ready to leave the campfire. I stood up, and that's the last thing I remember. The next thing I knew, Calvin Connors was over me with his sweater (which he'd dunked in water) trying to wake me up. He was so sweet! He was really concerned about me, and asked again and again what was wrong. I told him I'd be fine, so then he walked me to my cabin. I felt so terrible, like I was outside of my body. I could hear people talking to me but their voices were really far away. You know when someone wakes you up out of a dead sleep and you don't know where you are? That was me. I crawled into bed and pulled the covers over my head. Geez, I feel like I'm falling apart. I'm the counselor to twelve-year-olds, and they're more together than I am! It is so hard for me to keep up with them. Plus it's hot here and I can't drink the water. I haven't really felt all that well from the day I arrived. Part of me wants to go home because I feel so bad, but the other part of me wants to stay because Calvin is here. I'll just take it one day at a time. I think Calvin suspects something. He keeps saying, "You never eat anything!" I want him to see that I'm making an effort so I'll eat something, but just a little bit. Then he'll feel better and won't be watching me so closely at mealtimes, as he's starting to do.

In hindsight: Of course I was embarrassed to have passed out in front of the boy who kissed me! But I also recognized my having passed out as a sign my body was not doing so well—that I was tired, far too exhausted. It was evident even to me that I barely had the energy to keep up with twelve-year-olds—and that wasn't a good sign. But it was important to not let anyone know how I was feeling, because I was sure that if someone knew, I'd be sent home. By now I pretty much knew I was anorexic. My mother, who insisted that I see a therapist, thought I wasn't coping well with life and was stressed to the point of not eating. I'm certain she didn't know I was intentionally not eating.

I was pretty worried about why I was feeling so terrible, even though I was unwilling to see that food deprivation was key to that! Still, that I had passed out worried me. What if Calvin hadn't been around? What if the kids had found me instead? My solution: to be good and angry with myself for being so "weak." I vowed to never let that happen again. So once again, rather than seeing nutrition as a way to get better, I chose the path of denial and did what most anorexics do, which is to pacify those around them (so as to not have to eat). I played with my food a lot (so as to eat slowly and give the illusion I was eating). And I did eat when Calvin was around, and then skipped snacks or meals if he wasn't. Same thing at home at the dinner table. I had become a master at telling lies to cover up my not eating.

Yes, I did feel bad about myself. No one can lie and connive and try to pull the wool over someone's eyes without feeling bad about oneself. See, this is another sad outcome of having low self-worth. Again, it just keeps feeding itself sad and bad messages, causing your opinion of yourself to get even lower. As for my being a camp counselor, it made me feel bad, because there I was at a Christian church camp lying in the presence of God and a hundred twelve-year-olds. I was not all that proud of myself.

November (eleventh grade)

Dear Journal,

I've never been so tired in all of my life. And I'm such a space-case: I couldn't find anything I wanted to wear to school so I screamed, "I'm going to kill myself!" My mother came rushing back to my room and threatened that I had to go to the counselor instead of going to school. I refused, which made her even more upset. She called the school and told the counselor about what I had said. So then I apologized and told her that I would see the counselor later because I couldn't do it now. I had so much to do, from chemistry assignments that are totally gruesome, to lab and projects. I just can't keep up anymore. My mom thinks I'm depressed, but I don't think so. All this craziness is because I just have no energy. I mean I'm just totally zeroed out! I don't even have the energy to exercise at night, so I don't. The second I get home from school, I plop on the couch and fall asleep. When I wake up, I'm still tired, but I think it's because I wake up a thousand times every night. I don't think I've slept through an entire night for months now. Worse, I can barely eat anything. And I'm starting to throw up—and I don't know why. Even the thought of food makes me sick. The idea of putting anything into my mouth makes me want to gag. I've heard that not eating can make your stomach shrink. Maybe that's happened to me. But I didn't think it would hurt this bad. I don't know why this is happening, but it sure is scary. I think I need to go to the doctor. Maybe I have cancer or something.

In hindsight: Does this sound like a very sick girl to you? I was. Physically depleted, I was not only a basket case, but emotionally exhausted to the point of threatening suicide (which I did on more than one occasion—and for reasons even less serious than not finding something I wanted to wear to school that day). Though depleted—and hungry—still, I would not give in to eating a full meal. Sometimes I would cry, because I wanted to "cheat" so badly and wouldn't allow myself to eat. My body craved rest, but I didn't have time for rest: I was behind in everything. It was like I wanted to shout at my body, "C'mon. Get up, let's go. We have things to do."

As this journal entry shows, I was in a power struggle with myself. My body cried out for food, yet I refused to feed it. It cried out for rest, but I only pushed it harder. The result was a case of mononucleosis, an infection caused by the Epstein-Barr virus. Mono causes a fever, sore throat, headaches and white patches on the back of your throat, swollen glands in your neck. You are totally tired—and have no appetite!

There was no struggling with mononucleosis. It flat out

brought my world to a dead halt. With mono, I could do nothing but sleep. Frail—and suicidal—my mother and teachers watched my every move. Even I felt I might be falling apart: I cried all the time. If I didn't get the highest grade on a project, I cried. If someone looked at me the wrong way, I cried. If I thought someone was talking about me, I cried. Mono is no fun.

May (eleventh grade)

Dear Journal,

Great! Something else for me to totally stress out about. I might not pass. I've missed sixty-three days so far this year! (I even missed my prom.) The school policy says that if you miss more than three days in six weeks, you lose credits. So I wrote a letter to the editor of the newspaper protesting the school's attendance policy. I even talked to the principal today but he said that even though my grades are high, with the policy being as it is, the school might not be able to award me my credits. I'm really mad about it! I have worked way too hard for my grades this year. I'm still tired, but I've been able to exercise a little. It's getting nice outside again, so I have to start cutting back more on how much I'm eating. I haven't gained any weight, but there's still no way I'll be caught dead in shorts or a sundress the way I look right now. I bought a measuring tape so I can start measuring how big my waist is. When I stand in front of the mirror and put my hands around my waist, I can almost get my hands to touch. I can't wait to wear a belt again so people can see how small my waist has become. When

I wear my old belts now, I'll have to put the buckle in the first hole. Pretty soon I'll have to make a new hole—yeah! If I put my hands on my hips, my fingers almost touch. My goal is to wear a size 0! Skipping breakfast and lunch and working out with Mom's free weights have definitely made the difference.

In hindsight: My health now jeopardized to the point of my immune system being depleted, I was so run-down it was a struggle for me to even get to the bathroom. My doctor had prescribed steroids—and STILL I slept away the majority of the day. I hated that I didn't have the energy to fix my own meals, and I struggled to get down the soup and grilled cheese sandwiches my mom prepared for me. Because of being so sick, I lost a lot of weight. I was right at ninety pounds.

My mother by now was extremely worried about me. Because she had been diagnosed with diabetes, she was really nutrition-conscious and had lectured me on the importance of eating right. Because of her diabetes, as a family we didn't have a lot of candy or sugary snack foods in the house. And with her diabetes, there was an added attention on things like sugars, fats, carbohydrates and proteins, so it wasn't like I didn't know the importance—and effects—of nutrients in relation to their importance to the body. In short, I knew how essential it is to eat a healthful diet. No matter, I was reading everything I could get my hands on about how to lose even more weight. I even read books on eating disorders—and I did see the warnings of health risks. Of course, I didn't believe it when I read about the possibility of dying. I was stronger than the people in those books. I bravely convinced myself that "I know what I am doing."

Well, of course, I actually didn't. That I filtered out the warnings shows, in fact, how deep I was in denial. It's not that I ignored the voice in my head; it's that I couldn't hear the message that what I was doing wasn't a good thing. You see, at this stage of my eating disorder, "disease thinking" now deeply ingrained, I couldn't stop doing what I was doing. That I knew the way to feeling better (eating nutritiously) and didn't is a part of why an eating disorder is classified as a disease. If you remember back in the "A Word from the Authors" section, anorexia is classified as a disease because it has specific symptoms that can be identified, diagnosed and treated. In reading my journal entry back then, it's fair to say that I was deep in denial.

As a reader, surely you're asking, "Vanessa, why didn't you tell someone you needed and wanted help?" The answer is that I didn't want anyone to "bust" the deceit of my denial—which included lies about not only the extent of what I was doing and why, but all the ways it had taken a toll on me. Experts in the field confirm that a predictable outcome of any habit practiced over time is that emotional and physical dependency (which by the way, is the definition of addiction) sets in, and you begin to live your life around what you're doing. And so, you'll say—and do—most anything to keep doing what you're doing, including becoming "a professional liar" so that you can continue. In other words, you will spin a web of lies and deceit about your (strange and peculiar) actions so you can keep doing it. Once you've developed an emotional or physical dependency on what you're doing, the habit (disease) is now in command—and it commands you (to do and say anything that satisfies your habit). Certainly, I had to downplay the extent to which I was out of control or that doing what I'd been doing had driven me to say and/or do just about anything in order to satisfy my brain's "fear" that eating food would make me fat. In time, you don't know the difference between your brain's needs and your body's needs—a state referred to as "being in denial."

Does all this deception and denial make the user a bad person? No. If you were to ask almost anyone, "Would you like to starve yourself to the point of death?" undoubtedly their answer would be, "Of course not!" But in fact, denial is a symptom of the disease and a predictable stage of anorexia—and so compromising your health (and possibly dying) because of malnutrition is possible.

In reading my journal entries, it's easy for you to see that I was lying to myself about the harm I was causing myself by not eating. What about you? Have you ever convinced yourself that something was all right when deep inside you knew that you only felt this way because you had so given up trusting yourself to believe otherwise? Again, that's the power of a healthy sense of self. The flip side of that is, you guessed it: low self-worth.

November (twelfth grade)

Dear Journal,

What a drag! There are so many things to take care of in your senior year. I've got SATs coming up, senior pictures, college applications due, scholarship interviews, my job and tons of schoolwork. But I am so tired I don't see how I can get it all done. I just wish I could just go to sleep for a long, long time. I don't think I'll ever get caught up! The good news is that I haven't gained any weight, but still, I'm a size 2. People are starting to take notice! Even Jessica noticed! Today when I walked by her in class, she's like, "Nice jeans!" So that was cool! I've been getting looks from some of the other girls at school, too. It's like they're jealous because I'm not fat. The student council is putting on a fashion show for homecoming, and they've asked me to model! I can't wait for everyone to see how great I look! People may still talk about me, but I don't think they'll be able to make fun of me for the way I look anymore. I bet once everyone sees me on the stage looking fabulous in my clothes, they will wish they were me! It's great! I'm finally starting to feel like someone other people want to be like. Unfortunately, Mom is really watching me like a hawk at meal-times now, so I don't eat anything until dinner so at least she sees me eating. And my nightly exercise isn't going well at all. I have so much homework that by the time I get it done, I'm way too tired to exercise! I think I'm going to have to start doing other things like getting off on an earlier bus stop and walking the rest of the way home. Now that I finally got a job as a cashier, I'm going to buy some ankle weights to wear when I walk home. That has to make a difference in the calories I burn!

In hindsight: My twelfth-grade year was challenging for many reasons. There are so many things to do to close down this part of your life in preparation for the next phase. As for me, I also had a boyfriend for part of the year, and I spent a lot of my free time with him. That was a huge challenge, because one of his favorite things to do was eat out (I took home A LOT of food in doggie bags!). Spending time with him, still getting home-work done and working meant I didn't have as much time for exercise. And then there was my perception in my head that my boyfriend liked me because I was thin—which meant that if I didn't stay thin, he'd leave. So this was a stress—while self-induced—a stress, just the same. Stress is stress, right?

My health was spiraling dangerously out of control at this point. I started to lose my hair, because I didn't have enough nutrients in my body to make strong hair follicles. And because my iron level was so low, whenever I bumped into something, it left a huge bruise. By denying myself adequate amounts of food, I was putting myself into a "starvation mode," so my body was literally eating itself—using the muscle tissue as a food source. I wasn't sleeping well; I wasn't going to the bathroom (my body had next to no food to process); and I had little energy for more than the most basic activities. And I'd threatened suicide twice!

Luckily, my talking suicide alerted everyone—from my mother to teachers to my therapist—and everyone knew I was in serious trouble. Not being able to hide my problems meant that now I was forced to talk more frankly about what was going on with me.

January (twelfth grade)

Dear Journal,

I feel like I'm being ripped in half. I don't know which voice inside my head to listen to. Eating means I'll be fat and no one will want me to hang around with them. I'm unhappy now, too, but at least I'm skinny. People are finally noticing me and paying me compliments. I thought I would like people looking at me and being jealous, but now I'm not so sure. I don't know how much longer I can do this! What if they found out the truth about what I've been doing? What if they knew how unhappy I am? I think if anyone at school found out the truth about what I'm doing to my body, they would start making fun of me all over again! I can't stand this. The pressure to be perfect is getting to be too much. My stomach hurts all the time, I always have a headache, and I don't like waking up in the morning. I wonder what people would say about me if I died?

I just don't know how I'd kill myself. It seems like a lot of work, and I wouldn't want it to be painful. Today on my break at work, I walked around the pharmacy department, checking out every possible means there might be to end my life and the pain I'm feeling. I've heard kids at school say they had friends who overdosed on pills—but I don't remember what they used and how many pills you have to swallow at one time. Tomorrow I'll reread the labels and see if I can figure it out.

In hindsight: Because I was so depleted, I spent most of my time just coping one day at a time. Tired and overwhelmed, I cried a lot, because I felt a seventeen-year-old person should have things more under control, and I sure didn't. I didn't really have the energy to keep paying attention to how much I was eating and didn't have the energy to do any push-ups or sit-ups. It all felt like I was on a treadmill—and I wanted to get off. I began to wonder if anything—including working to stay thin and even living—was worth the effort. Still, that I had been practicing certain behaviors—starving myself, exercising and enemas—and lying for such a long time, I couldn't just stop. So I made "deals" with myself, promising that after a certain date, I'd stop: "I'll quit the day after Thanksgiving . . . Christmas . . . New Year's . . . Valentines . . . Mother's Day . . . my birthday." That date would come and go, so then I'd make a promise. That I couldn't even count on myself to keep a promise was a depressing realization, one that made me feel even more down on myself.

I did walk around the pharmacy department scrutinizing what "pill" might put an end to the emotional and physical pain I was feeling. That next day, I did try to kill myself. But in looking back, I know that I didn't really want to end my life; I was just so sick and tired of being sick and tired. I was in real need of medical and psychiatric help.

I'd planned out how to end my pain (and life). On a Saturday morning, my brothers were out with friends, my mother was at work, and I was home alone. I pulled out all of the things I would need to make all of my pain go away. In a daze, looking at these things—I started to cry. Panicked, I remembered I had my school counselor's home phone number in my backpack. She and I had talked about suicide before, and she had given me her number. At that point, I made a deal with God. I would look once. If I could put my hands on the piece of paper, I would call her. If I couldn't, that was the sign I'd go ahead with my plan.

I ran for my backpack. My fingers kept searching and searching until finally it closed in on the paper with my counselor's phone number. I was so thankful, I couldn't stop crying. I dialed my teacher, feeling like an idiot bothering her at home. The teacher didn't mind at all and talked with me for over an hour, until someone else came home.

This hadn't been my first brush with suicide, but it was the first time I was sure that angels were watching over me—and saved me from myself.

February (twelfth grade)

Dear Journal,

I got caught. Ever since I attempted suicide, Mom's been watching me night and day. While at school she searched my room and found my stash of diet pills. The moment I walked in from school she was right there at the door. I have never seen her so mad! With my diet pills in hand she demanded to know, "What is this?" I told her I didn't know. Before I knew it, my mother hauled me to the doctor's office and I was given a drug test—by way of jabbing my arm for blood. It was awful! I hate her for snooping around! Now what am I going to do? I've got to find a better place to hide the pills. Once home, all she did was lecture me about eating, so we had a big fight and went to bed mad. Now what? I wish I could tell my mom I was sorry and that I will stop doing what I'm doing. But I can't. This isn't at all what I thought would happen! I thought my mom would be proud that I was so disciplined and able to make sacrifices. But she's not! In fact, she's so mad right now, I don't know if she'll ever be able to trust me again. I have lied so much. I haven't meant to, but I had to cover up what I've been doing. I know if Mom knew what I'd been doing she would have tried to stop me. And then I would be fat for sure! I don't think she knows how important it is for me to be perfect. If I'm not, no one will like me. What am I supposed to do? No one cares if I'm smart or responsible. It seems like everybody at school only cares about what I look like. I know if I can look more perfect, they'll "get it" that I'm a wonderful person on the inside. Why is this so hard for people to understand?

In hindsight: Because taking the diet pills meant that I was barely eating, there wasn't enough food in my system to absorb the medication in these pills. As a result, I was edgy and jumpy, and my mood swings were really erratic. I was an emotional mess. Physically, I was skinny to the point that everyone around me was commenting about it—telling me I had to start eating, because I looked "emaciated," "awful" and like I'd "blow away in the wind"! But what I heard made me elated: My efforts were working. I was getting thin—which was music to my ears.

That my mother discovered the diet pills and took me in for a drug test is no doubt what saved my life. Even though I denied it, in my heart I knew I was a very sick girl, and medical intervention seemed like a huge relief. Even though I wouldn't have been able to say the words, I did long for someone to intervene, to rescue me. For sure, I couldn't stop what I was doing on my own.

This also put Mom and me on a new level. Rather than "policing" me, she emphasized how sick I had become. Mom cried for me because she was fearful. I cried for me learning of the damage I had done to my body.

Had my mom been able to afford it, I would have found myself in a residential treatment center. But she couldn't, so I was sent to therapy three to five days a week. I needed someone to help me confront what I was doing. I needed someone to make me responsible for my own behavior. And most important, I needed someone to listen to me and not judge me. My therapist insisted that I be candid, and so I began to disclose more and more about myself, and what I had been doing. This was one of the best things that ever happened in my recovery. I also started a new journal just for him—which allowed me to tell him things in the journal that I couldn't admit to working with him face-to-face.

I also began attending group therapy sessions for people with eating disorders. I did NOT want to go! But I had to, and for the first time, I saw other people like me. This group of people who needed acceptance from me accepted me. And I saw things that scared me, such as having tubes down their noses, because that was the only way they could eat. I saw some people who looked totally normal, and then I saw other people who looked like someone from a concentration camp. Disease-thinking being what it is, I was still in denial and thinking I didn't belong there. I decided to wait until the first break, and then I would leave. But I didn't. As people in the group started to talk, I realized I wasn't the only one who had some of the thoughts I did. For the first time in a long time, even though these people were strangers, I didn't feel alone. And so I began to think about the importance of "using" this help to get well.

June (twelfth grade)

Dear Journal,

I almost died today! My lower intestines stopped working, and I didn't know it. I ended up in the emergency room, because I could not eat or drink anything. I hadn't gone to the bathroom in so long that my body was starting to poison itself. You can't believe the number of tests I had to go through. Worse, I had a surgical procedure that was just awful. I lost twenty pounds in less than forty-eight hours. The doctors have tried to figure out how long it's been since I pooped, and the best we can guess is ten days to two weeks. It sounds bad, but I hadn't really noticed. My face was breaking out, but I thought it was a "period" thing. And I haven't been sleeping that well, but I thought that was just stress from final exams and graduation. But yesterday, I could not eat or drink anything. It's like I was so full on the inside that I could feel pressure at the back of my throat. So I got to go to the emergency room today. I could hardly believe it! I've got to get a hold of myself, because I'm falling apart. I had no idea that trying to lose weight could have such devastating effects on my body. I can't believe I did that to myself. I will do anything to get well! I mean it. I want to feel better. I just have to. I really don't want to die.

In hindsight: As a result of years of enema use, my body had become dependent on them to work. I couldn't go the bathroom without them. It took six months to retrain my body to eliminate waste on its own. The good news is that my body did begin to function normally again. The even better news is that I'm alive to tell about it!

Lying in the emergency room surrounded by strange machines, steel instruments and long plastic tubes, I realized I needed to stop what I was doing to myself for real—and for good. In the coming weeks, I attended a treatment program, and I regularly attended group sessions. Now motivated, I took an even closer look at those around me, noting that some people had permanent tubes going into their stomachs to keep them alive. Others were still at the early stages of anorexia. There were people there who were in their early teens and other people who were in their mid- to late forties. I looked around and saw that my future would be no different if I didn't get serious about recovery.

It was June of twelfth grade that became a turning point. Amazing, isn't it? Six years of pain and sheer hell, and still I kept on putting myself through all that pain for all those years. Like all diseases, this one didn't go away overnight just because I wanted it to. In fact, the toughest years still lie ahead: I had to put this disease that was strangling the life out of me into remission. Taking care of my health for the long term would mean that I needed new tools and needed to learn new life skills to return to being a normal girl.

I had to give up "dying for attention." If I was going to stay alive, then it no longer mattered what someone else thought of the size and shape of my body. That I put the focus on being healthy was all that mattered. In other words, I needed to believe in myself. In short, I had to love, honor and take care of the girl staring back at me in my mirror.

February (freshman year in college)

Dear Journal,

My dreams are starting to happen! I'm at college now. This is a new chapter in my life. My classes are in the morning, so I can go to my job in the afternoons. I love this level of learning, and I love my surroundings. I'm starting to know the real Vanessa. I'm still in therapy and finally giving myself permission NOT to think of thin as perfect! You might even say I have a new definition of perfect. I look around, and I see tall people and short ones, heavy-set and skinny ones, people with disabilities, even people who are older than my mother! No one really seems to pay any attention to anything but getting a degree. My professors seem to really like me. I feel as though each sees me as someone who has something to contribute. My therapist says I need to start keeping a new log where I put down all of my activities for a while. I think he's afraid I'll become so burdened with school that I'll start skipping meals again. I know I've lied to myself in the past, but I'm not going to do that this time. I want my life to be better, and I know the only way that can happen is if I'm healthy. I've changed my habits—which is good. For example, I don't work out before bed anymore. I get a couple of miles a day in walking around campus, and then on Tuesdays and Thursdays, I have aerobics class at the gym. That's enough. I didn't know that working out every day as I did in the past would hurt my body, but it did, since by doing that, I never gave it a chance to repair itself from all the strain and stress I put on it by exercising as intensely as I did.

In hindsight: College was one of the best things for me. For the first time in my life, I wasn't being made fun of for being smart. I worked on campus in the English department and enjoyed it. Also, for the first time in my life, I met people who—regardless of the size or shape of their bodies—accepted themselves and had positive self-images. It NEVER occurred to me that someone could be happy with herself if she wasn't thin! I loved this solid sense of confidence, and I wanted to be self-confident, too. I wanted to smile more, and did. As opposed to wanting others to be around me, I saw the importance of liking and accepting others for themselves. It wasn't "all about me." And, I found love. The love of my life, as a matter of fact. Waking up late, I had grabbed whatever clothes were at hand and, without makeup or hair brushed, dashed to class. This amazing boy had found me lovable—to my amazement, without looking thin and without makeup on! That was thirteen years ago! He remains the love of my life, helping and supporting me.

A New Sense of Self: My Life Today

Dear Reader,

Today my life is what you might call "normal." If you were to see me walking down the street, you'd never guess that at one time in my life, I suffered from anorexia. Nor would you guess that I was once a person who thought people couldn't love me unless I was thin. Getting to this place has been a struggle, and in truth, I've been to hell and back. But with treatment—and ongoing counseling—I'm proof that you can get better.

I've learned a lot from this harrowing experience. For one, I've learned that my worth is not up for grabs. My sense of self-worth and feelings of attractiveness are not dependent upon the number of pounds that register on my bathroom scale. I have a better respect for my body. I've learned the value of good health and the importance of nutrition in keeping my body (and mind) healthy. And so I leave you with these words: If you think that you're heading toward anorexia or bulimia, *get help right away.* You'll find some of those suggestions in the "Word from the Authors" section. Still, I want to remind you how important it is to reach out for help, to get the care—treatment—you need. Start now by keeping a journal. I can tell you that this is such a lifeline to getting outside of your head and to seeing your feelings for what they are. This can help you make better decisions about your health.

Stay in counseling. There's a good chance that you're going to need some help to sort out your distorted thoughts and to begin to think in better terms. Counseling can help you figure out how and why things are the way they are. For example, there came a time in my family when things were getting tight financially. That's when the boxes of food started coming in the mail from my grandma. I can remember my mom being so thankful when the boxes arrived. But I didn't feel thankful. I felt afraid. I didn't understand why we needed those boxes, and I sure didn't see how the food in them would be enough for four people. I wanted to be a good daughter, and because I was the oldest, secretly vowed to eat as little as possible so my younger brothers and mother could have more. Looking back now, it comes as no surprise that years later I would associate food with sacrifice and being a strong person. This new understanding, as something that contributed to my becoming anorexic, helped me move from my feelings of shame and guilt—and so I was able to move forward in getting well.

Be truthful with your counselor so that you are dealing with real issues. In counseling, things will come up that you can "heal" so as to continue to get better. As an example, as a child, my parents expected the house to be free of noise and free of conflict. If my brothers and I had a disagreement, there had better be no arguing or fighting. The first time I hurt myself was when I was four. I can remember being so mad at my mother that I took her hairbrush and hit myself on top of the head over and over again until my skull went numb. By the time I was done with my "fit," all of my anger was gone. But over time, the brush wasn't enough, and the headache I'd give myself wasn't worth it. I started to look for something else that I could use that would have the same effect. I needed a way to get out my anger without crying and screaming—because it did hurt. That's when I jabbed myself with the scissors. I then discovered that the sight of blood made me scared and took the anger away. Self-mutilation, as I said in one of the "In Hindsight" sections, is by far the darkest secret I had. It took me a long, long time before I told the counselor about it. Too bad, because the moment I did, the counselor helped me learn how to remove the shame and get on with healthful living.

Commit to learning new skills that promote being healthy. Read all you can on staying physically and emotionally healthy. Read books that inspire you to be as whole, loving and content as you can be. This is actually how I found—and made absolutely sure (!!) I met—Dr. Bettie and Jennifer Youngs. I love the *Taste Berries for Teens* series and found them really good. I began seeing how important they are to young people gaining a more realistic view of themselves—and those around them. In these books, the many stories deal with real issues about real teens and about real life. You see, far too often we imagine that others have life better—when in reality, each and every one of us struggles with common issues. Gaining an understanding of our own needs, wants and desires; making friendships and getting along with others; setting and achieving goals that are important to our own lives; and discovering that we are loving and lovable—all are things each and every human being finds important. The stories in the *Taste Berries for Teens* series show and tell about the journeys that young people take to discover how to have these valued things—but not at the risk of losing health or emotional well-being. You're not alone. So don't struggle alone. Read up on how others your age are going about finding meaning, purpose, direction and being content within their own skin. It can help you feel less alone, and be more happy and content. Believe me, learning how to cope with your emotions is a job in and of itself.

I have had to admit that, in my life, I have been so unable to cope with my emotions that I have practiced an eating disorder (and intentionally cut myself) to take out my anger on myself. But no longer. I've moved forward in my life. Since high school, I attended and graduated from college. I am a young teacher now. I love it and find it really fulfilling. I am also happily married.

In closing, I'd like to tell you that you can be happy without being perfect—and yes, as cliché as it sounds, you're "perfect enough" as is. Keep telling yourself this until you "get it." I did—which is why I'm alive! I'm learning that self-worth is not about gaining the approval of others but of striving to do one's best in life, and feeling grateful and content about that. And here's something else I've discovered: When you do that, others find you very appealing. To own yourself, to like yourself, to have a sense of being whole, is very cool. Have the courage to like yourself. Yes, improve yourself all you can, but never at the risk of your own well-being. Be a taste berry to others, yes. But never forget that you owe it to yourself to be one for yourself: Care about yourself. Love yourself. A lot.

Sincerely, Vanessa Vega

Teen Talk: Weighing In on Body-Image Issues

My "Wrestle" with Anorexia

When most people think of eating disorders, a picture comes to mind of a person—most always a girl—who is emaciated, rail thin or who looks like a skeleton. This picture is not necessarily accurate. Someone who is anorexic may not be skinny—or be a girl. I know, because as a wrestler I've done some really stupid things to get and keep my weight where I wanted it to be (as do many of the wrestlers I know).

My first bout with anorexia was as a freshman. As a wrestler, I needed to maintain a certain weight in order to qualify for a certain weight class. By eating next to nothing for weeks on end (first to qualify and then to stay in a weight grouping) I did manage to stay in the weight class I wanted. But because I was starving myself to death, my body wasn't getting the nutrition it needed. As a result, I felt awful and got really weak. So then, I'd end up not winning some of the key matches anyway.

I realized I needed to keep my weight down, but I couldn't sacrifice strength, energy and endurance. Starving myself wasn't the answer. So I looked for a better way to accomplish my goal, which was how to fuel my body to keep it strong and healthy while still not gaining weight. So I learned some things about nutrition and discovered some amazing things. For example, I can still keep my weight down, and my energy up, when I eat foods that are high in protein and low in fat and carbohydrates. And I did the food-combining thing, where you eat "groupings" of food, and basically, one food helps you digest and metabolize the other, so you still get the energy and nutrient benefit of the food.

Overall, I discovered that by eating sensibly, I could lose as much weight as my friend who risked becoming bulimic. He'd eat and then stick his finger down his throat to throw up what he ate. Well, he lost matches, too, and it was because he just got too weak (from the lack of nutrition). Having struggled with the weight-issue thing for three years, I'm sympathetic toward those who are fighting bulimia and anorexia. Having been there, I know a little something of the price they're paying for it. It's not worth it. As for me, I've decided that nothing, not friends nor championship trophies, is worth sacrificing my own health.

Jacob Worley, 17

Skinny Is "In" at My School

At my school, the "in crowd" is a skinny bunch, so everyone feels that being skinny is a requirement to be a part of that group (which it is). Anyone wishing to be accepted by the group has to conform. Most will do whatever they can to get thin—starve themselves, take over-the-counter diet pills or laxatives, and things like that to help them get or stay skinny. I know, because I was once a member of the "in crowd" at my school.

To stay thin, I did the binge-and-purge thing, a terribly gross habit. After I'd done this for about five months, I became bulimic. I was bingeing and purging all the time, and then I couldn't stop. I battled bulimia for three long years. For me, the consequences were terrible. I had to drop out of school—because not eating made it impossible to concentrate (I failed all but two classes!)—and because I was too sick to come to school on a daily basis. I failed three of my classes just because there was an automatic "drop from class" upon a certain number of days missed. But even if I'd been allowed to make up the course work, I wouldn't have been able to. I was in and out of the hospital a lot during those times; it was always one thing after another. Like, I was walking down the hall and passed out (because I had become anemic! It was so embarrassing. Twice the school had to call an ambulance, and I had to be taken to the hospital!).

It took a long time to get beyond bulimia. I had to see a nutritionist to help restore my body. I saw a therapist (twice a week the first year of treatment) and also attended a crisis center for teens once a week (I still do attend). Being "skinny" is so not worth it. I mean, like, do the other kids in the group care about me now? Not even. If you're in the group, great. When you're not, then you're history. Gosh, does that sound harsh? Well, yeah, it is. So you really have to think long and hard about the price you're willing to pay for being "one of the group."

The price I paid was really high. First of all, being bulimic is NO FUN! In addition to going through all the nastiness of bingeing and purging, I lost out on three years of high school, years that should have been fun—but weren't. I spent so much of my time coping with myself. It seemed to me that my whole life revolved around my illness—well actually, it did. I was tired and felt sick and sickly half the time. Well actually, for more than half the time. And I missed out on getting a good education. Right now if I were sitting in a college classroom, I don't feel that I could compete. But fun, health and learning weren't the only loss. That I actually did what I did (because bulimia is not for the faint of heart!), well, I'm still pretty down on myself for all that. My shame and guilt are still pretty high. So I've strapped myself with issues that I really would rather not have to deal with—but I have to if I want to get beyond this. And I do. I know the seriousness of bulimia; it's no cakewalk.

Jessica Convoy, 18

Building Muscle Is Not About Lifting Your Fork Less . . .

For guys, muscles are the things that get attention. I'd always wanted great muscles, and when they didn't just automatically appear, I decided to do something. I got a membership at the gym. In the gym you hear things like, "You've got to watch what you eat: No sugar; no pasta; no . . ." When I heard this, I took it to mean, "Lift the weights more and your fork less." So I went to the gym every chance I got and controlled everything I ate. Well, I've since learned a thing or two about food. First of all, building muscle is not about limiting the amount of food you eat. It's about eating less of some types of food but definitely eating more of others.

When you think about it, this is a nifty theory. Hearing in the gym that you can "feed your body for performance," I realized it could mean you could feed the muscles to get them to bulge; feed the brain to get it to think; and feed the body for high energy. The body, I've learned, is an amazing machine. But here's the deal: You can't starve it into shape; you have to feed it to get these results. So when I hear people trying to achieve some specific result for their body by starving it, I know they need to learn just how the body works. Even if you try to starve it, your body is smart, and it's going to do something to protect itself. Like I know that if the body is being starved, it will literally start feeding on its own tissues to stay alive. No thanks—I'd just as soon feed it some real food.

Raoul Thurman, 17

"Waifs in Skimpy Clothing . . ."

When I hear the phrases, "scarf and barf, binge and purge," I instantly think of some of my friends, because I know more than a few who obsess about the way they look. Their total focus is "thinner is the winner." They really want the attention of others—and who doesn't want attention? Personally, I think one of the greatest contributing factors to anorexia and bulimia is the media and entertainment industry. On television, waifs parade around in skimpy clothing and are surrounded by admiring followers. But I also think you have to think for yourself. I mean, look around. Most normal people do not look like waifs, and you get really bad reviews from everyone if you parade around in skimpy clothing. So letting the media set the standard for what you're to look like and then feeling bad about yourself as a result, is just plain dumb. You've got to think for yourself. You've got to be yourself. P.S.: And just WHO is the media, anyway?

Jackie Taylor, 17

Would You Sacrifice Your Health for Someone Else?

It's sad to think that anyone would compromise her own health simply because she wanted to look a certain way to gain someone else's approval. But it happens; I see it every day at my school. Maybe if they went to a hospital and saw the extreme results of anorexia and bulimia, they wouldn't risk their own health. To not take care of your own body and health is total craziness. It's negligence of the worst kind.

Meghan McKinney, 16

"Lean and Mean Machine": I Used Steroids to Build Muscle Mass

When you're trying to build muscle, looking "sculpted" is the deal. I'd heard that some guys would go so far as to use steroids in order to build muscle mass. That was my deal. Steroids, I've learned, are dangerous. I'm now on a kidney dialysis machine, because I've hurt my kidneys by using steroids. My only goal was to be "a lean and mean machine." Now I'm dependent on a machine to clean the toxins from my body. It's a horrible price to pay. So think about it. The body needs nutrients: The body is a living thing, a "machine" that needs fuel—good fuel. Better learn how to operate it, is what I say. Need convincing? Come see me.

Chad Bartlow, 18

Great Makeup + Great Lighting + Good Camera Angles + ($$$) Hype = A "Model"

When I see models staring back from the billboards and in magazine ads, I know the real truth about their good looks: It comes from camera angles and makeup. Yes, this is true. Wash these girls down and put them in regular clothes, and guess what—they'd look like you and me. I also know that while models look "perfect," behind the scenes there is the real chance of a heartbreak story about an eating disorder. I know; I've been obsessed for years.

Everyone in my family has a weight problem, so I knew at a young age that I didn't want to be fat. Obesity is my biggest fear. So to make sure I'd never be fat, I'd go days without eating. When I did eat, it would be only fruits, vegetables and bread. I developed an eating disorder. I look back at old pictures of myself and wonder how I could have done that to my body. I realize now that being that thin was not attractive, and that it messes up your body's metabolism—which affects everything else. The good news is that I've gotten help and am doing better now. While I still fall into old habits of not eating, at least I now catch myself. I know how unhealthful this choice can be. And I no longer care about the eating-disorder case up there on the billboard. This is my life and my health.

Mona Villarreal, 16

Even Famous People Do It

I have always liked looking at movie and fashion magazines for the latest styles. What I saw on those pages were tall, super-skinny women with no curves. The models never had curly hair or braces, and they surely never had a pimple! These women are supposed to be examples of "perfection." I believed that because the models looked the way they did, their lives were perfect. I wanted my life to be perfect, and so I tried to be like them. I straightened out my naturally curly hair and talked my mom into getting me contacts. I counted the days until my braces came off, and I dieted. When Princess Diana died, the magazines had a different story to tell. She wasn't happy. She had an eating disorder and cut herself in private. Angelina Jolie, Johnny Depp and Christina Ricci, all have admitted to cutting themselves. Why don't magazines ever tell people that side of the story? Why aren't there ever stories about famous people and their problems? To look at them, you'd never think models or celebrities have ever been in rehab or have to talk to a therapist. But this isn't true. Like the rest of us (and maybe even more so), they have had their struggles. So if we would hear more about this, then people like me wouldn't feel so alone. I'm learning that NO ONE has a perfect life. I wish magazines wouldn't make us think models do.

Galen Hall, 16

"Potentially" Beautiful

Whenever I think of anorexia or bulimia, I think of a "potentially" beautiful girl. I say "potentially beautiful," because I find it hard to believe that anyone could think she would be beautiful by getting so thin you could see her bones through her clothes. That person not only looks emaciated, but she makes others feel sorry for her: Is she battling a rare blood or bone disease, or what? Rarely do you think that person's thinking is simply so distorted that they're personally starving themselves to death. I see it all around me. I even had a male friend who battled anorexia. Luckily, it was only for a short time, so while he did lose a lot of weight, he got in touch with himself before it was too late. I think it was a stupid thing for him to do. He now feels that way, too.

Jeremy Bevill, 16

Eating Disorders: A Cry for Help!

Young people are repeatedly being subjected to brainwashing messages about weight. Both anorexia and bulimia are proof that some people are willing to take a chance on killing themselves for the sake of being "slim-thin." I honestly can't see how depriving myself of food could be considered a good thing. But individuals with eating disorders have a distorted body image: What they see in the mirror is not always what they believe they see. I do understand anorexia. I've been close to being anorexic many times. Personally, I think that while anorexia and bulimia are diseases that can be fatal, they are a cry for help, too. I hope the media starts being more responsible in showing the world that "rail thin" is not healthful. I have never seen a model whose weight looked like a healthful thing. I hope that one day, young girls will realize that there is more to life than a physical appearance that says, "See how thin I can be!"

Windy Lopez, 15

"A '10' When Walking Down the Hall Together . . ."

Anytime I hear about someone having an eating disorder, I have to ask, "What is she thinking?" And yet, it's easy for me to judge. I think back to a summer that I spent trying to lose weight. There was a guy I liked who was very cool. I wanted to be thinner so we'd look like a "10" when we were walking down the hall together. That was my motivation for losing weight: I'd picture us walking down the hall together. Hello? For the sake of impressing classmates—if my being thin would improve the picture of the two of us walking down the hall together—I was willing to work my way into a disease? Hello! Time for a reality check! Do I want to be a "10"? You bet, but I'm going to determine that standard. No one else is going to set it for me. These days, my attitude toward others is, "Love me as is, or leave."

Kelly Diaz, 16

Skeleton Thin Is No Joke

Once I was joking around with my friend about these teenage girls I saw on television who looked to me like they were totally anorexic. To this, my friend told me about her struggles with bulimia. I apologized for my insensitive comments, and then she told me that when you're rail thin, you get a lot of positive feedback for being thin—which keeps you mired in the painful times of what you're doing to stay that thin. So from her comments, I realized that the pain of living inside an eating disorder is overshadowed by the end result of weight loss. So what that means is that peer scrutiny will always keep teens wanting to lose weight. Only a really positive sense of self is going to keep someone from being a victim of an eating disorder.

Octavia Pittman, 19

You Can't Pressure Me

I don't feel too much pressure to look a certain way, because I know that no one will ever be "perfect." I think we get this very warped idea from the movies (though I've yet to look at someone on the screen and think, "that is a PERFECT person!"). On magazines, the people look so flawless, and it makes you want to look like them—but you also know that if you spent the day at the hairdressers and the makeup counter, and someone gave you the most beautiful, colorful and trendy clothes, and if the lighting was set to highlight your best features, well, hey, you'd have a real good shot of looking every bit as cool as the model on the magazine or in the ads.

Still, good looks are one thing, but to starve yourself and then develop an eating disorder just so people consider you good-looking, well, that sounds a little warped to me. I'm thinking that when enough people learn the price of this "thinner is the winner" stupidity, that maybe we will begin to buy, for real, the notion that everyone is beautiful—just as is. I mean, enough already!

Anita Jones, 17

I'm Not into Pain

What struck me the most about Vanessa Vega's ordeal was the self-mutilation. I can relate. I did it for three years. The first time I hurt myself was in the seventh grade. I hated everything in my life—mostly myself. I was disgusted at the way I looked. When I tried to tell others what I was feeling, they always told me, "Oh, it's just a phase. You'll grow out of it." I didn't want to grow out of it. That would take too long. Angry and disgusted, one day I cut myself across my arm. Then I saw the blood. I felt panic. Then, amazingly, my hate went away—like it does when you cry really hard. I was ashamed of myself for doing it. Still, I had found a way to overcome my feelings without hurting anyone else. I hadn't yelled at anyone. I hadn't made my mother mad. I had gotten rid of all of my frustration, and the only one who knew it was me. It took me three years of counseling to stop this "destructive" thinking. I've learned to take care of myself and to associate my sense of personal self-worth with being willing and able to do that.

Brianna Lewis, 16

The Maudsely Program

I was an anorexic for six years. I was rail thin, and I thought I was pretty—even though the price I paid for being so skinny was that I always felt sickly, and I had sores and bruises covering my body, plus my hair was falling out in clumps. At the dinner table—which was always a battle—my parents demanded that I eat. But I would sit there, play with my food and literally wring the grease out of a pizza slice to avoid eating the grease. I would do the same with toast at breakfast.

When you're anorexic, you will do anything to avoid gaining weight. Yes, it's a head game, but, of course, you're starving yourself to death, so it's a huge physical problem—to say the least. In the six years I was an anorexic, I was hospitalized six times. To help me break free of it, I was treated with antidepressants, individual and group therapy, and on four occasions during this six-year period was given fluids intravenously. Once, because of potassium depletion, I was rushed to the hospital in shock and suffering from seizures. I'm still getting help, but now I'm involved in a special program called the Maudsely Program and doing pretty well. I do know that I have to be serious, because I'll die if I don't. It's all about self-worth.

Roxy Burke, 17

Part 7

Cool Attitudes: The Art of Being Cool

Our generosity toward others is key to our positive experiences in the world.

—Marianne Williamson

If I have lost confidence in myself, I have the universe against me.

—Ralph Waldo Emerson

Character is what God and the angels know of us; reputation is what men and women think of us.

—Horace Mann

Talents are best nurtured in solitude; character is best formed in the stormy billows of the world.

—Goethe

Proof is always in the strength of our character.

—La Rochefoucauld

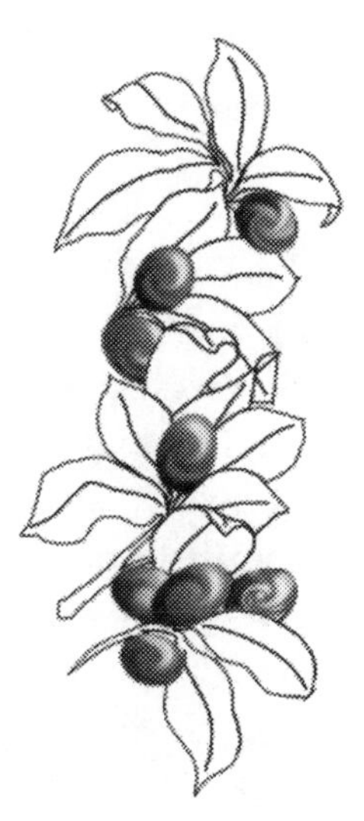

A Word from the Authors

"Cool"—is there anyone who doesn't want to be cool? The answer, of course, is a no-brainer: No! Everyone wants to be cool. Especially teens. To be seen as cool—to be considered a person who is "with it," "hip," "popular," "on top of things," "in the know," "present with presence," "liked," "admired"—is a totally good thing. Just ask any teenager!

But what is "cool" and what does it take to possess it? What is it about being cool that makes whatever one must do to be seen by others in this light worth it? Why do you think we're fascinated by those who are? Is being cool important to everyone—or does it just seem that way? Good questions. In this unit, we look for the answers. Here you'll find stories from teens such as yourself who tell about a time or circumstance in which the heavens opened up and cool was bestowed! Or taken away! Or placed in jeopardy! Before we get to the stories, take a moment to think a little bit about the art of getting to cool. Why do you think it's important? Is it for the attention: to have all eyes fall upon YOU as you enter the student center or walk to the front of the room? Is it for gratification, sort of an "I worked hard to get others to notice me, and it's working"? Is it about "pecking order"—an air of "I am better than you, so eat your heart out"?

Aside from its state of importance, what are the attributes of cool? Is it about having the "best" hair, dressing in the latest fashions or being talented? Is it about being an athlete, a cheerleader, possessing a quick wit—or a funny bone? Is it having great confidence or an incredible sense of style? It may be all of those things, of course. And here's a question worth thinking over: Can someone be cool and not even know it?

In working with teens on this unit, we discovered that while there was total agreement on the importance of cool ("It's totally important"), there is disagreement on just what makes someone cool. In one school, for example, being an athlete, cheerleader or pep squad member make for automatic membership in what teen Berry Wilson from San Mateo, California, calls the "Cool Club." In another school, those who are more likely to be inducted into what Amber Lesperance's (whose story is profiled in this unit) friends dubbed the "Club of Cool" are those who showcase a particular talent—such as having formed their own band; or are seen for their leadership skills, whether it's being a class officer or heading their school's Future Leaders of America (or some other organization or activity). It can also mean being seen by their peers as "super helpful and friendly," or having a sense of individualism. But while there is some disagreement as to the credentials for "who is cool," there is no disagreement that while cool has an upside, it can also have a downside. Perhaps sixteen-year-old Lannie Lockwood described it best when she said, "Knowing that all eyes are on you can be a burden, because the pressure is always on for looking and being your best. On some days, that's just great. But on other days, you just feel like schlepping through the day. If you're known as your school's 'most cool,' that is not allowed. You need to keep up appearances—even when you'd rather not. If you don't, someone else will take your place." Hmmmmmmm. Interesting point.

What about you—are you cool? If a "Who is cool?" poll was taken at your school—by secret ballot, of course—would you be on it? Try this exercise: Write down the names of ten people in your school you consider to be the most cool. (If you are home-schooled or simply wish to try this exercise out on another group to which you belong—such as an organization or a community team you play on—no problem.) Then, next to each person's name, give the reason you believe that person is cool. Now take a look at what you identified as the reason for each person being cool. In looking over your list, does any trait or characteristic stand out—for example, appearance, attitudes or talent? If so, that can tell you a lot about the values your school or group holds important for membership in the Cool Club.

Okay, here's the really important question: Did you include yourself on the list? Do you see yourself as cool? Why, or why not? You see, sometimes we consider others cool but not ourselves. Why is that? The little exercise you just went through is one we do all the time with teen groups around the country. What we notice is a consistency in the way teens respond to the questions. For example, when we ask teens if they feel their peers consider them cool, many will say, "No way." When we ask why they believe this is so, invariably teens will respond: "I'm seen as average," or "Others think of me as a 'geek.'" When we ask them to give a reason for why they feel this way, teens who called themselves "just average" explain, "Because I'm more or less invisible." When asked, "Why do you think others think of you as a geek?" the typical response goes something like: "Because I wear glasses," or "I wear braces," or "I'm seen as a brain" or "I'm shy, so no one really knows me."

And here's an eye-opener for you: Many teens who said they didn't think their peers would include them on the Cool Club list were in fact on the list! And in many cases the very reason a teen gave for thinking he or she wouldn't be on the list was the very reason he or she MADE the list! As an example, those who said, ". . . because I wear glasses" were often seen as having exceptionally pretty eyes, or as having a great sense of style because of the color or style of frames chosen. The person with braces was seen as having "a great face." The person who thought he or she was too smart was seen as cool precisely because he or she was smart. Even being shy was an endearing quality. Many times it was this shy person whom others thought knew himself or herself the most. And get this! Many of the "most popular" are not always on the list, nor do these particular teens always list themselves. Some teens, even those who you might consider to be exceptionally hip or with it, feel too insecure to think that others might see them in this light.

Does all this surprise you? It shouldn't, but it was one of the reasons we had a lot of fun doing this unit. In the following stories, you'll read about other teens who talk candidly about what they learned on the road to cool, as well as from those who say they personally think of themselves as cool—even if others do not. Not that this is enough. Everyone knows that "cool—in your head" is not enough! If you are cool, but then have to drop your confidence once you arrive at the doorsteps of school, that's got to be a real letdown.

So what does it take to get to cool? Here, from your peers, is a Top Ten list of what it takes:

1. The willingness to stand apart, whether to lead or to exercise individualism.
2. Being really sure of yourself (self-confidence).
3. Having a personal sense of style.
4. Possessing a talent and having an "I'm going for it" attitude about that, such as "I AM going to be a rock star"; or "This weekend I'm going on a Habitat for Humanity house build."
5. Being someone who is "going places" because he or she is current or stays up on things, such as "Kenny always wears the latest hairstyle"; or "Raianna always knows what's up with the latest software gadget."

6. Being a considerate and genuinely nice human being.
7. Having "gorgeous" hair.
8. Having friends—enough to serve as "groupies of one's own."
9. Being witty, funny and easy going.
10. Thinking of yourself as cool!

Yes, cool can be about wearing a school athletic uniform or having the best hairstyle ever. But it is also about an inner confidence, a willingness to establish an identity of one's own, having sight of one's talent or an ability to lead. Summed up, "cool" is this: living consciously.

Knowing that there are many roads that lead to cool should help you decide this: That others think you are cool is great. That you decide you are cool is even better. And that's what being a taste berry is all about. Just as you like and are supportive of the talents and attributes of others, you simply must be accepting of your own style and persona as well. In a nutshell: Like yourself. One of the great secrets of cool is this: It is an "attitude." Like many of the teens discovered in this unit, while you may think that cool is bestowed upon you by others, more often than not, this is an attribute in which you do have a say. Remember, voting for yourself is always an option. The lesson is a longstanding one: Always be on good terms with the face in the mirror.

❤ *Taste berries to you, Bettie and Jennifer Youngs*

Jocks Are Automatically Cool

It's not making the football team that makes for cool as much as developing a stronger personality that seems to come with the territory.

—Pete Morris, 15

I knew if I made the football team I would automatically become cool. All the guys on the football team had the best girlfriends. They got invited to the best parties. When it came to grades, the teachers always gave the athletes the benefit of the doubt. The jocks just had the best lives.

All summer long, I did all I could to get in top physical condition. I did yard and handyman jobs around the neighborhood. I worked out. I ran. I ate a healthful diet. I definitely wanted to make the football team come fall.

The day of football tryouts arrived. I walked into the locker room, ready to suit up. The first person I saw was Mike Connors, the captain of the team. He was talking to one of the trainers. The previous year, Mike had been voted Mr. Football, and as a result got to escort Marla Hendricks (the homecoming queen) at the football parade. He ended up becoming her boyfriend. (I told you football players get the best girls.) I looked around the locker room; we were all there. Those who had made the team every year, along with the wannabes—first-timers like me wanting to make the team. You could just tell by looking at each guy if he'd played before, because there was a certain confidence about him. A confidence that I would soon have.

As I was putting my stuff in my locker, I overheard Mike Connors talking about Nick Corrigan. I didn't know Nick well, but I was surprised to see that he was going out for football. He was a small guy, a studious type, and didn't appear to be very strong. I doubted he had much of a chance of making the team.

Apparently, Mike felt that way, too. Looking in Nick's direction (and not caring if everyone overheard him), Mike said, "He ought to save himself and us the trouble. He'll do nothing but waste room on the field." Nick did hear the comment, but said nothing. I felt bad for Nick—and relieved they weren't making fun of me.

The tryouts were long and grueling. I was glad I'd spent the summer getting in good condition. Still, I was exhausted at the end of every scrimmage. But I stuck to it. I knew it was worth it. And I was hopeful I'd make the team, because with every passing week I could feel I was getting better. Even Nick was improving. But that didn't stop Mike from making fun of him every chance he got. Every day Nick endured name-calling like "wimp, wuz and bones," or worse. Always, there was a prank being played on him, like a foot stuck out to intentionally trip him when the coach called him onto the playing field. But Nick paid little attention and seemed to take things in stride, like he expected harassment. And could handle it. I still doubted his ability to make the team, but Nick kept right on showing up and working hard. Then tryouts came to an end, and the coaches told us we did a good job and had worked hard—and that results would be posted on the gym door the next morning.

I got to school early the next day and headed straight for the gym. My heart racing, I looked at the list: Mike, Chris, Brian, Adam and Nick . . . Nick had actually made the team! I was surprised, but knew he was deserving. I continued down the list: Ryan, Alan, Sean and Pete! I had made the team. I was ecstatic.

Finally, I had a shot at being a cool and popular guy!

So then came the regular days of routine practice. Once again, Mike set out to harass Nick—only this time they were going to include me, too. Mike and the older guys were standing in a circle. They called me over. So happy to get a nod from them to be included in whatever they were up to, like a good player I went over. They said there was an initiation all the new players had to "pass," and my "test" was to go grab Nick's helmet and throw it in the toilet. With all eyes watching, like a good sport, I did. I went over, opened up Nick's locker, took his helmet and put it in the toilet. "Good job!" Mike said, laughing. We all waited around for Nick to discover his helmet in the toilet. Sure enough, Nick opened his locker and right off the bat noticed his helmet was missing. "All right, where's my helmet?" Nick called out. Acting like nothing happened, we continued discussing the upcoming game. Suddenly, Brian Samuels yelled, "Why is there a helmet in the stool?"

So then Nick went over to investigate, found his helmet, fished it out, took it to the sink, ran water over it and without saying a word, dropped it on his head. Heading for the field, he walked past Mike and said, ever so coolly, "Simple minds need simple entertainment. I'm glad I can make your day." Just like that. No hard feelings, no foul language, just a straight finger-in-your-chest funny, but to the point, put-down. It was a great comeback! Everyone laughed, Mike included. Standing up to Mike was the best thing Nick could have done: It was the last time he got harassed by Mike.

As for me, just because I made the team didn't automatically make me as cool as I'd thought it would. The girls didn't suddenly come running, and the teachers didn't necessarily think I deserved straight A's. All in all, I'd have to say that life pretty much remained the same—except for the fact that I was always dead-tired, bruised and limping. Oh yes, and I found myself doing homework in the wee hours of the morning. Sometimes the team returned home so late from the away games that I was up until midnight getting everything done. Not that I'm not happy being on the team. Especially when we win—that is very cool. And I really like the camaraderie with the guys on the team; there is a lot to being seen as "one of us." But as for cool, I'd say that it wasn't making the football team that makes for "cool" as much as developing a stronger personality that seems to come with the territory of playing. I do feel more confident. As for Nick, what I've learned about him is that he possessed cool even before coming out for football. Small or not, he has loads of confidence—which is probably why, even being small, he decided to go out for the team. It's probably why he made the team in the first place, as well. I'll bet the coaches spotted his confidence and knew they could work with it.

Certainly, the girls spot something in him. While he's not dating a cheerleader, Nick has managed something the rest of us guys are still trying to figure out: All the girls in school like him. They all talk to him and feel so comfortable around him. You can tell because when they stand beside him, they'll lay their heads on his shoulders, or brush his hair away from his face, things like that. Do you know what I would give to have a girl feel that comfortable around me? For starters, I'd let her wear my football jacket. Luckily, I now have one!

Pete Morris, 15

Invisible No More

Being shy puts a damper on being cool: Being too timid to put yourself "out there" does little to increase the numbers of those who come flocking to you. You've got to get out of your little cocoon.

—Shelly Tomkins, 16

Like everyone else, I really wanted to be cool. But I wasn't. In fact, I was probably further away from cool than anyone I knew! I didn't rank with the nerds or anything, but in seventh, eighth and ninth grades, no one knew I existed. I'd like to think that my biggest problem was that I was shy. Being shy really puts a damper on being cool. If you're too timid to put yourself "out there," no one is going to know that you're even alive.

While my mother says I was just born shy, I'm not sure my entire problem was genetic. I was afraid of the "out there" part, because I didn't want to not know how to act and then have everyone make fun of me. Some of the kids at our school can be pretty mean, especially the popular crowd. Like sometimes they'll look at someone, roll their eyes and do this clicking sound with their tongues—kind of like a snake does to warn he'd like you to disappear or else he'll strike. If someone did that to me, I'd want to slink away as fast as I could.

And there's something else, too. It's hard to move from one group to another. In my school there are the "cool" kids, the "brains," the "jocks," the "normal, average" crowd, the "nerds" and "geeks." My "ranking" fell somewhere in between the crowd that when someone mentions their name, others say "Who?" or when trying to bring me to mind ask, "What does she look like?"

The price I pay for not standing out is that basically I'm invisible. Being invisible is a no-man's land for sure. I was seldom "picked"—such as when teams were selected for class projects or to work in groups, go to the library, things like that. I was one of those kids the teacher had to pair up with someone—which meant with one of the other "left outs." Or, if I was the last and only one left without a partner (which happened to me a lot), then the teacher would have to assign me to a group who already was coupled up. So then I became the "third wheel," and that sucked, too. Being invisible also meant that I was never invited to special gatherings or birthday parties, and never asked along to just "hang out" with others on the weekends. And it's not like my phone was ringing off the hook: When the phone rang at my house, I didn't even think twice about it being for me. No one called for me, not even classmates who needed someone to fill him or her in on a makeup homework assignment.

Then came tenth grade. I was standing in the lunch line—alone. I don't know why someone seems like such an easy target when she's alone, but she is. Several kids ahead of me stood Serena Thompson—one of the "coolest kids"—with her entourage. Serena turned to see how long the line was and for some unknown reason, looked me up and down, rolled her eyes, clicked her tongue and remarked in the most catty way I'd ever heard, "Now there's a work of art." The others turned to look at me, and everyone, probably wanting to suck up to Serena, laughed. So then I thought maybe being "left out" wasn't as bad as being "rejected" or being made fun of.

Then came third hour. Lo and behold, the moment I walked into my English class, there sat Serena. "Hey, it's the work of art," she mocked, and again those around her snickered. At that point, I was pretty much bracing myself for having the worst school year of my entire life. I hurriedly took a seat well behind her. No need to let this girl fire off any more sarcasm at me.

Within moments, the teacher handed us each a nametag and told us to write our name on it and stick it to our shirt. "Just for today!" she assured everyone who objected, thinking it was nerdy. She wore one herself: "Ms. Marc," it read. "Okay," she said, "We're going to start out with a little exercise to get acquainted." Then came the words I dreaded: "Pick a partner." This was followed by, "You will each be introducing your partner to the class, telling the class four things about that person. We'll use a timer; you each have five minutes to gather this information. You then have one minute to introduce this person to the class, sharing what you've learned about the person."

The exercise was supposed to be a kind of "icebreaker," a bonding experience. But I'd already counted the number of kids in the class—and there was an odd number of students. Someone would be left without a partner! You guessed it—that person was me! Talk about wanting to disappear. Seeing that I was "left out," the teacher glanced at my nametag and said, "Shelley, you'll be in charge of the timer. Class, if any of you have any questions, ask Shelley. Whatever she says goes." Serena looked at me and smiled sweetly.

At first I thought, *Oh great! Everyone can see through this: the teacher had to rescue me and there I would sit holding this stupid little egg timer—looking like a total geek.* Before I could feel even more pathetic, someone yelled, "I have a question. . . ." But before that student could ask it, Ms. Marc said, "Any and all questions, ask Shelley." And then, pandemonium broke out. Everyone, it seemed, had questions. "Can we make up questions of our own, or do we have to ask those on the list?" "What if we already know each other?" "What if one minute isn't enough?" "Ask Shelley. It's all up to her," Ms. Marc replied. Practically everyone had a million questions, and no one could complete their introductions within the allotted time, so everyone begged me for favors. "I just need a little more time—pleeeassse?" I was quite popular! I loved it. By the end of the class period, everyone knew my name!

When I went to bed that night, I was still on a high. I thought about how smart it was of Ms. Marc to have planned an exercise that had drawn everyone together. No one was left out. But the key had been that everyone had to interact with everyone else. And that had made all the difference. The walls had been broken down. Without the walls, we were all one. This made me reconsider the importance of putting myself "out there" instead of always hiding in my own cocoon. From that time on, everyone in class smiled at me—which made class fun. In return, I smiled more, too. And everyone seemed friendlier from that time on.

This "new me" spilled over into my school year. I can't say I became one of the cool crowd or that I was suddenly popular, but from that day on, I never sat alone at lunch. As for Serena Thompson, I've not won her over completely, but at least she no longer sees me as a scapegoat for her rolling eyes and runaway tongue! Being outgoing is definitely a part of being cool. I'm trying to really work on not being so shy, because if you're too timid to put yourself "out there," then it's not like others are going to come flocking to you. I don't want to be "invisible" any longer. I'm doing all I can to break out of my little cocoon. I plan on being cool.

Shelly Tomkins, 16

"It Girl"

I'm mean only when I hang out with my group—because they expect everyone to act mean. But this is not cool, and I know it.

—Ling Bahl, 16

I was the quarterback's girlfriend. And president of my class. And a varsity cheerleader. Everyone knew I was the "It Girl" of our school.

My boyfriend and I, his arm around me, walked into the cafeteria. I could just feel all eyes upon me, envious I'm sure. My boyfriend and I sat at our usual lunch table—a table where all twenty-six of the football players and cheerleaders squeezed in, no matter how tight. Better to be uncomfortable than to be seen sitting elsewhere.

No one but our group dared sit with us. We were superior to everyone else. We could giggle and poke fun at anyone and everyone, and not care if they heard us or not. No one was as cool as we were, so they expected to feel inferior. It's just the way things were. No one dared question it, either. If you weren't a part of us, then you were one of "them." That's the way it worked: "Us" versus "Them."

So we're sitting there and being cool, and along comes Cassie Rann. Cassie was new to the school by two weeks, and as of yet was neither an "Us" nor "Them." But until you're one of us, then you're not. Guess she didn't understand the rules, because Cassie came over to our table, pointed to the possible open seat and asked if she could sit down. We all stared at her until we realized she was serious. Then we all laughed and told her to get lost. How dare anyone who wasn't a part of our group ask to sit with us? At that point Cassie told us there weren't any other seats left at any other table and that she had to sit somewhere. Like we cared there was nowhere else for her to sit? Not! Once again she looked at the open space by me where Monica Jordan had been sitting, but she had to leave early because of a meeting with the counselor. Thinking that maybe she was just going to sit there, I reached down, picked up my backpack and put it on the seat. Everyone laughed and then scooted together, ensuring there was no open space left at the table. Surprised and with a look of dejection written all over her face, Cassie turned to look for a seat elsewhere.

I did feel bad, especially seeing how hurt she looked as she walked away. I was sure it must feel terrible to have others be so rude to you. Especially since she hadn't said or done anything wrong—yet, we had treated her as though she was a contagious disease.

The next day there was a note sticking out of my locker. It was from Cassie. *"Thanks for giving me a dose of my own medicine,"* the note read. *"As you know, I'm new to the school. In my old school I was just like you, the 'It Girl.' And I, too, treated others just like you treated me yesterday. I have to be honest and tell you it feels really awful, and I thank you for showing me how that feels. I hope never to treat someone that way again. P.S.—When you and I did the library paper together, I saw a completely different side to you, so your actions yesterday took me by surprise. But I know it's because you felt supported by the group. I understand. Just want you to know I forgive you. Love, Cassie."*

Forgive me? I laughed, crumbled up the paper and went to class. But throughout the day, I thought about what she had said. She was right. What gives me the right to treat others this way? Though a cheerleader with a football player as my boyfriend, and most especially as president of my class, when it comes right down to it, I'm just a girl who has learned to be mean to others. And the group I hang with reinforces this behavior. When I am one-on-one with others, I never treat them in that manner. Cassie was right: There is an entirely different side to me. I am mean only when I hang out with my group—because they expect everyone to act mean. But this is not cool, and I know it. The people who really are cool are girls like Marissa and Tina and Carly—they are nice to everyone. They are comfortable with themselves. They are more true to themselves than I am.

I can't go back to that day and erase my actions. But I can change what I do from now on, and treat people with kindness and respect. I did apologize to Cassie. She graciously accepted my apology. As for my friends, they wondered what had come over me. Peer pressure is tough. But life goes on.

A year has passed. I'm not a cheerleader this year, but Cassie is. My quarterback boyfriend graduated and is attending a university many states away. He says he is dating a girl on campus. I am now that girl coming into the cafeteria looking for a spot to sit. Cassie, a very cool cheerleader who is also a very cool person, can be found sitting anywhere and everywhere. Much more "real" than me, she plays no favorites. Having set a new standard, she's collecting a crowd who thinks her brand of "It Girl" is cool. She's fast becoming everyone's favorite friend. Seems that in my school, the criteria for being an "It Girl" has changed.

Yes, I've been dethroned. Funny how that works. But I'm having more fun than ever before. But I am still looking for a boyfriend!

Ling Bahl, 16

Carpe Diem!

I've discovered that being in a leadership position isn't always about "doing"—sometimes it's a simple matter of "being."

—Buck Plevyak, 17

When I hear a friend complaining about anything I always say, "*Carpe diem,* Dude!" I mean, no sense in worrying yourself to death. Life is going to happen; you may as well use the opportunity to do what you can with it. Not that I've completely mastered this myself. I mean, sometimes I mutter these words as incentive while I'm rubbing my eyes because I've just dragged myself out of bed, grabbed something from my closet and headed out the door. Always, I'm hoping that I'm not wearing my shorts inside out or walking around with a streamer of toilet paper sticking out of my shoe! I confess there are even a few moments during the school day when I seem not to conquer the overpowering urge to place my arm on the desk, lay my head down and nod off, dreaming of meeting Kelly Clarkson. But always I don't get too far off from my number one goal in life, which is to always "*carpe diem*" (seize the day)!

I do this in lots of ways. The first way is that I'm blessed with a great personality—an "up" perspective on just about everything! I'm not saying I haven't had some trying times, because I have. But my preference is to look at life from the "cup is half full"—versus half empty—perspective. Because I see life from this vantage point, I'm able to say that I have great parents, fantastic friends and that I attend an excellent school with incredible teachers. I'm able to say that my life is fun and filled with laughter. As for cool—well, even if no one else sees me as cool (which I cannot imagine!)—I see myself as cool.

My personal philosophy of "*carpe diem*" is just one of the many reasons I was inspired to run for junior-class president. It was a tough competition with lots of good candidates vying for the office. As you'd expect, I, Buck Plevyak, won! And so, once back from my most utterly insane summer, I set out to begin the presidency. I was so looking forward to being "the Prez," because that is a position that can really do a lot for anyone's image of cool. Of course, I knew how much good I could do from this platform for the image of the school as well! I mean, a president has a lot of power, right? So I could make a lot of changes. I was just sure I could turn the school—and the students—around, making it a place of unlimited excitement!

Seizing the day, I sat down and wrote a short and sweet little memorandum about what I felt was needed to make the school a hot little place in which to hang out during the day. I then posted it on the board in the student center for all to see.

It was a sweet weekend—most of it spent dreaming about how being president would mean that practically all the girls would be vying for me to squire them to many school activities. Looking more dapper than even I could imagine, that following Monday morning I strutted into school, looking forward to being big man on campus. Well, I have to tell you, things didn't necessarily turn out as planned that day. I discovered that no one really wanted me to set him or her straight on too much of anything. I mean, the student body didn't sit quietly at my feet while I enlightened them with a new vision for a new millennium. In fact, I learned they wanted me to do a lot of listening. Whether I liked it or not, I had to concern myself with even those classmates I wouldn't normally associate (or necessarily think their perspective mattered). But I learned I couldn't just listen to a chosen few. I'd been elected by the mass, to represent the mass—and therefore had to consider the mass. And so I had to learn the art of randomly striking up conversations, if for no other reason than to be seen as friendly and outgoing to everyone. I also learned that it's not enough to care about others; they have to know you care—you have to communicate it. For this insight, I am most thankful. I now treat everyone in the student body with absolute respect! Each and every day. I do my best to encourage, support and inspire my fellow classmates so that each one has a totally enjoyable school-day experience.

The essence of cool, I've discovered, is this: Being in a leadership position isn't always about "doing"—sometimes it's a simple matter of "being." So I'm "seizing the day" in doing just that! In so doing, I'm becoming a cool person to everyone on campus. Even I think so!

So remember the name—because someday you're going to see it again. It may be on the billboards at the movies, running as a U.S. senator, or it may be as a famous novelist! I'm not exactly sure, but you can count on it being something cool! Because I'm one cool dude. And that, my friend, is the way it is!

Buck Plevyak, 17

My Friends Said I Was "Annoying"!

If you want to be cool, you must discern which quirks of yours are socially acceptable and which are not. Then, work really hard at getting rid of the obnoxious and annoying ones. Because if you don't, your friends are going to be rid of you.

—Kim Holcombe, 17

If you want to be cool, you have to be well-liked, which means that you have to make sure you don't do things that anger or offend people. I have firsthand experience with how not to do this. In my freshman year of high school, I was obnoxiously loud and a very annoying sort of person. I can't say that I made a decision to be obnoxious and loud, but I do remember making the decision to express my opinions—and as forcibly and as loudly as I could. If someone didn't agree with me, then I'd simply berate and belittle that person. Let's just say I had too many embarrassing moments to even count, and everyone basically stayed as far away from me as they could. I have worked for three long years to overcome that reputation, and to be perfectly honest, I'm still not all that popular. But at least I have some friends who decided to overlook the fact that I was one of the most annoying freshmen in history.

So when you hear the cliché "just be yourself," well, that may not be the best advice. I mean, if you are as loud and obnoxious as I was, then you'd better not be yourself. Getting to cool means you keep checking to see if there is anything you need to do to improve yourself. You need to keep asking if others want to pal around with you. That's a simple test, but a good one. If you find that not too many people are standing in line to be your friend, then you need to make some changes. For example, if you're not a good listener, then you're going to have to change that. Everyone wants to talk about him- or herself, so be a good listener, and you'll be liked. If you're shy, you're going to have to find ways to put yourself out there. Get out of your shell. Nobody can get to know you if you don't come out of your shell. If you're bossy or like to be in control of everything all the time, then stop that. And if you do things that are socially unacceptable, for sure, that has to go. For example, yelling at people because they don't agree with you is not cool, nor is doing something equally embarrassing, like I did in ninth grade when I threw a whole glass of water on a boy. Not only did I get him wet, but I drenched the three people sitting next to him as well. No one likes to be drenched, and needless to say, those three people didn't like me for a long, long time. Cheating off someone's paper is annoying, as is budging in line whether in the cafeteria or at the movies. Not cool behavior!

Things like that. It's pretty much common sense. I'd sum up cool this way: If you want to be cool, you must discern which quirks of yours are socially acceptable and which are not. Then, really work hard at getting rid of the obnoxious and annoying ones. Because if you don't, your friends are going to be rid of you. And that's not cool.

Kim Holcombe, 17

Club Cool: Outsider on the Inside

Cool is not just about appearance. It is an attitude. Cool is in your head. Cool is not just for a few; we can all be cool. And we are.

—Amber Lesperance, 15

There were six girls at my school who thought of themselves as more cool than anyone else. These girls, "Club Cool" as they called themselves, literally took over the school. They bossed everyone around. They made up the rules as to "who" was who, and what was "in" or not. But I was okay with it, because I was one of them.

I still don't know for certain if the five other girls treated each other equally or not. I do know that for me, membership in Club Cool meant that I was number six—in other words, the lowest ranking of the members. But like I said, I don't know if everyone else shared a number-one billing or if there was a hierarchy among them, too—a number one, two, three, four, and a fifth-place position. I do know that I had to do whatever they wanted me to—"or else." "Or else" could mean anything from not being able to sit with them at "their" lunch table, to not being invited to come over to one of their houses to listen to a latest CD.

Lowest person on the food chain in Club Cool or not, I liked being seen as one of the coolest girls at school. So I willingly did what I was told. As an example, Club Cool girls wore makeup everyday. Nail polish was a requirement. On pep assembly days, our nails were painted in school colors—every other nail being one of the three different school colors, followed by in-between nails being striped in all three colors. No exceptions. We even had rules for the way our hair was worn. The predominant style was a ponytail—and it had to be really high up on your head. There had to be two ribbons around it. Not one. Two. Period. I thought the "rules" were stupid, but if that's what it took to be a member of Club Cool, then I'd do it.

There were some things that I didn't like about being a member, but I considered it a sacrifice. For example, I didn't appreciate it that the other girls would sometimes take my things—lipstick, nail polish, paper tablets, pencils and so on, but there wasn't much I could do about it. They expected me to share eye shadow, and sometimes I'd have to hand over a lipstick and be just fine with the fact that I might not get it back. That bugged me, but I never did say anything.

I had to do other things to "earn" membership-in-good-standing as well. They said I could stay being their friend as long as I did their homework—especially big papers and things—whenever they requested it. No matter that I also had the same big projects. But again, I did what they asked, even though the more of their homework I did, the more they asked me to do. No one returned the favor, as I discovered one day when I desperately needed help with one of my projects. Panicky, I told them I needed help. All refused to help me! That stung.

Then one day as I was doing a history project for one of the girls, the song "Anthem" by Good Charlotte was playing on the radio. As I listened to the lyrics, everything became clear: I wasn't really a friend and they weren't mine. I wasn't "in" the group; I wasn't one of them at all. They were only letting me hang out with them. I was an outsider—on the inside, for a while. I was only being used. These girls weren't special. They were just snots! Disgusted, I looked at the paper I was working on, crumpled it up and threw it in the garbage! And to think that I'd given up my really good friends to be a part of this group!

I told the girls I couldn't continue doing their homework. So they told me "good-bye"! They've since chosen someone to replace me. I don't envy her one bit. I know she's busy doing everyone's homework and wearing goofy-looking fingernails. I told my old friends that I was sorry about the way I treated them, and that I wanted to be their friend once again. They took me back but never let me forget what a "monster" and "sissy" I'd become in working so hard to be a member in Club Cool.

Having been an outsider on the inside, I know that just because you're popular does not mean you are a cool person. Cool is not just about appearance. It is an attitude. Cool is in your head. Which means that cool is not just for a few who set themselves apart and then treat others rudely so that you're intimidated into feeling small. We can all be cool. And we are.

Amber Lesperance, 15

How Cool Is Britney Spears?

I think you can work too hard at being cool—which isn't cool. I mean, what was Britney Spears thinking when she ran off in the middle of the morning to get married?

—Gideon McKenzie, 18

How far will you go to be considered cool? I mean, think of Britney Spears. I ask you, is Britney Spears cool? I mean, she's pretty and all, but does it seem to you like she's working way too hard at trying to be cool? See, I think you can work too hard at being cool—which isn't cool. What was Britney thinking when she ran off in the middle of the morning to get married? And to "just a friend," no less? How much sense does it take to say to yourself: "I'm Britney Spears: Everyone knows me by my first name only! I'm on top of the world: I'm beautiful; successful beyond my wildest imagination; every guy (maybe with the exception of Justin Timberlake) wants to go out with me. So what can I do to be seen as even more cool? I know, I'll get married in Las Vegas—with an unknown limo driver walking me down the aisle. I'll marry for the fun of it—it doesn't matter that marriage is a holy thing, nor that it should be saved for the love of my life. Tomorrow I'll say, 'Oh, it was just a mistake! I just wanted to have a little fun. It's not like I was serious or anything!'" I mean, c'mon. Does she think the whole world is going to think of her as "more cool"? Personally, I think they'll think of her as either a fool or else they'll say, "Poor Britney. She's over the edge. She came back from her break too soon."

Don't get me wrong: I am sympathetic to Britney Spears. It's not like I can't relate. People will say and do almost anything if they think it makes them appear cool these days. Like just recently a group of my friends and I were hanging out at the local Wal-Mart. One of the guys suggested that we go steal something. "You're totally crazy," I told him. "There are cameras everywhere and signs in the bathrooms that warn you against shoplifting. And why on earth would you do such a thing?" My rebuff didn't faze him. "Oh, please," he replied. "Those signs aren't real. I bet the cameras aren't even turned on. C'mon, it'll be cool. Can you just imagine how the guys will laugh when tomorrow we tell them what we did?" The other guy with us bit right away. "Yeah, c'mon. Let's hit the CDs," and off he went. "No way, man. I'm not about to do something dumb like jacking a CD." As both guys headed off for the music aisle, one said, "Go home to your mommy."

I left the store.

The next day, my friends weren't at school. Or the next day. Or the day after that. I tried to figure out what happened to them. "Oh man, you don't know? They got busted for trying to steal some DVDs. Their parents have to pay over two thousand dollars in fines and they are going to court. Seems that the police watched them on camera until they pocketed several discs and then arrested them. I wish I could have been there—it would have been cool!"

Had I stayed, I too would be in court and having to pay money, whether or not I stole any items. I'd be either listed as an accomplice or explaining myself a million times why I wasn't. Always, I'm faced with friends who want to do pranks, everything from "TPing" someone's house to letting the air out of someone's tires. Like Britney, who got married "for fun" and then dismissed it as a "mistake," my friends say some of their wacky (and sometimes illegal) actions are just "for fun" and when found out, admit it was a "mistake." It seems that no one is thinking too much about whether or not such things are just fundamentally wrong. I am not saying I'm an angel; it's hard to always do the right thing when it seems like everyone around me is rewarded for doing something outrageous. One of my teachers told me that a true test of character is doing the right thing even when no one else is looking. It takes a strong person to be like that. Sometimes I don't think I can be that strong. But I'm working on it. I tell myself that if the little voice inside my head tells me it's wrong, it probably is. So I keep reminding myself to "think, think, think." I want to be cool, but I won't jeopardize my reputation or good name to do it. Nor will you ever find that I've run off to Las Vegas to marry a friend "for fun." Not cool.

Gideon McKenzie, 18

Assistant Coach

If you feel your self-esteem needs a boost, do something for others. You'll help them and feel good about yourself. And that is cool. Very cool.

—Shire Feingold, 16

I best learned about "cool" when, for a class, we had to choose a community service project. But what to do? Then one day as I was helping my little sister get signed up for Little League, I saw an application for assistant coach. I thought back to the days when I played on a basketball league and remembered how much I enjoyed it. I really looked up to my coach and thought he was cool. And I'd always wanted to volunteer my time to a worthy cause. "Shire Feingold, Assistant Coach": *It's perfect*, I thought.

I applied and was accepted, so on Wednesday nights at seven, I show up at the gym of my old elementary school. When I enter that gym, all the smiling faces swarm around. It's a magical feeling. There I am, surrounded by fifth- and sixth-grade girls. I tell them to prepare to get sweaty, learn a few moves and have a lot of fun. The girls are so eager to learn and improve their skills. Some of them seem to get the moves right away, and some have to really work at it. I've developed a system whereby the girls with the best skills help the newcomers learn them. They love this approach. When anyone learns something new or does a cool move, the "student" is pleased and the "teacher" is proud. Always, they are quick to congratulate each other and say what a great job someone did.

Then comes game day. On Saturday, all the hard work and sweat on Wednesday pays off. The girls go nose-to-nose against another recreational team. Sometimes we win and sometimes we lose. Either way, the girls come out winners. They try their hardest and have fun; that's the whole idea.

Being assistant coach for my little sister's recreational basketball team, I've certainly "given back." Whatever it is a particular girl needs—some extra time to get a move down, a compliment, extra hair elastic or even a hug—I'm there to provide it. When I see a girl is having a bad day, I take the time to go over to spend a few moments and see if I can help her feel a little better about things. Whether helping the girls learn a new skill or helping them feel better about themselves, all are good ways to boost their self-esteem. These girls look up to me as a friend, mentor and as assistant coach. I love it.

While coaching may have started out as a way to get community service credits, it has become so much more. It has satisfied my need to do something good for others. The season is going to be over in a month, and I am truly going to miss these girls. I know I've had a positive impact on them, and that is a pretty cool feeling. I would recommend to anyone out there who feels like they'd like to be needed—or feel their self-esteem is in need of a boost—to go do something for others. You'll help them and feel good about yourself. And that is cool. Very cool.

Shire Feingold, 16

Dominica

Cool is having empathy for others. Should you not understand the other person's words, just keep in mind that smiling and being polite is a universal language.

—Heather Christie, 15

Being a foreigner in a new country is a painful experience if you don't have at least one friend. I learned this when my family moved to the United States in the middle of my eighth-grade year. I really missed my old friends a lot. I missed them all the more because I found it difficult to make new friends in the new school I attended. In my old school in Spain I had so many friends and was considered popular. But in America I had no one. Everyone looked at me, but looked at me as an outsider. I felt really lonely. And alone.

I survived eighth grade, but not by much. Kids would make fun of my accent and the fact that I couldn't read very well. When I would mispronounce a word, they would giggle and laugh out loud. Knowing how important it is to be able to communicate with people, I worked really hard at mastering English. That helped me with words but not to gain the friends I longed to have. I tried to be patient and take everything in stride—at least in the beginning. I thought my not having friends had to do with me. Because my English wasn't all that good, I thought maybe others couldn't understand me. This made me all the more homesick. On some days I missed my homeland so much that I could almost smell the pastries in the bustling outdoor markets.

One day toward the end of the year, I walked into my math class. There was a new girl, and she was sitting in my seat. I smiled at her and without telling her she was in my assigned seat, I took an empty seat nearby. Just then a really popular girl,

Cindy, walked in. Noticing the new girl, she looked her over and then made a remark about the jeans she was wearing. The new girl was wearing a pair of bright-yellow jeans, and most of the kids just wore denim blue ones. The new girl said nothing, just sat there as quiet as a stone. "What's the matter, you can't talk either? What is this, a school for foreigners?" Cindy then rudely asked. Obviously, her comment was aimed at not only the new girl, but me as well. Upset, I instantly started talking to the new girl, basically telling her not to worry about a rude, smart-mouthed girl such as Cindy. The new girl's face brightened and she quickly thanked me for speaking in my native tongue, Spanish. I had been so upset by Cindy's comment, I didn't realize that I had resorted to my native language!

So that was our first bond. Having been in her shoes, I know how nice it must have been to find someone who communicated with her in her own language. After class, I immediately went up and welcomed her to school. She said her name was Dominica and she was from Mexico. She said she couldn't understand a word of what the girl in the "uniform" had said to her. I told her everything would be okay. I told her how I had been attending this school for only a year, and that I would look out for her and help her through everything.

Dominica and I became fast friends, talking about our homelands as well as our new lives here in America. In the beginning we talked about most things in Spanish, but as she learned more and more English (which I helped her with as much as I could), we talked only in English. So finally, I have a friend. Dominica is a good friend, someone who is kind, nice and courteous.

Now that I've been in this country a little longer, I have other friends besides Dominica. Dominica has made other friends, too. But I think sometimes your classmates don't understand how tough it is to be new and "different." Just think what it would feel like if your parents moved to a foreign country and you were faced with everything being new and different. You would naturally miss all that you had left behind. And if the new people you met while being abroad weren't polite or treated you as though you didn't belong, imagine what a terrible feeling that would be. That's what I faced. It's what Dominica faced. I don't think that's cool. I think cool is having empathy for others if they are new to a situation. If you can't always understand the other person's words, just keep in mind that smiling and being polite is a universal language.

Heather Christie, 15

Toddling Brain

Cool is living one day at a time.

—Lannie Freeman, 16

In eighth grade I learned that I have depression. I was put on medication to help my body produce the chemicals I need so that the world doesn't seem as though it is covered with a heavy black cloud. But even with the medication, my depression got worse, so the doctor put me on even more medication. As a result of the side effects of the medication, such as always being sleepy and feeling nauseous, I had to stop going to school. So then I started being homeschooled. But that meant that I didn't get to see my friends. I told my parents how much I missed everyone, so then the doctor reduced my medication so that I could attend regular school again. The rest of the year went by fine, and I didn't have any major problems.

Does all that seem like a drag to you? It is. But there is nothing I can do. I'd like nothing better than to not have depression be a part of my life, but it is. Mine is what they call an "imbalanced brain." I have the responsibility to always keep watch over it—like a toddler.

Always, I was hopeful that one morning I would wake up and my ordeal would all be over. Just before my ninth-grade year, I was thinking that maybe my dream had come true. So ninth grade came and because I was feeling happy, I went off my medication. I was always "nervous," but I coped and things seemed okay. I joined a sports team and did okay. I even had no problem taking my pool class—which I was really nervous about. The medication I was taking made me put on weight. A lot of weight. When tenth grade started, I didn't go out for any sports, because I was too heavy to compete. I continued to get good grades, but I spent a lot of time alone. I just wasn't really social. That only made the problem worse. I got really heavy. The heavier I became, the shyer I was about hanging around with my friends. I lost confidence that I could hang out as a friend or have a boyfriend without having a panic attack. A panic attack is scary to me. I think that would be scary for the other person, and I'd be embarrassed.

Isolating myself meant that I got even more depressed. One night, I was so despondent that I tried to overdose. That I had once again sunk so deep into depression scared my parents. It scared me, too.

I was then hospitalized. I stayed there for a while, and they finally released me on the promise that I'd see a counselor on a weekly basis and take my medicine every day. I was told I still had depression—and that I also suffered from "social anxiety." So that's the way my life goes. I just have to accept the fact that my depression may come back at different times in life. As a result, my goal is no longer to beat depression, but rather to manage it. I wish I didn't have this burden. But I do. So when I think about cool, the first thing that comes to mind is acting normal so I'm not thought of as different. That's tough to do when your problem is not in your head, but rather an imbalance in your body's chemical system.

So I'm taking things one day at a time. Living one day at a time is cool. I've spent a lot of time in and out of hospitals over the years. I've talked to a lot of people who say, "Live your life one day at a time—and be thankful for each day." I'm learning to adapt. And that's cool, too. I'm hoping to go to college and find a career in an area where I can keep learning about how to care for myself. I'd like to help others who share my problem. So that's my definition of cool: adapting. Which for me means that I am taking good care of myself and wanting to help others do the same.

Lannie Freeman, 16

I'm Just as Cool as You . . .

Individuality and creativity are about expression of self. What makes someone cool is his or her willingness to look deep into the interior of a person before judging.

—Erika Slate, 18

I rank in the top 15 percent of my class. I've been inducted into my state's honor society as well as the National Honor Society. I've been awarded a full scholarship into a college honors program in a university. Community service is high on my list of priorities. I've organized road cleanups and raised money for local charities, and had a cat- and dog-food drive for a local animal shelter. Still, one of my best accomplishments came last year when I was elected to the highest office in an organization I've been a part of since I was twelve. I was selected to be the "Worthy Advisor of the North Scituate Assembly of the International Order of the Rainbow for Girls," an order of the Masons designed for teen girls. The goal is to promote community service, strengthen public speaking ability and develop leadership skills for young girls ages twelve to twenty. I am devoted to my church and can always be found in its youth group Sunday nights. Every summer I serve as a counselor for the recreation program in my town. The kids love me.

I tell you these things not only because I am so very proud of them, but to make a point. So often I hear, "Why does a thoughtful, intelligent and really nice girl such as yourself dress as you do?" Which makes me ask in return, "What do you see when you look at me? Is your first impression only about the way the tips of my hair are dyed different colors? Does my spiked jewelry scare you? Does my looking different than you make you think I have a personality disorder? I may not fit your idea of 'ideal,' but I am, as you say, a thoughtful, intelligent and really nice girl."

Individuality and creativity are about expression of self. Just because someone may seem a little bit different on the outside doesn't always mean they are rebelling on the inside. I am proud of myself and what I have accomplished so far in life at the young age of eighteen. So I pass on to all who read this: Accomplishments and goals speak for themselves. But so does your attitude of acceptance. I am me. It's what makes me cool. What makes you cool is your willingness to look deep into the interior of a person—which is exactly where traits such as being "thoughtful, intelligent and a really nice girl" reside.

Erika Slate, 18

Teen Talk: "I Would Be Cool, If . . ."

. . . **I Had a Boyfriend:** I'd be cooler if it weren't for the fact that I lack a boyfriend. At my school the girls who have boyfriends are always seen as cooler than those without boyfriends. Same for boys with girlfriends—they're also seen as more cool than those who are not a couple. All of my friends have boyfriends, and they're pretty cool (which is surprising, because they chose them from the guys who attend our school). I don't know why it is, but a lot of times the guys from other schools are much more good-looking and act better than the ones at your own school! Anyway, I've looked over the rest of the guys—those who don't have a girlfriend—and you know, I don't see myself with any of them. Everyone says, "Oh, one day the right one will come along." Yeah, yeah, yeah! I'm waiting! Hello—how about now? I'm already fourteen.

AlbyAnne Sheldon, 14

. . . **My Teeth Weren't So Crooked:** If I had straight teeth, then I'd be cool. But I'm smart and I have pretty hair, so I'm not a total write-off. The dentist says I need braces "real bad," but I don't see that happening any time soon. My mother has a job and it doesn't cover all the expenses we have, so a dentist bill isn't a good thing. My stepfather says my having braces aren't his responsibility—and that my father should pay for them. But my father is unemployed, and I'm certain my getting braces isn't anything he cares about. I even asked him. He told me if I wanted braces, I should get a job and earn the money myself. Well, I'm fifteen. Jobs available to fifteen-year-olds really won't cover the expense of dental bills the size of braces. So since braces aren't in the picture, I have to learn how to smile so my teeth won't show. I've been working really hard on it. I already have a couple of different ones that seem to be working out okay. I also have a couple of ones that are a little lame.

Jessica Brennan, 15

. . . I Hadn't Been Born with a Shy Gene: I'd be cool if I weren't so shy. If I weren't so shy, everyone at school would know what I was like—which is a totally nice person. At least my close friends know what I'm like. We have our own definition of "cool"—and that's cool.

Karla Esponda, 16

. . . My Life Wasn't Controlled by the Freaky Little Addict in My Head: I'd be cool if I could get myself together. I'm fighting addiction. Addiction is totally awful—there is nothing cool about it. I've been using for three years and trying really hard to stop. I've been in two drug rehab programs. Just because you've been in a drug program doesn't mean your problem goes away. Even after you stop using drugs, the after-effects—and cravings—are still there. They call these "PAWS," which stands for Post Acute Withdrawal Syndrome. What this means is that you can think you're just fine and then one day, your skin will start crawling. It feels sort of like you've got a million ants crawling up and down your entire body. Well, it drives you really crazy. When that happens to me, and then I see someone smoking or smell pot, then my brain just screams for some of it, too. So stopping drugs may sound like an easy thing to do for those who have never used or never had to fight an addiction, but for me it's like my whole life is controlled from some little freak inside of my head who totally refuses to let me have my life back. I feel owned, and I hate that. I'm working really hard at staying sober and drug-free, but addiction is a terrible burden. I did drugs to be cool. Truth is, there's nothing cool about it. I'll be cool when I get the real me back.

Isaac Renolds, 14

. . . You Believed That I Already Am! What keeps me from being cool is in someone else's mind, because it's not in mine. I'm cool, and I have no doubts about it. My theory is that if people don't think you're cool, it's probably because they don't know you.

Tanner Swindell, 17

. . . I Didn't Have LONER Stamped on My Forehead: I'm really quiet. My mother says it's just a part of my personality and that I shouldn't worry about it. So what that means is that I won't grow out of it. Now that's a depressing thought—because being quiet sure puts a cramp on others wanting to be your friend. For one, you feel alone all the time—well, actually you ARE alone all the time. I sit alone at lunchtime and at school assemblies; I walk all alone to class. It sucks. Worse, when someone glances in my direction, I feel as though I have the word "LONER" stamped across my forehead. There is this terrible sinking feeling that happens, and if I'm close to a girl's bathroom, I duck into it so it's not so obvious I'm alone. Having some friends would do a lot for my image of cool!

Shelby Amos, 13

. . . **My Boy Thinks I Am:** I gave birth to a baby boy my sophomore year. Quite frankly, it's more important to me that he thinks I'm cool rather than if my classmates do. To my infant son, it doesn't matter how I dress or with whom I hang out. I once worried about what everyone thought of me. My hair had to be just perfect. My nails were always just so. But becoming a parent has changed my priorities: My worries are bigger and more complicated now. Because I am a mother, I have to constantly make sure my son is okay: Does he have good care while I'm at school or working? Is he healthy? Will his father be there for him when I can't be? Things like that. So for me, being cool is being a good mother.

Rebekah Molina, 16

. . . **You Knew the Meaning of Cool:** Personally, I don't think the kids at my school know anything about being cool. I mean, everybody has their own notions, but it seems to me they all take a different road. Do all roads lead to cool? I don't think so. The kids at school would find me cool if it weren't for the fact that the way you dress is like the number-one sign of being cool. Now how dumb—okay, "limiting"—is that? Luckily, I have a lot of friends, and we have a lot of fun. I just accept the fact that I'm not going to be considered "cool" at school, but I'm cool enough for my friends. For me, that counts a lot.

Amanda Singh, 13

. . . **I Didn't Walk Around in Uncomfortable Steve Madden High Heels:** Personally, I believe we all secretly long to be cool, whether we admit it or not. I think it's just a matter of defining cool. Once I thought it was about my appearance. Every morning I religiously followed my self-imposed thirty-minute shower and performed the ultra-exfoliate to my moisture-drained-hair routine. It was very important to me whether or not I had the cutest Roxy backpack, the latest MAC eye shadow, and the softest and shiniest hair. Now that I am in high school I realize that looks don't matter as much as you think. Your friends are still going to love you regardless of a pimple on your forehead. Cool is not waking up at 5:30 a.m. or walking around in uncomfortable Steve Madden high heels. Cool is rolling out of bed ten minutes before walking out the door, wearing a fluffy sweatshirt, UGGs and a ponytail. Cool, I've discovered, is being comfortable—in your normal, natural self.

Melissa Miller, 17

. . . I Stay Just as I Am: A lot of being cool is in your head. If you think that you're just fine as you are, and if everything is going your way, then you're cool. You don't have to be a football star or have a nice ride to be cool. Wake up, acknowledge that life is great—then you know you're cool. To me, you are only cool if you think you are. It does not matter what other people think. If people think you are cool and you don't feel that way, then you aren't going to believe it. The only thing that matters is the way you feel about yourself. Try it. You'll see that if you're grateful just to be alive, then you'll feel cool. Consider yourself a together-enough person, then others will think of you this way, too.

Bryan Granger, 17

. . . I Didn't Waste Time Wanting to Be Cool: Being cool is great, but is it worth it? Most of the kids at my school who are cool—or think of themselves as cool—spend a lot of time trying to convince others they are. If being "cool" means less time for getting good grades so that I can go to college, then I'll save it for later. Besides, cool is not a one-time thing. You can choose to step on or off the "cool" merry-go-round. If I sacrifice being cool right now for getting a good education, I'm not going to be as cool as I want to be later.

Isai Alvardo, 16

. . . I Could Go to a Football Game and Not Care Where or with Whom I Sit: I believe that being cool is one of those abstract things that everyone wants but doesn't really know what it is. What is cool? Is it always having someone to talk to? Is it having a saved seat at lunch? Is it fitting into the "right" crowd, or having your phone constantly ringing? To me, being cool is being able to go to a football game and not having to worry about who you are sitting with. Cool is feeling like you fit in. So pretend that you do. Just go with it.

Whitney Williamson, 15

. . . I Save "Cool" for Later: There is a group of kids at school who think that if others see them getting into trouble, then they'll become famous around school and everyone will know who they are. Some teens think that skipping classes makes them cool. They believe that having a "big" attitude will make them cool. Wearing "cool" clothes is the big deal. I'd like to be seen as cool, but not by doing the same things. I want to be me and express myself, but not in these ways. So for now, no one pays any attention to me, but that's okay. I'll be cool later. The first eighteen years of your life are only the first eighteen.

Diana Gomez, 16

. . . I Remind You to Tell All Freedom Fighters, "Thank You": My good friend Anthony has always been sort of a "big brother." I was definitely caught off guard when he told me he was joining the army. After the six weeks of basic training and then being stationed for a while in Texas, like so many brave men and women, Anthony was sent to the war in Iraq. I talked to Anthony the other night and told him how thankful I was that he and so many like him were protecting freedom throughout the world. "You're welcome," he said and then added, "It is so good to hear someone actually say this." Anthony—American hero—will be coming home soon. Like my father, Nicholas Samouris, who served in the U.S. Navy, Nick and so many have put their lives on the line in the name of freedom. They are all American heroes—and they are definitely cool. So to me, "cool" is telling all veterans, "Thank you."

Stephanie Samouris, 16

. . . I Didn't Want to Be a Free Spirit: My desire to be true to myself keeps me from being seen as cool. I don't really associate with the so-called cool crowd. I am a free spirit and a happy person. I don't like others dictating how I'm supposed to act or what I'm to value. I have a lot of fun. I'm not into girls, and couldn't care less about the cars and lifestyles of the rich and famous. I'm cool because I set my own standards; I'm true to myself. It's enough.

Henry Manyseng, 18

. . . I Didn't Have to Put On a Happy Face: It's a lot of pressure to be cool. I suppose most kids at my school would say that the cool people are the cheerleaders. They always look like they're happy. I know that sometimes they have a bad day, but because they have so much pressure on them, they just put on a happy face and hold their real feelings in. So half the time they're just being phony. Who needs it? I couldn't put on a happy face when I wasn't happy. Honestly, I don't know how the cheerleaders do it.

Maribel Rizo, 16

. . . Only I Could Stay Out of Trouble: I don't go out of my way to get noticed. I don't care what people say or think about me. I try not to get caught up in the idea of being popular. Instead, I try to focus more on my schoolwork and playing sports. A lot of people know who I am because I am an athlete. I hang out with a lot of popular people, but I don't think that makes me cool. I just try to be true to myself. If people notice me for doing that, then that's great. I hang out with my friends and try to stay out of trouble—which in and of itself is a big job. Sometimes that's "cool" enough.

Alvin Thompson, 17

. . . I Act Like a Real-Life Person: I'm on the drill team at school and have lots of friends, but I don't care about the things that would make me popular. I don't consider myself better than anyone else. Instead, I try to hang out with everyone and to treat everyone fairly. To me, being "cool" is about character, more of an inward quality than an outward one. Being a nice person, someone who is friendly and willing to speak to others regardless of who they are, well, that's cool. Cool is about being a human being and acting like one. It's all about taking this journey together. No use in pretending we're in it alone.

Lauren Welch, 16

... **All Ethnic Groups Were More Accepting of Others:** In my school there are a lot of different ethnic groups. Mostly, kids from the same ethnic group hang out with each other. Being popular or what is cool or not is sort of based on what is important to the ethnic group you're a part of. Because the kids divide themselves into these different ethnic groups, what is cool to one group may or may not be to another. It can be pretty limiting.

Yesenia Fuentes, 17

... **Those Who Made the Rules for Cool Thought of Me as Cool:** In my opinion, cool isn't all that important. I would like to be popular, but the kids who determine that aren't personal friends of mine. Besides, it's just an arbitrary thing. The few who set themselves apart as cool judge others whom they know little about. They feel they are better than others and look down on them when they don't follow along. I mean, it's all just a matter of "pack" behavior. No thanks. I don't worry about being cool, because I don't think I need to make an impression on people who I won't hang out with after graduation. I'm trying to keep it simple: I only care what my close friends think of me. That's the important cool. And it's enough.

Windy Lopez, 15

... **I Keep My Great Personality:** Everyone thinks that to be popular you must be beautiful or that you have to have bulging muscles. I think it's more important to be nice and to have a good personality. Looks are secondary to who you really are on the inside. Most of the time those who think of themselves as cool think they're better than everyone else and act superior. Instead, I'd rather have friends and get along with people in a genuine way. I want people to know me as someone who is nice, generous and outgoing, rather than be someone who is always being talked about.

Sharayah Darter, 17

. . . I Cared What Others Thought: It doesn't matter to me who other people think is cool. It's a very temporary thing. Think about it: After graduation, everyone will go on his or her separate way. Some people will go to college, work or get married. No one is going to remember why someone was cool. School should be a place where everyone wants to learn, and where people develop a sense of who they are and what they want to be. Spending your time doing whatever you have to do to be seen as cool is a waste of time. In my mind, being "cool" is overrated, but then I also think school is.

Jessica Taylor, 16

. . . I Remember the Importance of Being a Good Friend: Friends are an important part of being cool. I have a lot of friends. The nice thing about mine is that I can count on them and I can trust them. And they're really fun to be around. We get along, and we don't get mad or talk behind each other's back. Nor do we tell each other's secrets. I know that I can talk to them when I have problems and know that they will listen. And that is very cool. None of my friends are backstabbers who talk about you behind your back. When one of us is feeling bad, we cheer each other up. Also, when one of us gets a good grade on a project or gets an award, each of us will congratulate the other. That is very cool, too. Just as having a friend is important, so is being a good friend. That way you have someone to talk to besides your family, and you won't be alone at school. Even by having one friend, you start making more, and this builds your confidence in being more social. So, like I said, friends are a big part of being cool.

Jazmin Gomez, 13

Part 8

Dear Dr. Youngs: What Should I Do About . . .

When you do not know a thing, to allow that you do not know it: this is knowledge.

—Confucius

Keep knocking and the joy inside will eventually open a window and look out to see who's there.

—Rumi

I would rather live in a world where my life is surrounded by mystery than live in a world so small that my mind could comprehend it.

—Harry Emerson Fosdick

Life is a contact sport.

—Anonymous

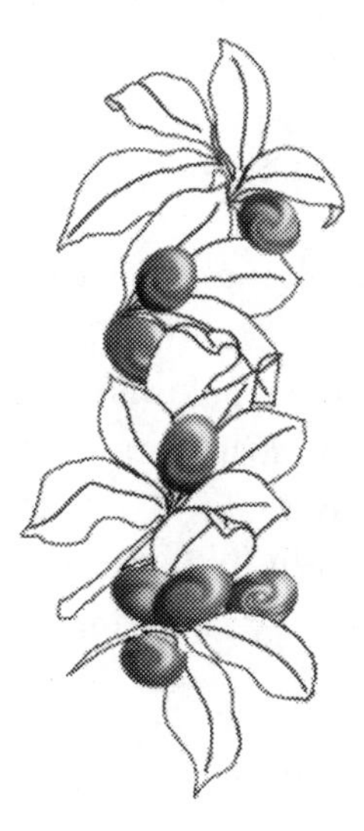

A Word from Dr. Youngs

As they say, "Life is a contact sport." And a lot of contact at that. There is always something going on, always something happening. Most of the time, it's all good! But sometimes life doles out some real challenges. At those times, it can be really helpful to talk with others about these issues. This can help you better understand the nature of the problem as well as help you gain a better understanding in how to best go about working through it.

I've worked with teens for many years, as an educator of middle school and high school students, and also as a speaker within schools and in other various youth group settings. In addition, I hear from thousands and thousands of teens via the letters and e-mails they send me in hopes of being published in our *Taste Berries for Teens* series. From all this contact, I know that as you are making your way through the many adventures of being a teen, issues come up. Especially in workshop settings, I notice the benefits of laying the question on the table. For example, I've always found that when one teen asks a question, practically the entire group—guys and girls—in unison say, "Good question. I wonder about that, too." Then, once I've given advice on how to best go about things, once again the audience joins in, saying things like,

"Oh, that could work," or "Good point, I hadn't thought of that," or "Something else he/she can do is. . . ."

Outside "insight" can be good. And that's the goal of this unit. I invited teens to send me a question he or she most wanted to know how to resolve. Though space does not allow me to answer all of your questions, I thought you might be interested in knowing the kinds of issues typical in the teen years. Here is a sampling of the kinds of questions I received.

- A kid at school has threatened to "kick my butt." What can I do?
- I really would like to have a boy/girlfriend. Nothing I've done so far seems to be working. Is there something I'm doing wrong?
- A nasty rumor is circulating around about me. What can I do to clean up my reputation?
- How do I convince my parents to loosen up the rules?
- My good friend has started flirting with my boy/girlfriend. How do I find out if anything is going on between them?
- What is the secret to being popular?
- I get teased about the way I look (hair, weight, complexion, clothes). What can I do?
- How can I have more friends?
- I'm being pressured to have sex. What's the best line to use to say "no"?
- My good friend is using drugs (or drinking). It's really messing up my friend's life, as he/she's starting to be in trouble all the time. What can I do to help my friend?
- Someone I thought was my friend has started backstabbing me. How do I get him/her to stop?
- I feel down all the time. Is that normal?
- My boy/girlfriend is always giving me ultimatums. How do I get him/her to back off—without breaking up?
- I know kids who are diagnosed with things with weird

names such as bipolar, anorexia, bulimia, dyslexia or ADD. Sometimes I feel down and have really weird thoughts. How do I find out if anything is wrong with me—if one of those "labels" applies to me?

- What can I do to convince my friend to just be my friend?
- Several months ago my grandma (grandpa/friend/classmate/pet) died. I can't stop thinking about it. I'm sad, and I cry all the time. What can I do to make the sadness go away?
- There is a rumor going around at school about me. It feels creepy to walk down the halls having everyone stare in my direction. Moving to another state or changing schools is out of the question. What can I do?
- I started a rumor around school, and everyone knows I did it. Now no one wants to be my friend. How can I repair things?
- My parents always want to know what's going on between my friends and me. They even call their parents to check on things. I get embarrassed and my friends don't like it. What can I do to make them stop—and to trust me more?
- My mother/father yells at me all the time. How can I get them to talk to me like a normal person?
- I'm going to be getting a really low grade in a class at school. My parents are going to be really upset. How can I make sure I don't get put on restriction?

Can you relate to these issues? Most teens can. Though trying times are a part of life and painful feelings are part of trying times, sometimes it can all start to feel overwhelming. The goal is to take positive action in coping with difficult situations and feelings. If you don't, then even small things can seem paralyzing. But sometimes the challenges—and the feelings they create—are just too much to handle on your own. Reaching out for help is a sign of strength. Rather than suffer alone or resort to doing things that are self-destructive, I urge you to confide in someone you can trust. This is especially true if you are afraid of someone, or are feeling really down and depressed.

I also encourage you to keep a journal. When you're going through a tough time—such as a breakup, a family crisis, or even if you can't pinpoint what's bothering you, but know something isn't sitting well with you—keeping a running account of what's going on and how you feel about it is really helpful. Journaling is a great way to get your thoughts out of your head and onto paper. Not only is this an excellent way to "talk to someone" (because you are expressing yourself), but it is also an excellent way to SEE how you are handling things. This can help you decide if you can manage this problem/issue on your own, or if you need to turn to a counselor, or your mom or dad, for help and support in getting to the other side.

So here are selected issues I've chosen from the many I've received, and my responses to them. As you may recall, in my book *Taste Berries for Teens #3: Short Stories and Encouragement on Life, Love, Friends and the Face in the Mirror,* I did a similar unit. In the months that followed, I received much mail from teens asking for the name and address of a particular teen. "Send me so-and-so's name, and I'll write that person and tell him or her how to handle things," you wrote. Know that for safety, security and legal reasons, I never give out anyone's name or address. Still, thanks for your concern and generosity. It's always nice to know that there are others who have discovered the secrets of being cool, caring and courageous, and are willing to coach, comfort and guide other teens as they work through the problem times of life. This is EXACTLY the definition of a taste berry, and no one knows how to help others sweeten life's joys and ease the bitterness of a disappointment, or to lighten the burden of a heartache, more than teens. Always, always, teens know how to "be there" for their family and friends.

❤ *Taste berries to you, Bettie Youngs*

What Is the Best "Line" to Use When Being Pressured for Sex?

Dear Dr. Youngs,

I'm sorta feeling blackmailed. My boyfriend says if I don't have sex with him he's going to get a new girlfriend. Part of me wants to have sex with him just to get it out of the way so he won't leave me. But I don't want to do anything morally bad; my youth pastor says it's wrong to have sex before marriage. I'm afraid that if I say "yes," I might end up with some terrible disease. He brags about having had sex with other girls at my school and the one nearby. What if I got pregnant? There is a girl at my school who is pregnant right now, and she said she was having protected sex but it failed. Plus, her boyfriend told her the same thing about leaving if she didn't have sex with him, but he dumped her anyway! I'm really confused about what to do. What is the best line to use to get him to stop pressuring me?

Meghan Ambers, 15

Dear Meghan,

Don't be confused. First of all, sex is never something to "get out of the way." It's the exact opposite: to be saved for the most special person of all. Stand your ground on the reasons you state so clearly in your letter. You already know what you must do. So that you can take a good look at your own thinking, let me point out why you needn't be confused at all:

***NO** to sex:*

- ❤ Premarital sex is against my faith.
- ❤ I could contract a disease; my boyfriend has sex with others.

- I don't want to get pregnant (protected sex sometimes fails).
- If I give in to having sex with him, it's because I feel pressured.
- I am being blackmailed; my boyfriend says if I don't have sex with him, he'll get a new girlfriend.
- I don't trust his word: If I have sex with him so he'll stick around, it may not mean he will. It didn't work for a girl I know.

All these reasons point to "no sex." Stand your ground. Casual sex is not a bargaining chip. If he is unwilling to respect your decision, respect your feelings by asking yourself: *Am I willing to overlook my true feelings just so my boyfriend can count me among those with whom he's had sex?* The best line to use with your boyfriend is this: "I am NOT going to have sex with you, and I do not want you to pressure me about it anymore." If he is a good guy, he'll respect your decision. If he continues to pressure you for sex, use this line: "Because you won't respect my feelings, I'm booting your butt out of my life. Bye." P.S. If you feel you cannot say these words in person, put them in a letter and hand it to him—in person. If this doesn't work, talk with your school counselor.

❤ *Taste berries to you, Bettie Youngs*

I Was Caught Cheating; How Do I Earn Back the Teacher's Trust?

Dear Dr. Youngs,

I was caught cheating in my English class today. I used to be one of my teacher's favorite students, but I can't be now. I feel bad, and I'm really embarrassed. What can I do that will help my teacher trust me again?

Nate Wilheim, 16

Dear Nate,

You are going to have to prove to your teacher that you've changed your ways. Make an appointment with your teacher to speak to her in private. Apologize and let her know that you realize what you did was wrong, and that you want to earn back her trust. Say something along these lines: "I'm sorry that I resorted to cheating on the test. I know it was wrong. I feel really bad, and I'm really embarrassed, too. I also know that by cheating, I've lost credibility with you. I want to apologize for my actions and ask if you'll give me a chance to prove that you can trust me again. You've always thought of me as a good student, and that's always been important to me. I'd like you to trust me again. I want you to know that you can count on me to never cheat again. I also want to know if there is any way I can redo the work or do some extra credit project to make up for the zero because of my having cheated on this test?"

If your teacher allows you to redo the work, make sure you do your very best. If he/she doesn't allow you to make up the credit you've lost, then you'll have to live with that consequence. Earning back trust once you've lost it is not going to happen overnight; it may take some time, as it should. But I think if you apologize for your behavior and show your teacher that you regret what you've done, because you know it was wrong, then I'm confident you will be one of your teacher's favorite students again. If you feel that you simply cannot sit down with her face-to-face, then write her a letter. At that point she will no doubt ask you to come in and talk things over, but at least she will have learned of your sincere willingness to make things right. And Nathan, don't forget the bigger lesson in all this: Trust is at stake in almost everything we do. Being trustworthy is a character trait that speaks so loudly it enters a room before you do.

❤ *Taste berries to you, Bettie Youngs*

What Is the Best Way to Get a Bully to Back Off?

Dear Dr. Youngs,

Today at school a friend and I were sitting at a table in the cafeteria. Three guys came over and said, "You're at our table. You have ten seconds to move your butts" (he used the other word for butt along with saying the "f" word a lot of times). So my friend and I got up and left, because we didn't want to start anything. The next day, my friends and I were at a totally different table, and the same thing happened again. Same guys. So maybe we should've stood our ground the first time. Maybe giving in made these guys think we could be pushed around. I don't want to get beaten up or anything, but I don't want to look like a wimp either. What is the best way to get a bully to back down?

Brad Whitney, 15

Dear Brad,

I get a lot of mail (from both guys and girls) about the many ways teens are bullied by their peers. Dealing with bullies is often daunting, but there is a way to put a stop to it. There are two levels to this: you and school policy. As for you: Always look for peaceful ways to avoid a confrontation (which you did when the bullies claimed your table in the cafeteria). As with your decision that day, some things are generally not worth disputing, as an example, teasing; do your best to ignore it. If you feel the bully is relatively harmless (in other words, if you stand your ground, the degree of your being challenged is minimal), then stand your ground by saying something assertive like: "We're not moving. Get lost." The next time the trio comes sauntering over to your table, try saying this: "How can it be that every table we sit at is your table? Look, we gave up the table yesterday. We are not doing it today. You can leave us alone, you can sit here with us, or you can get into it with us over a silly table."

HOWEVER, if the bullying is beyond friendly teasing—if anyone threatens you verbally or physically, do not fight back. Pushing, hitting, spitting—things like that—are never allowable from the bully or you. Once this behavior starts, it most generally escalates and someone could get hurt. This is where "Level Two" comes in: Anytime you feel there is the very real probability of things getting emotionally heated (swearing, name-calling) or physical in any way, then it is your right and even your duty to report it to an authority figure—such as the principal or a counselor. This lets the bully (and those who see this sort of behavior) know it will not be tolerated or go unpunished. This can save you or someone else from being victimized again. I also suggest you look into whether your school has a peer-to-peer intervention program, mediation program or peer-to-peer support program. Many schools do, and it is a good way to get outside help.

So often teens feel they must tolerate a bully. You don't and you shouldn't. No one wants to live in a world where bullies can berate others at will. Also, many teens feel that to "blow the whistle" on a bully will only make matters worse for them. Those days, by and large, are over. Most all schools have elaborate school policy spelling out the school's responsibility to create a safe environment for all students. This includes putting a halt to "half-grown" bullies who will—if we allow them to think we are not looking out for the welfare of all—grow up to be bigger and bolder bullies. It is your responsibility to help create safe schools—which, by the way, is a big contribution toward creating world peace. Say "no" to drugs. Say "no" to being bullied.

❤ *Taste berries to you, Bettie Youngs*

How Do I Go from Girl-Shy to a Girl's Guy?

Dear Dr. Youngs,

I've never been the kind of person who could just strike up a conversation with girls. Even when I'm talking to my guy friends, if a girl comes over, I just clam up. I just don't know what to say; I can't seem to think of anything that a girl would find interesting. I'm sure small talk about football scores is boring to girls, and that's mostly what I talk about with the guys. But my friends seem to have no problems talking to girls. How do they do that?

Michael Mills, 16

Dear Michael,

Many teens feel as you do: awkward about having all eyes and attention focused on you. Here's the plan to go from girl-shy to a girl's guy:

- Be a good listener. This is not just ho-hum advice. Everyone appreciates being listened to. It shows you are paying attention; it makes the other person feel valued. To a girl, listening shows you respect her.
- Make eye contact. Don't just put your chin down and stare at the floor. No one will think you're listening. Look at the person doing the talking. Try it. Girls looooove eye contact.
- Don't just stand or sit there listening, feeling shy and nerdy. Join the conversation. Even better, be the one who starts a conversation. You're probably right about sport scores being boring to most girls. Unless there's an upcoming school athletic event—in which you can get away with saying something like, "How do you think we'll do in the game Friday against school XYZ?"—then go with something

more "worldly." There are many things going on in the world, and everyone wants to hear about them. Do you go to movies? If so, talk about what you saw and why a particular movie was or wasn't good. Do you watch TV specials? If so, use them as conversation starters. So your entering a conversation might run something like this: "Did anyone see (you fill in the blank—"the Grammys last night" or "the president's State of the Union address")? It was so awesome/terrible because. . . ." DO NOT ask the question if you haven't seen any of these, because someone is going to answer your question with "no," and then you'll put yourself in the position of feeling stupid for having asked the question. The point is, you need to be able to jump right into talking about something that happened of which you can offer an opinion—and are willing to hear the opinion of others (which takes you right back to gaining acceptance because others are seeing you as a good listener). Girls like guys who have a broad range of interests.

- ❤ When you're speaking, look around at the various people in the group, paying attention to the person who is most likely to have a response. For example, another movie buff is likely to add something along the lines: "I saw *21 Grams.* It was wild. Did you know that Sean Penn won a Golden Globe award for that role? I thought he was even better in *Mystic River,* and I'm betting he'll win the Academy Award for best actor in *Mystic River.* At least I hope he does. Did anyone else see it?" You see—YOU have started a conversation. Girls *really* like a guy who can hold a good conversation.
- ❤ Smile when you speak. Relax and enjoy yourself. If you smile when you speak, others will smile even though they haven't a clue why they are smiling. BUT, because they are smiling, they will assume it's because they like and accept you! Girls looooove a guy with a great smile!
- ❤ Believe in yourself, Michael. Confidence starts there. Even

the class nerd is going to be liked if he can put himself in the position of getting others to talk with each other. It's one of the greatest secrets of popularity: to get others to join together on things. And girls, by nature, like it when people feel like family.

- ❤ Tell your heart to keep an eye on the girls. Translated: If a particular special someone was in the group conversation, and she hadn't yet seen a particular movie discussed, here's your chance to catch up with her later—via in person or a note—and invite her to see it. This is how Romeo got started: one date at a time. Girls like a take-charge sort of guy!

So start with that, Michael. The more you do this, the easier it will get. Don't worry if at first you feel a bit awkward. Everyone feels that way. But as you come out of your shell, you're sure to find that the girls will take more interest in you! One good conversation at a time. Good luck, and from time to time, let me know how you're doing.

❤ *Taste berries to you, Bettie Youngs*

Is It Ever Right to Rat on a Friend?

Dear Dr. Youngs,

I've discovered that my very best friend is stealing money from the purses stored in the lockers in gym class at school. I actually saw her open two lockers (most of the girls don't lock their lockers) and hurriedly go through the wallets. I am so shocked. But I don't know what to do. I did talk to her. She told me to "forget about it." That's not possible. It's wrong to steal even if the other girls really should have locked their lockers. I think my friend is taking money from other places as well. Some kids leave money in their lockers for lunch and things. And there is a "community jar" in the library where teens drop in loose change—pennies, nickels and dimes—in case someone needs to "borrow" a dime for a book that is a day late or something. Last week, "reward" signs were posted all around school for the "Book Bandit" as well as "Locker Pick-Pocketer." I feel really bad that this is going on and even worse that I've discovered that my friend is a thief. Should I just keep this a secret or what? I hate to rat on a friend.

Nicole Vargas, 16

Dear Nicole,

Think of your school as a small community. Everyone must look out for everyone—which is the intention behind the community jar in the library. In a community, everyone has to work together to ensure safety for everyone—or in this case, to protect the freedom of everyone getting to both deposit and take out money from the community jar. You sound like a good friend. Yes, you are her friend, but aren't you also a friend to others in your school community? You are protecting her, but are you willing to protect the others as well? Besides, you've already given your friend a chance to change her ways. Go to the head counselor and ask if you can speak with him or her confidentially (meaning your friend will not be told that you are the person reporting her as the thief). Tell what you know. Don't make any assumptions that your friend is stealing anything other than what you have witnessed firsthand. After you have done this, then you can "forget about it." You are not ratting on a friend. You are doing your part in making your school a place where trust and honesty can flourish.

❤ *Taste berries to you, Bettie Youngs*

How Can I Stop My Stepfather from "Flirting" with Me?

Dear Dr. Youngs,

My mother and stepfather have been married for ten months. My mom loves this guy a whole lot and tells me how lucky we are to be a "family." What she doesn't know is that he's been doing things that make me really uncomfortable. Like he'll do the laundry and then put my underwear on the top of the pile of folded things. Rather than leaving my laundry outside my door or on my bed or dresser, he'll hand it to me. I feel really embarrassed, and I don't like it one bit. I stopped putting my underwear in the laundry room, even though Mom gets on my case for leaving dirty clothes in my room, but sometimes I just forget things in the dryer. He does other things, too, like he'll come to the kitchen—wearing only his boxers—and make small talk when I'm fixing a sandwich late at night. Gross! I don't know if he's being suggestive or just trying to be "one of the family." He always volunteers to take me to school in the mornings, and in the car tells me how pretty I look, stuff like that. It embarrasses me, and I don't like it. He just gives me the creeps. I don't feel like I can tell my mother these things, because she loves him, and I don't want to ruin her life. What should I do?

Brianna McMillan, 15

Dear Brianna,

You *must not* keep your feelings a secret from your mother. She needs to know about what is going on and would expect you to bring these things to her attention. It is her responsibility to protect you, and she will. Someone has to get your "new" stepfather's attention and let him know that his actions are not appropriate, that people are watching, and he will not get away with anything. He needs to be confronted by someone in an authoritarian role, either your mother, your biological father (if available and willing) or a counselor. The behavior has to stop, firm boundaries established, family counseling started and written agreements established that will ensure the environment is safe and non-hostile. The sooner you talk with your mother, the sooner changes will be made that keep your "new" family a healthy family. Your mother, too, will not feel okay about your new stepfather wearing just underwear in your presence, and she will put a stop to that. As for other things, such as your not wanting him to give you a ride to school, when your mother learns that this makes you feel uneasy, she will no doubt put a stop to it as well. If you feel that your mother has not taken all the steps necessary to change your stepfather's advances toward you and that things haven't changed for the better, then file a complaint with the police for inappropriate sexual behavior. You don't have to prove anything, just file the complaint. Do not procrastinate: Talk with your mom ASAP.

P.S. If you feel you cannot talk with your mother, then talk with your school counselor. He or she will know how to best handle things or refer you to someone who can.

❤ *Taste berries to you, Bettie Youngs*

What Can I Say to a Friend Who Has Lost Someone?

Dear Dr. Youngs,

My friend's mother recently died. I'm pretty freaked out by the whole thing, so I can only imagine how hard it is for her. My friend is back at school now, but she's really quiet. Many of the kids at school—especially the boys—are sort of pretending nothing happened. Is that the best way to help her? She looks so sad. I don't know if I should say, "I'm sorry about your mother," or if that will only make her cry. I wish I could do something to help—give her some advice or some magic words to make her feel better, but I don't know what to say. What can I do to help my friend?

Eva Leffer, 16

Dear Eva,

Friends often don't know what to say when someone has suffered a tragedy as overwhelming as having lost a parent. Pretending that nothing happened isn't good, nor is saying nothing. This can make the person who is grieving feel alone, or as though no can cares. As a friend, try this approach:

❤ Be a good listener. And be generous with your time. It's so important to be able to talk about our feelings. Make it easy for your friend to talk to you.

❤ Show that you care. It's okay to say things such as, "How are you doing today?" Don't say, "I know what you're going through." We can imagine what it's like, but we can never trade places with the person who has experienced loss.

❤ Let her talk about things. If and when the topic of her mother comes up, ask to see a picture of her mother. Let her talk about her mother and share special memories with you.

❤ Be okay with your friend expressing sadness and sorrow. Should she cry, be okay with her tears. Don't say, "Please don't cry." Say, "It's okay to cry."

❤ Especially in the first few weeks, just "be there" for her. If you feel that your friend is "too sad"—or if you feel that she is depressed—then talk with the school counselor and tell him or her of your concern for your friend. The counselor will be able to decide if your friend needs the help of a counselor or therapist to help her cope with the loss of her beloved mother.

I'd say your friend is most fortunate to have you; you sound like a true taste berry! That's what friends are for!

❤ *Taste berries to you, Bettie Youngs*

How Do I Convince My Parents I Need Plastic Surgery?

Dear Dr. Youngs,

I need and want plastic surgery. My dad said absolutely not, and my mother is against the idea, though she did take me to the doctor so we could have a talk with him. My problem is that I've been overweight all my life, and I'm really tired of it. I've been watching a medical makeover show on television, and, wow, you should see some of the "after" pictures of some of these people! I mean, there are some people who are almost ugly, but after they've had plastic surgery, they look great. (My parents don't know it, but I've written in to the television show hoping that I'll get selected for a "complete makeover.") I've already decided what I want to change: The first thing I want is liposuction. The doctor says I still must lose between fifty and sixty-five pounds to be where I'm supposed to be, so liposuction would be a really big help to get rid of the weight. The next thing I want is to have all the loose skin on my body removed. I've recently lost thirty-one pounds, and as a result, I have a lot of loose skin. It's really ugly, and I want it removed. I told the doctor that I hated all the loose skin, but he told me my skin would "settle"—like in six months! I want it to look perfect now. And maybe a chin implant. My nose is okay. But my chin is sort of flat, so I'd be better looking with a bigger chin. I'll start with those things. But like I said, my parents are not on the same page with this. Please help me convince them to let me do this. I really want a great-looking body, and they don't have any idea how awful it is to be young and fat.

Ashley Feldman, 16

Dear Ashley,

I agree with your parents. Plastic surgery is not to be taken lightly; it is not without risks. And it is very expensive. Still, the doctor and your parents are saying "no" because it is not the best approach to "fixing" being overweight. Liposuction is not a procedure used for weight loss. Liposuction, often referred to as "body sculpting," is often used to remove pockets of fat from areas such as legs and thighs, but it is not for removing weight from all over the body. As it relates to weighing what a girl your age with your frame (bone size and structure) should, nothing can help you achieve good health more than a diet that is designed to help you lose the appropriate amount of weight within an appropriate amount of time. A word of caution here though: Please follow a sensible weight-loss program, one that is recommended and overseen by your doctor, or someone trained in the field of nutrition. All dieting is stressful for the body and must be done carefully, and under the guidance of someone trained in the field. Exercise is also a good way to help you lose weight, and to help your skin regain elasticity and tone.

As for your loose skin, the doctor is giving you the best advice possible: You need to give your skin time to shrink. It may take your body anywhere from six weeks to six months to do this. Ashley, my advice to you would be to forget about the adults you see on a taped television show. First, these folks ARE adults, which means their bodies are not, like yours, still developing. At sixteen, you don't really know what your "final body" will look like. Second, these shows are edited, meaning as a viewer, you are not seeing the entire process of going from "before" to "after." And, for sure, you are not going to be seeing the person who had surgery when the healing process didn't go as planned—such as the pain involved, scars from the surgery or bad results (you don't always know how your body will heal from the trauma of surgery). I say this not to scare you, but to give you a more realistic view of the full range of possibilities that can result from cosmetic surgery.

As for your desire to be "perfect"—Ashley, there is no such thing. Each and every year for the rest of your life, your body will change. It really is best to adopt an attitude of going for good health; do all you can to achieve a "great-looking body" through good nutrition, exercise and being a happy person. For now, concentrate on your weight loss. Under the guidance of your family doctor (or nutritionist), set a realistic goal to lose the amount of weight you and your doctor say is best for you, and focus on that. As for the chin implant, maybe do a wait-and-see until you are twenty, just to see what nature does between now and then. Please write in three months, and let me know how you are doing.

❤ *Taste berries to you, Bettie Youngs*

What Can I Say to a Friend to Get Him to Stop Using Drugs?

Dear Dr. Youngs,

I think my friend Tommy has a drug problem. He's always smoked pot, but I think he must be doing other stuff. He won't tell me what, but he sure is changing. He's starting to miss a lot of school, and when he is here, he sleeps in most all his classes. On some days he hasn't showered, and his clothes aren't always clean. I worry he's become hooked. I just don't want him to fall apart. What can I say to him that will get him to stop using drugs?

Mike Truman, 16

Dear Mike,

Unfortunately, words alone won't get your friend to stop using. It sounds like Tommy is already chemically dependent. Someone who is chemically dependent cannot stop using through willpower. Tommy needs to get help to break the cycle of addiction. What's more, Tommy needs to do more than just not use drugs; otherwise, he won't stay clean and sober. Depending on what he's using or how long he's been using, Tommy will need to make a commitment to attend either substance abuse counseling or an in-house treatment program. Even after that, he'll need to work a recovery program.

You can't force him to get help, but you can suggest it. You can also ask a counselor to help do what is called an intervention. This is where four to six concerned people come together and talk to Tommy, sharing their concerns and trying to convince him he needs help to stop using. The sooner your friend gets help, the better—otherwise his drug use will grow more and more destructive. Talk with your school counselor and share your concerns for your friend. This is not betraying Tommy or causing trouble for him. It's acting out of care and concern to get the direction and facts that you need in order to help him. Tommy can get better and turn his life around if he stops using and starts working on his recovery. He's fortunate to have a friend like you who is concerned enough to try and get him the help he needs. Hopefully he will.

❤ *Taste berries to you, Bettie Youngs*

Appendix A

WHO GETS YOUR VOTE FOR:

Best TITLE of Poem: ____________________

____

____

Most Interesting Subject Matter: ____________

____

____

____

Overall BEST POET—$100 cash prize winner: ____________

____

____

After you've voted, send this form to:

Taste Berries for Teens Poetry Contest
Box 2588
Del Mar, CA 92014

All entries must be received by December 15, 2004, to be eligible. To find out the winners, visit our Web site: *tasteberries forteens.com.*

Tell us who you are:

Name ______________________________

E-mail ______________________________

Age______________________________

Street Address ______________________________

____

State ______________ Zip code ______________

Appendix B

About our books for teens (for more information, visit *www.tasteberriesforteens.com*).

365 Days of Taste-Berry Inspiration for Teens. A collection of 365 affirmations by teens. Each day provides a reminder of the power of love, friendship, courage, integrity, compassion, kindness, service, forgiveness, perseverance and the many other taste-berry traits and qualities that create meaning, purpose and success. Uplifting, motivating and practical, these taste-berry thoughts are sure to remind teens of their highest ideals and personal best.

Taste Berries for Teens: Inspirational Short Stories and Encouragement on Life, Love, Friendships and Tough Issues. This international best seller of inspirational stories by teens for teens offers encouragement and advice about understanding self and friends; helps teens consider how to best search for a career; how to make a difference at home, in the community and throughout the world.

Taste Berries for Teens Journal: My Thoughts on Life, Love and Making a Difference. Journaling is a powerful tool to process feelings. Probing questions stimulate thinking about self and life from relationships to feelings. A "most favorite" journal for teens.

More Taste Berries for Teens: A Second Collection of Inspirational Short Stories and Encouragement on Life, Love, Friendships and Tough Issues. This book of inspirational stories by teens for teens offers encouragement and advice about understanding love and relationships; understanding how embarrassing moments can teach us valuable lessons; and more. A real favorite with teens.

Taste Berries for Teens #3: Inspirational Short Stories on Life, Love, Friends and the Face in the Mirror. This 2003 *Best Teen Book World Storytelling* Prize award winner offers one-hundred-plus inspirational stories by teens for teens offering encouragement and advice to gain perspective on the ups and downs of life; learning how to maneuver the maze of friendships—making, keeping and sometimes leaving; learning the "love behind the rules" at home; and coping with tough and challenging times.

A Taste-Berry Teen's Guide to Managing the Stress and Pressures of

Life. This skill book (with stories by teens for teens), provides eighteen practical tools and exercises to understand what stress is and isn't, and how to turn it to one's advantage.

A Taste-Berry Teen's Guide to Setting & Achieving Goals. This skill book (with stories by teens) helps teens to think about their goals in relationship to their personality, aptitudes, hobbies and interests; and to identify, set and reach goals in nine important areas. A 2003 *Forward* magazine's Gold Winner for Best Book for Teens.

A Teen's Guide to Living Drug-Free. This comprehensive book is written for teens grades six to twelve, but it is a tremendous help for anyone—young adults, parents and professionals included—who wants to gain a thorough understanding of chemical dependency. It offers insight on how to best help teens stay (or get) drug-free; help friends who are using; understand and work through relapse; find and select treatment programs; understand the road to recovery; as well as work through issues that lead to using.

Feeling Great, Looking Hot & Loving Yourself: Health, Fitness and Beauty for Teens. This health, fitness and beauty book helps the teen gain inner confidence and self-assurance, and to understand these essential attitudes of "beauty"—inside and out. Also discussed are ways to best care for teen skin, hair and personal hygiene. Very popular with teens.

12 Months of Faith: A Devotional Journal for Teens. This daily devotional supports teens in learning and living their faith, and helps them see the importance of setting aside quiet time each day to grow their faith.

A Teen's Guide to Christian Living: Practical Answers to Tough Questions About God and Faith. This book helps teens understand the principles of Christian living, and to find answers to questions, such as, "Does God have a plan for my life?" "Does God care who my friends are?" and "Does God love me—no matter what I've done?"

Living the 10 Commandments in NEW Times. Throughout these pages, you'll take a walk through each of God's laws and learn of God's love behind each one, and gain a better understanding of why and how each commandment guards something that is of the greatest importance to your welfare. Discover how each law is not only the basis for moral and spiritual conduct, but perfectly formulated common sense showing us how to live interdependently and in harmony with each other.

About the Authors

Bettie B. Youngs, Ph.D., Ed.D., is a Pulitzer Prize–nominated author of thirty books translated into twenty-four languages. She is a former teacher of the year, university professor and executive director of Instruction and Professional Development, Inc. A long-acknowledged expert on family and teen issues, Dr. Youngs has frequently appeared on *The Good Morning Show, NBC Nightly News, CNN* and *Oprah. USA Today,* the *Washington Post, US News & World Report, Working Woman, Family Circle, Parents Magazine, Woman's Day* and the National Association for Secondary School Principals (NASSP) have all recognized her work. Her acclaimed books include the best-selling *Taste Berries for Teens* series including: *Taste Berries for Teens: Inspirational Short Stories and Encouragement on Life, Love, Friendship and Tough Issues; Safeguarding Your Teenager from the Dragons of Life; A Teen's Guide to Living Drug-Free; A Teen's Guide to Christian Living: Practical Answers to Tough Questions About God and Faith; 12 Months of Faith: A Devotional Journal for Teens; Living the 10 Commandments in New Times;* the Pulitzer-nominated *Gifts of the Heart: Stories That Celebrate Life's Defining Moments;* the award-winning *Values from the Heartland* and *Taste-Berry Tales: Stories to Lift the Spirit, Fill the Heart and Feed the Soul.* Dr. Youngs is the author of a number of videocassette programs and is the co-author of the nationally acclaimed *Parents on Board,* a video-based training program to help schools and parents work together to increase student achievement.

Jennifer Leigh Youngs is the author of *Feeling Great, Looking Hot & Loving Yourself: Health, Fitness and Beauty for Teens,* and coauthor of the *Taste Berries for Teens* series. Jennifer is a former Miss Teen California finalist, and a Rotary International Goodwill Ambassador and Exchange Scholar. She serves on a number of advisory boards for teens and is a Youth Coordinator for Airline Ambassadors, an international organization affiliated with the United Nations that involves youth in programs to build cross-cultural friendships; escorts children to hospitals for medical care and orphans to new homes; and delivers humanitarian aid to those in need worldwide.

To contact the authors, write to:
Youngs, Youngs & Associates
3060 Racetrack View Drive, Suites 100-103
Del Mar, CA 92014

www.tasteberriesforteens.com

What Others Are Saying About This Book . . .

"I once struggled with math. Then a math teacher, Mrs. Jacobson, came along and believed in me when I couldn't. It was a taste-berry action that changed my life. Though I am an actress, I graduated UCLA summa cum laude, with a degree in Mathematics—and have since coauthored a new theorem. Math really can be a fun subject, and I encourage all of you to face it without fear. If any of you would like some help, please visit my Web site (see page 98 of this book!), and when you e-mail me, mention that you got it from this book, *Taste Berries for Teens #4.* I always enjoy passing along any (taste-berry) gift that was once given to me!"

—Danica McKellar, 29
actress from TV's
The Wonder Years and *The West Wing*

"I love this book! Reading it made me laugh and it made me cry, too. But more important, it made me feel less alone."

—Malia Moriarty, 16
Southbridge, Massachusetts

"I think all teens—adults, too—should read this book. That way we can all know, without guessing, what experiences teens really face, and see how dramatic and traumatic teen life is. As for me, I feel better now. I don't feel as 'odd' or 'strange' or 'alone' as I'd secretly felt before."

—Tom Whitt, 17
Detroit, Michigan

"I was so amazingly surprised to find that other teens feel exactly as I do. Reading this book lifted my spirits, and it can do the same for you."

—Melyssa Boone, 17
Millbrook, Alabama

"People sort of don't take seriously how difficult some days can be to get through for teens. Being a teen is not as carefree and easy as many may think. That's why the *Taste Berries* books are so good. They're about real teens having a 'real' experience. I love these books. And this new one is the best ever!"

—Nikeylla Willams-Harris, 14
Alameda, California

"I love reading the *Taste Berries* books. And this new one is just great! The stories from other teens help me see my own life better. That's why I was able to write the story *The Secrets I Hide.* I once thought they were 'secrets' and that I had to 'hide' them. Now I can talk about what's going on in my life. Because practically everybody's got something they're worried or embarrassed about. Reading these books helps you feel 'okay' and 'normal.' What a relief! Best of all, now I know what I can do to solve—or at least better manage—some things going on in my life."

—Kay Linn, 15
Irvington, New Jersey

"One of the many reasons I love the *Taste Berry* books is that as a result of reading them, I've decided to be a writer. In reading the stories of other teens, I realize that I can write, too. I just showed my teacher a story I wrote for your new book, and she said I was an 'extraordinary' writer. It feels really cool that she said this—but I believe her! My mom told me that all I have to do is set goals and keep at it. I'm going to! I plan on seeing my next story in your next book!"

—Jenna Witham, 12
Portland, Oregon

"I'm 14 years old, and writing to you from jail. I've been here for 9 months. A friend gave me *365 Days of Taste Berry Inspiration for Teens,* and I think it is really inspiring. I love it. It's really helping me cope with my problems. But mostly, it's helping me want to be a better person."

—Tyler Edmonds, 14
Starkville, Mississippi

"Hi again! It's me! I love the new book! I have the whole collection, and what's cool is that because every teenager thinks she's 'in love,' these books can really help you get a handle on your emotions. I think it's important to 'own' yourself more than most teens do, and these books really help you do that."

—Roxann Baca, 16
Clint, Texas

"I love the Taste Berry books. They're really interesting and really cool. But they're helpful, too. Because of reading them, I've decided what I want to do in life—which is to be a singer! I've decided that I'm capable of starting a charity—and know exactly what issue I'm going to support. Now that I've made these decisions, I feel really much better about myself and not so unimportant as I used to feel. And after reading this great book, I have an even better outlook on life. Thanks for that!"

—Hanan Dumas, 13
Richmond, British Columbia, Canada